D1570452

ARTHUR ANDERSEN'S GLOBAL LESSONS IN ACTIVITY-BASED MANAGEMENT

ARTHUR ANDERSEN'S GLOBAL LESSONS IN ACTIVITY-BASED MANAGEMENT

Edited by

Steve Player
and
Roberto Lacerda

JOHN WILEY & SONS, INC.

New York • Chichester • Weinheim • Brisbane • Toronto • Singapore

This book is printed on acid-free paper. ∞

Copyright © 1999 by Arthur Andersen. All rights reserved.
Published by John Wiley & Sons, Inc.
Published simultaneously in Canada.

This publication is designed to provide accurate and authoritative information in regard
to the subject matter covered. It is sold with the understanding that the publisher is not
engaged in rendering legal, accounting, or other professional services. If legal advice or
other expert assistance is required, the services of a competent professional person
should be sought.

Library of Congress Cataloging-in-Publication Data:

Arthur Andersen's global lessons in activity-based management / [compiled and edited
by] Steve Player and Roberto Lacerda.
    p. cm.
   Includes index.
   ISBN 0-471-36288-3 (cl. : alk. paper)
   1. Activity-based costing Case studies.   2. Managerial accounting Case studies.
I. Player, Steve, 1958–   . II. Lacerda, Roberto.   III. Title: Global lessons in
activity-based management.
HF5686.C8A74 1999
658.15′11—dc21   99-30532
                                                        CIP

Printed in the United States of America.

10 9 8 7 6 5 4 3 2 1

Dedication

This book is dedicated to Lydia, David, Emily,
and Cole Player and Jacqueline, Carolina, and Patricia Lacerda.

This book could not have been completed without their patience and support.
The work for our clients takes us to all corners of the globe, but wherever we are,
the love and understanding of our families sustains and encourages us.

CONTENTS

FOREWORD

It is becoming increasingly clear that companies can no longer plan and control their way to the future. Today's global marketplace is a fast changing world. To survive, organizations need to operate with flexible strategies that can counter competitive threats and capture new opportunities as they arise. They must respond rapidly to changing customer needs, eliminate all unnecessary costs, and share knowledge and best practices. None of this can be done effectively without devolving power and responsibility to the front line. But this is easier said than done.

Traditional accounting and budgeting systems act as a barrier to such changes as they reinforce the centralized command and control business model. This is hardly surprising, as this is precisely what they were designed to do over 75 years ago. Financial accounting systems and their costing derivatives (such as standard costing) are now seriously out of kilter with the needs of today's operating managers. And this situation can only get worse as SG&A costs account for an increasing share of the overall cost burden.

Fortunately, like an old western movie, the cavalry has arrived just in time in the guise of activity-based management (ABM). After a hesitant start in the early 1990s when ABC was largely seen as just a better way of allocating the same costs, the more strategically focused ABM has blown through the accounting corridors of power like a breath of fresh air. It has enabled managers to see costs and profits in a new light. ABM is the missing key that unlocks the door to empowerment and rapid value-based decision making.

True empowerment means that managers must have the freedom to act *and* the capability to make the right decisions. One without the other renders the so-called empowered manager impotent; alas, so many companies provide the freedom but not the capability. This needed capability relies upon fast, relevant information, and this is exactly what ABM is designed to provide. As many organizations have discovered, ABM is a real source of competitive advantage.

Think of it this way. Which company would you prefer to work for or invest in? One that knows the profitability of its products, markets, customers, segments, and channels (after charging all support costs), or one that does not? One that knows the causes of its costs or one that does not? One that can identify those activities that add value or one that cannot? One that knows how to improve its processes, or one that does not? The answer should be obvious and the solution compelling.

Let's focus on just one of these issues facing businesses today—customer profitability. Few companies know which customers (or segments) are profitable after accounting for all the costs of serving them (e.g., marketing, sales, order processing, distribution, service, debt collection, and management time). Indeed, many studies have shown that a small percentage of customers produce the vast majority of profits. But imagine that you have customer profitability information at your fingertips and you are able to work out a strategy for turning unprofitable customers into profitable ones or, if necessary, unloading your unprofitable customers on to your competitors. The overall profit impact can be enormous. Such is the power of ABM.

This is not a hyperbole. As this excellent book illustrates, many companies around the world have now embraced ABM with great success. And major software vendors are beginning to provide the appropriate systems to harness the full potential of ABM and integrate its output with financial systems. All of this signals that ABM is reaching critical mass; the period of experimentation is over. Many organizations will now be making profound commitments as they adopt ABM as their major decision-support system, running alongside the financial accounting process (but by no means inferior to it).

Those organizations that have not yet recognized the benefits of ABM will need to catch up rapidly. And there is no better way to do this than to read this book. *Arthur Andersen's Global Lessons in Activity-Based Management* provides a wealth of information where it matters—from the experience of real companies worldwide.

My recent work with the Consortium for Advanced Manufacturing-International (CAM-I) sponsored *Beyond Budgeting Round Table* has provided yet another perspective on performance management systems—one that bridges measures and behavior. Measures drive behavior, but as our initial work has clearly shown, traditional accounting measures drive the *wrong behavior.* Nowhere is this more obvious than within functions, departments, or cost centers (i.e., R&D, marketing, IT, and accounting), where costs become an *entitlement* to be maintained or increased in the annual budgeting process.

Only by applying *value-adding* tests can these activity costs be justified. If the activities do not add value to operating units or cannot be justified by reference to strategic or regulatory requirements, they should be eliminated.

ABM is the way forward. There is little doubt the practice of management accounting is undergoing a period of rapid change. Hard-pressed operating managers do not need piles of irrelevant reports that tell them detailed departmental costs above or below budget. What they need is information that tells them what action is needed to improve the performance of markets, customers, products, and processes. ABM enables managers to focus on solutions. This book will help them use ABM to understand these solutions and how to implement them successfully.

Jeremy Hope
Co-author of *Competing in the Third Wave* and *Transforming the Bottom Line* (both published by the Harvard Business School Press, Boston)

PREFACE

Four years ago we wrote of the power of activity-based management (ABM) in *Activity-Based Management: Arthur Andersen's Lessons from the ABM Battlefield.* That book (recently updated with a second edition by John Wiley & Sons) showed how ABM could be implemented successfully. Its acceptance in the marketplace was far greater than we could have hoped. Its case studies, however, were predominantly U.S.-headquartered companies. What amazed us was the demand for the book around the globe.

Editions were translated and released in Portuguese, Korean, and Japanese. Selected articles appeared in French and German. Our travel demands increased dramatically. What we found was not only a thirst for the lessons learned but also some powerful examples of excellent work.

As the case studies in this book will show, ABM is a global tool that works. From banks in Brazil to production plants in France, ABM can help any organization. *Global Lessons* illustrates how companies understand the work performed in their organizations. It shows how to become more profitable and effective.

Part One begins by supplying some basics. Those just getting started will want to spend time in Chapter 1 reviewing the tools and techniques of implementing ABM.

Chapter 2 is a bit more advanced. It provides some key points from our research into the Best Practices in ABM. Arthur Andersen has played a key role in this research, which has been produced jointly with the American Productivity & Quality Center (APQC), the Consortium for Advanced Manufacturing-International (CAM-I), and individual study sponsors and partner companies. In Fall 1999, Phase 4 of the Arthur Andersen–APQC study of Best Practices in ABM will be launched.

Chapter 3 addresses the rapidly evolving systems being built to support ABC applications. While PC-based solutions have been available for 10 years, there is currently a convergence on ABC applications. This comes from enterprise requirements planning suppliers such as SAP, PeopleSoft, Oracle, Baan, and J. D. Edwards. All are enhancing their functionality to improve the return on investment they provide to enhance the post-Y2K value proposition. The functionality of online analytical processing (OLAP) tools such as Hyperion Solutions Essbase and the recent edition of Microsoft OLAP are rapidly increasing to better enable their support of ABC. The PC-based tools are also continuing to advance, with many accepting venture capital money to speed developments. Those groups are also teaming, as seen by SAP's investment in ABC Technologies, Armstrong Laing's alliance with J. D. Edwards, and the acquisition of Sapling by Hyperion Solutions.

Chapter 4 concludes the first part by focusing on the results. ABM tools and techniques, best practices, and software are only as good as the decision making information they produce. Chapter 4 focuses on the reporting output and the impact that OLAP technology is having on reporting.

Part Two focuses on case studies—sharing what happened to real people when implementing at real companies. Each chapter features a case study authored by local implementation teams. The cases and industry designations are noted as follows:

Chapter	Country	Company	Industry
5	Brazil	Banco Real	Banking
6	Brazil	CTBC Telecom	Telecommunications
7	Brazil	Multibrás Electrodomésticos	Manufacturing
8	Canada	Alcan Smelters and Chemicals	Manufacturing
9	Canada	Finning International Inc.	Service, Distribution, Leasing
10	Canada	Clarica	Insurance
11	France	AscoForge Safe	Manufacturing
12	Mexico	Grupo Casa Autrey	Distribution
13	The Netherlands	Hallmark Greeting Cards	Consumer Products
14	Portugal	Portugal Telecom	Telecommunications
15	United States	American Seating	Manufacturing
16	United States	Manco	Manufacturing
17	United States	National Council on Compensation Insurance	Services Insurance
18	United States	Tampa Electric Company	Utility

The appendix contains a special section on benchmarking the finance and accounting functions, then a vignette on the German-based company Leybold Systems GmbH, and the CAM-I glossary of terms.

In his 1954 book, *The Practice of Management,* Peter Drucker said the way to understand an enterprise is by analyzing its activities. This book shows how companies around the globe are doing just that. We hope this book sets readers on the way to success in their organizations.

Please contact us with your feedback, comments, or questions.

Roberto Lacerda
(55-11) 5181.2444
roberto.s.d.lacerda@br.arthurandersen.com

Steve Player
(214) 741-8789
r.steven.player@us.arthurandersen.com

ACKNOWLEDGMENTS

We gratefully acknowledge the clients of Arthur Andersen who allowed us to tell their story. Their willingness to share not only their successes but also their pains, their frustrations, and the lessons they learned have made this book possible. Our appreciation to Alcan Aluminum, American Seating, Asco-Forge Safe, Banco Real, CTBC Telecom, Finning International (Canada), Grupo Casa Autrey, Hallmark Greeting Cards, Leybold Systems, Manco, Multibrás Electrodomésticos, Clarica, National Council of Compensation Insurance, Portugal Telecom, and Tampa Electric Company.

Thanks to Sheck Cho and Joyce Ting of John Wiley & Sons for their patience and diligence in turning our words into this product. We would also like to thank our research partners the American Productivity & Quality Center, the Consortium for Advanced Manufacturing-International, and the Institute of Management Accountants.

Thanks also goes to Barry Brinker, executive editor of *International Journal of Strategic Cost Management,* for his helpful comments on the chapters, and to Carol Cobble of Armstrong Laing for her assistance with some of the case studies. We appreciate the ongoing support of our practice leaders Pat Dolan, Luis Alberto Tredicce, Chuck Ketteman, Steve Hronec, and Chuck Marx of Arthur Andersen and their suggestions in improving the drafts. Additionally, we would like to thank the Brazilian marketing team, Heloisa H. Montes and Marcia C. Pinto, for their coordination of the cases and support with clients.

We also extend our thanks to the members of Arthur Andersen from offices around the world for taking the time to capture and contribute the lessons they have learned. Documenting success stories from seven countries emphasizes the strength of cost management worldwide. As editors, we appreciate the significant contributions made by: John Anderlic, Juarez Lopez de Araújo, Arthur Azevedo, Margarida Bajanca, Pedro Alba Bayarri, Michelle Behrenwald, Nuno Belo, João Carlos Brega, James D. Castille, Jay Collins, Nick Curcuru, Joseph P. Donnelly, Jóse Luis Santos Azevedo Filho, Ruy de Campos Filho, Victor Gilman, Willy G. Hartung, Randolf Holst, Matthew W. Kolb, Heidi A. Labritz, Isabelle Lacombe, Michel Maisonneuve, Andrew Marchus, Mitch Max, Olivier Meltzer, Stephane Mercier, Hein ter Meulen, Alan Peretz, Carlos Eduardo Rocha, Paulo Salgado, Robert J. Savage, Francisco Silva, Scott W. Smith, Dennis Sparacino, Henri Tcheng,

Clodomarcio Tosi, Sanjay K. Upmanyu, Gerald F. Veccio, and Gema Moreno Vega.

A special thanks goes to Paige Dawson, whose professionalism and diligence are world class. She is a driving force behind not only this book but our entire practice. We also thank Robin Baumgartner, Stacie Rivard, Megan Salch, and Chris Stier for their assistance with this publication.

PART ONE

Foundations and Trends in Activity-Based Management

1

TOOLS AND TECHNIQUES FOR IMPLEMENTING ACTIVITY-BASED MANAGEMENT

Randolf Holst and Robert J. Savage

Activity-based costing (ABC) and activity-based management (ABM) have received accolades in the 1990s and will continue to grow rapidly in utility and application into the 21st century. In the private sector, thousands of companies have adopted activity-based costing and management approaches to control cost, grow revenue, and help improve business performance. These efforts are taking place in companies such as Hallmark, Tampa Electric Company, John Deere, American Express Inc., and the U.S. Postal Service, and span a broad range of organizations in size, focus, and diversity. Local and national public sector organizations are also beginning to apply activity-based cost management (ABCM) for purposes of reinventing government, as they attempt to become both more efficient and more effective in supplying services to taxpayers.

Gaining the full benefits of ABCM lies with assessing, designing, and implementing the underlying data collection and analysis system. Effective ABCM systems focus on providing information on the strategic business issues facing the organization as well as meeting the operating data requirements of the organization's decision makers.

Achieving a robust, effective ABCM design begins with the initial planning phase of the implementation and continues through the development of ongoing improvements and adjustments to the system as an organization's needs change.

KEY DIFFERENCES BETWEEN ABC AND ABM

Significant confusion regarding the semantics and acronyms associated with activity-based information exists. To clarify these issues, the Consortium for Advanced Manufacturing-International (CAM-I) initiated the development of a comprehensive glossary of ABC/ABM terms. (See Glossary.)

Activity-based costing is defined as a methodology that measures the cost and performance of activities, resources, and cost objects. Specifically, resources are assigned to activities based upon consumption rates and activities are assigned

3

to cost objects, again based on consumption. ABC recognizes the causal relationships of cost drivers to activities.

Activity-based management is subsequently defined by CAM-I as a discipline that focuses on the management of activities as the route to improving the value received by the customer and the profit achieved by providing this value. ABM includes cost driver analysis, activity analysis, and performance measurement, drawing on ABC as its major source of data.

In simple terms, ABC is used to answer the question "What do things cost?" while ABM, employing a process view, is concerned with what factors cause costs to occur. Using ABC data, ABM focuses on how to redirect and improve the use of resources to increase the value created for customers and other stakeholders.

USES AND BENEFITS OF ABM

ABM refers to the entire set of management actions initiated on a better information basis with activity-based cost information. Organizations implement ABM for different reasons. They believe ABM will help them make better decisions, improve performance, and earn more money on deployed assets. As suggested by Exhibit 1.1, companies in many situations can find value in ABM information. Some of the specific uses of ABM in organizations today include attribute analysis, strategic decision making, benchmarking, operations analysis, profitability/pricing analysis, and process improvement.

Attribute analysis classifies and combines cost and performance data into manageable, controllable clusters. ABC/ABM systems can use many different attribute or "data tags" for specific cost. Data attributes allow a company to perform analysis on many different dimensions of a management problem using the same basic warehouse of data.

Strategic analysis explores various ways a company can create and sustain a competitive advantage in the marketplace. Emphasizing long-term objectives and challenges, strategic analysis seeks to impact future costs and improve future profitability by clarifying the cost of various cost objects such as products, customers, and channels. Strategic analysis emphasizes future opportunities and challenges, using a combination of both physical and financial measures to explore the impact of alternative strategic positions.

For example, the ABM initiative at Hewlett-Packard North American Distribution Organization provides both strategic and operational information including full customer segment costing, full and simpler product costing, and targeting of improvement opportunities.[1]

Benchmarking is a methodology that identifies an activity as the standard, or benchmark, by which a similar activity will be judged. It is used to assist managers in identifying a process or technique to increase the effectiveness or effi-

EXHIBIT 1.1   General Uses of ABM Information

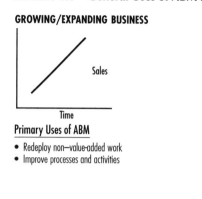

GROWING/EXPANDING BUSINESS

Sales

Time

Primary Uses of ABM

- Redeploy non–value-added work
- Improve processes and activities

NO GROWTH/FLAT BUSINESS

Sales

Time

Primary Uses of ABM

- To identify non–value-added cost
- To set priorities for improvement and effect improvement
- To isolate/eliminate cost drivers
- To determine product/service costs

DECLINING OPERATIONS

Sales

Time

Primary Uses of ABM

- To cut cost
- Downsize
- Effect layoffs

CAPACITY CONSTRAINED

Sales

Time

Primary Uses of ABM

- To determine product/service cost
- To make product/service decisions
- To determine activity capacity (bottlenecks)

Source: Reprinted by permission of John Wiley & Sons, John A. Miller, *Implementing Activity-Based Management in Daily Operations*, copyright ©1996, John Wiley & Sons, p. 26.

ciency of an activity. ABM supports internal, industry/competitive, and best-in-class benchmarking.

For example, ABM has been applied successfully within AT&T's Business Communications Services (BCS) to support its benchmarking efforts. In this case, unit costs are used as metrics for benchmarking internal work groups as well as comparing the BCS to other billing centers. Work groups more cost efficient at performing an activity can share information with other internal groups and billing centers. By having access to reliable cost data, management can investigate cost discrepancies and more effectively plan process improvements to achieve cost reductions.[2]

Operations analysis seeks to identify, measure, and improve current performance of key processes and operations within a firm. Areas where ABM is useful include "what-if" analysis, project management, creation and use of activity-based performance measures, capacity management, constraint analysis, and process-based costing.

Profitability/pricing analysis is a key area for any company. ABM assists a company in analyzing the costs and benefits of products and processes in both the "as-is" and postimprovement "to-be" scenarios. ABM also supports prelaunch analysis and improvement of product profitability.

Process improvement lies at the heart of modern management techniques. Focused on identifying the causes of variation, waste, and inefficiency, process improvement includes both incremental and quantum change efforts to increase the value created per resources consumed by an organization. Uses being made of ABM for process improvement include business process modeling, total quality initiatives, business process reengineering, and analysis of outsourcing and shared service opportunities.

The Pennzoil Production and Exploration Company (PEPCO) used ABM as a key measurement tool to identify costs by process and to support its reengineering efforts. To keep pace with lower crude and natural gas prices and slowing North American operations, PEPCO needed to find ways to reengineer existing processes to streamline and improve efficiency.[3]

ABM provided the data for Pennzoil to change the cost structure of its exploration and production efforts. It achieved this by determining what resources actually were required to support its properties based on current operation. In addition, the reengineering link enabled the company to consider those same properties and determine how it could best meet its economic objectives with fewer resources through a variety of operations improvement analyses.

ABM is used to support a broad array of management initiatives to help organizations create more value for their customers while reducing the cost of operations.

ABM IMPLEMENTATION STEPS

Whether applied on a small scale to a specific area of an organization, such as a department, function, or applications, or used for a large-scale implementation in a specific plant or applied simultaneously to several plants, facilities, departments, or functions, there is no one right way to implement ABM. In fact, the general steps involved in taking a holistic approach to ABM implementation can be expressed in a number of ways and can be performed in different sequence.

While each ABCM project is unique, an organization's actual implementation plan will likely include most or all seven steps outlined in Exhibit 1.2, although not necessarily in the exact order presented. While organizations can modify the sequence and emphasis placed on these steps to meet the needs of a particular situation, these activities are recommended as a guide for implementing activity-based initiatives.

EXHIBIT 1.2   ABCM Project Implementation Steps

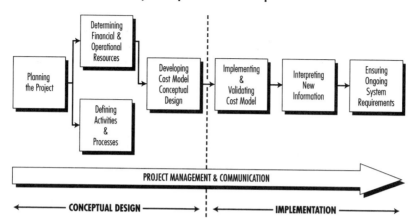

1. Planning the Project

While the planning phase of an ABCM implementation represents only a small part of the total time and effort of an ABCM initiative, it has a major impact on the overall success of the implementation. Key objectives in the planning phase are:

- Identifying the business imperative
- Confirming objectives and scope of the project
- Identifying and educating key stakeholders and sponsors
- Organizing and educating project teams
- Developing implementation work plans and schedules

Communication, top management and sponsor support, and the education of project teams regarding the objectives and benefits of the ABCM system lay the foundation for downstream acceptance and use of the activity-based information. No matter how good the underlying ABCM information is, it will have little or no value to the organization if it is not accepted and used effectively.

During the planning phase, core tools and techniques utilized to improve the effectiveness of the overall implementation include agreed-on project objectives and scope, a project team, and ABCM education and training.

Agreed-on Project Objectives and Scope

The ultimate success of the ABCM implementation requires consensus and clarity of overarching objectives to align efforts and resources efficiently and effectively. Objectives frame the design and implementation of the ABCM cost and reporting structures.

When the objectives are well defined (i.e., to improve the accuracy of cost estimates for customized product offerings, or the cost of serving customers), ABCM designers and users should develop targeted, precise definitions of required data and how the resulting information will be used.

Project Team

Developing a cross-functional perspective and application of ABCM begins with the project team. It is imperative that the team include key individuals from various functional and management levels if the ABCM project is to be seen as more than just another finance initiative.

While team structures can and do vary, several basic roles need to be assigned if the ABCM project is to proceed smoothly. A typical project structure might include: project sponsor, steering committee, project manager, functional or departmental business experts, a core team, and a project analyst. This structure assigns accountability and responsibility for the ABCM results to all levels of management. This project team structure can be a major factor in removing existing barriers and communicating the strategic goals of the ABCM system. Finally, it provides *top-down* communication of individual accountability for the project results and emphasizes senior management involvement.

ABCM Education and Training

Training is an important tool of implementation because much of the analysis is different from the analysis used in traditional cost accounting. Three levels of education and training must be considered early in any ABCM project: (1) senior management, (2) users, and (3) project team members. Each of these groups and their unique educational needs should be specifically addressed for the ABCM project to be successful. The extent of training will vary depending on the existing skills and knowledge of various participants as well as their degree of interaction with or dependence on the system.

2. Determining Financial and Operational Resources

Activity costs are calculated by determining the cost of the resources consumed by the performance of the activity. An important step in ABCM implementation, therefore, is to understand and define the operational and financial resources consumed by an activity, such as equipment, technology, facilities, materials, labor, supplies, and any other items used in the performance of a specific activity. The objectives of the resource analysis phase of the ABCM initiative are understanding the organization's financial and operational resources and identifying the resource drivers.

General Ledger and Payroll Information

The general ledger is the primary source of cost information for the ABC model. Most ledgers are structured in a hierarchy of accounts and subaccounts. Typical accounts might include labor, depreciation, occupancy, and material. Subaccounts contain more detailed account information; for instance, labor subaccounts might be contract labor, benefits, overtime, and vacation.

Payroll information is needed when it becomes necessary to identify unique labor classifications for a given cost center. For example, if tool and die repair machinists and machine operators were in the same cost center, then the payroll system would be used to differentiate the resources, so that their cost would be assigned to their respective activities.

Labor and Nonlabor Resource Templates

The key data elements of operation resources are departmental labor and nonlabor costs. A typical labor template might include the labor classification, compensation level, skill level, department, hours worked, or percent of time by activity. This template does not need to include individual names but should instead focus on general types of labor used, where it is deployed, and the activities and outcomes it supports.

In a related way, nonlabor templates can be developed that identify the placement, cost, capacity, and current use of material, equipment, occupancy, supplies, and related support costs. To the extent possible, nonlabor costs should be directly assigned to activities that consume them. Creating data tables will improve the efficiency and usefulness of the ABCM database, serving as a support for both implementation and maintenance of the ABCM system.

Resource Hierarchy

Classifying resources by assigning attributes and organizing them into a hierarchy provides a useful way of viewing information and making decisions. This is depicted in Exhibit 1.3. The exhibit illustrates how resources are classified and consumed by different levels of the service parts operations of a major automobile manufacturer. Identifying the outputs at each level of the organization, as well as the type and number of resources consumed, is a key technique of ABCM system design.

3. Defining Activities and Processes

In the cost model conceptual design step, activities and activity drivers must be identified. Regardless of an organization's size or number of employees, an almost unlimited set of activities might be selected.

Driven by defined goals and required information, the choice and number of

EXHIBIT 1.3   ABC Classification of Resource Costs

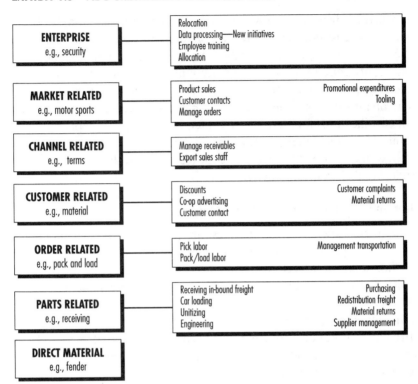

activities will vary based on the use of the information. For instance, detailed definitions of activities often are not necessary to improve product cost accuracy or decision making. More detailed activity cost data is necessary for operation managers who want to use this information to better manage resources.

A process is then defined as a collection of related activities. The objectives served by activity and process analysis include the following: identifying activities and business, identifying processes, defining outputs and output measures, defining activity attributes, and identifying activity cost drivers.

Several core tools and techniques typically used in this effort are discussed in the following subsections.

Universal Classification Scheme

The Universal Process Classification Scheme can be used to assist in classifying the activities within an organization into the correct business processes.[4] The scheme, illustrated in Exhibit 1.4, contains 13 business processes that apply to almost any organization in any market.

The first seven processes are operating processes companies follow to de-

EXHIBIT 1.4   Universal Process Classification Scheme

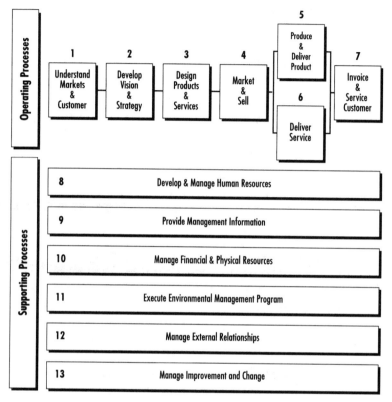

Source: Arthur Andersen and International Benchmarking Clearinghouse.

velop and move products and services to market. These processes include understanding markets and customers, designing products and services, and marketing and selling. The last six processes are management and support processes that make it possible for the organization to perform its operating processes effectively. These processes include human resources management, information systems management, and finance and accounting.

Organizations use the process classification scheme for different purposes such as determining the scope of their ABCM analysis or for benchmarking purposes. The scope will be dictated by the organization's objectives and the questions it wants to answer based on the ABCM information.

Activity Dictionary

An activity dictionary is an absolutely critical tool in any ABCM project. It is a comprehensive listing of all definitive activities including descriptions, attribute tags (if any), cost drivers, suppliers, customers, and any input and output measures. The dictionary also serves as an effective communication tool when activity analysis worksheets are distributed to employees.

Activity Analysis Worksheets

Once the activity dictionary is completed, the next step is to gather information from the organization's employees regarding how much time they spend on each major activity. This step is usually performed using activity analysis worksheets. Activity data can be derived from a variety of different sources including operational records, brainstorming, procedures manuals, quality studies, job descriptions, labor reports, process charts, interviews, and workshops. The method chosen depends on the amount of time available to complete the work as well as the resources (people and software) dedicated to activity identification and analysis at the individual level.

Activity Attribute Analysis

Organizations interested in using ABCM for performance improvement can use grading methods to evaluate the activities that contribute to the output of goods and services. These grading methods assess whether the activities are necessary, if they support critical strategic success factors, or if they are performed efficiently. Using activity attribute analysis creates an orderly way of reporting. Attributes quantify different aspects of business processes, providing multiple views with which to focus, prioritize, analyze, and measure organizational efforts and outcomes.

Process Mapping

Process mapping involves documenting the sequence of steps different functional units undertake to convert inputs to outputs for a specific process or subprocess. A process map shows the units involved in the process, the steps performed, and the key decisions made.

ABCM process maps are used to define the sequence of activities in an organization and the associated cost per activity. This alignment of activity-based data with the process flows provides organizations with important information about improvement opportunities.

Process Overview Form

To help analyze and organize process mapping efforts, organizations can use a process overview form. The process overview form lists the process and its associated vital information such as the mission, inputs, outputs, departments, and performance measures.

4. Developing a Cost Model Conceptual Design

The conceptual design phase is probably the most critical stage, because the model design determines what data are to be included and how the results will be used. The ABCM system must be designed to meet the needs and requirements of the organization. The purpose and use of the system will drive both the amount of information to be collected and the detail to which it must be obtained.

Core tools and techniques used to improve the effectiveness of this step include system design considerations, converting the general ledger and payroll detail into resource cost elements, and cost-flow diagrams.

System Design Considerations

In a product or service cost application, the minimum base information that must be collected on a forward-looking basis for a specified period of time (i.e., month, quarter, year) includes:

- Actual resources expended
- How people spend their time on activities
- How machine time is spent on activities
- How facilities were used on or supported activities
- How other costs were traced to activities
- Counts of activity outputs
- How activity outputs were consumed by the cost objects identified

In addition to this minimum base information requirement for product/service costing, counts and measures of activity performance, cost drivers, and benchmarks often are required for process improvement–related applications. Other issues to be considered in developing a cost model conceptual design include accuracy, frequency of update, and relevance.

The level of accuracy required by the ABCM system is dependent on the objectives of the project and limited by the accuracy and availability of the data entering the system. Frequency update is largely a function of the ABCM's purpose and use. For an ABCM system to be useful, its focus must be on the important aspects of the organization, at a level relevant to the improvement efforts and for decision making.

Converting the General Ledger and Payroll Detail to Resource Cost Elements

The next step in developing an ABCM system is to determine the organization's current labor-based activities and costs as well as the resources it consumes.

This begins with an in-depth review of the general ledger and payroll system for labor-based costs. These two systems provide the cost data for the ABCM model. The payroll system comes into play when labor within a cost center needs to be uniquely defined, something the ledger usually does not provide.

Cost-Flow Diagram

The cost-flow diagram is a graphical depiction of the way resources, activities, and processes flow within an organization to produce outputs. The cost-flow model depicts the operational relationships as they exist at a specific point in time and as such should be updated as conditions dictate.

It is easier to make sense of the cost model flow on paper, which can then be used as the basis to create input data files for the ABC system software. Approximately 75 percent of all data elements identified by the cost-flow diagram are nonfinancial, including driver and output volume by activity.

5. Implementing and Validating the Cost Model

The next major step in the ABCM project is to implement and then validate the cost model. After the data have been gathered and organized, and the conceptual design completed, the organization is ready to input the data into a software model. The objectives pursued during this stage reflect its executable nature and the need to reaffirm the conceptual design through application and validation. The objectives of this implementation stage include importing data into the cost model and validating cost model data.

Achieving these objectives requires the use of a set of core tools and techniques that emphasize the reliability of the cost data, specifically structuring data in the cost model, importing data into the cost model, and validating cost model data.

Structuring Data in the Cost Model

Loading the ABCM software model generally involves creating definitions and structures within the software for resources, activities, and the cost objects. The links for these structures are created by defining the driver relationships and their quantities consumed. Similarly, the relationship of activities to other activities, as well as activities to cost objects, must be defined within the software.

This task is accomplished by entering the information into the software application to define the relationships and the values underlying the relationships (e.g., driver quantities). A typical example of an ABCM model structure is presented in Exhibit 1.5.

EXHIBIT 1.5   ABCM Model Structure

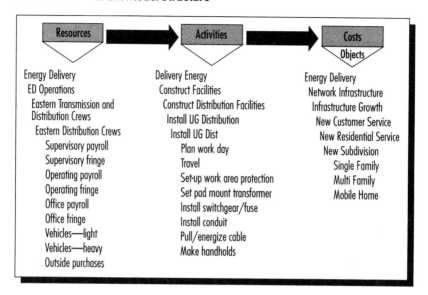

Importing Data into the Cost Model

Once the structure of the cost model has been created, the data can be loaded. There is always a cost associated with entering the data, but this cost varies with the design of the system and the data sources. The two basic ways to load data into the system are through (1) automated downloads and (2) manual entry.

In most instances, commercially available ABCM software permits operational and financial data to be imported from other information systems. The electronic transfer of data is ideal when data already exists in an electronic format that is compatible with, or easily converted to, the ABCM model format.

The most time consuming, yet most flexible, alternative to inputting data into the ABCM database is manually keying the information directly into the system. As a general rule, however, an automated interface should be employed whenever possible.

Validating Cost Model Data

Once the ABCM software model is built and the data loaded, it is necessary to verify all elements of the system to ensure the model is accurate and the underlying database contains the defined data elements in the correct format and structure required for ongoing use.

The core team must be very sensitive to any system results that do not make intuitive sense. The team must rigorously test the validity of any counterintuitive results or, in other words, perform a "sanity check." Reconciliation of the model includes validation of resource, activity, and cost object data.

6. Interpreting the New Information

Once ABCM results are released, no one is likely to remain neutral about them. Given that ABCM provides a very different view of costs, the results should be analyzed with an emphasis on using them for improvement opportunities rather than having to defend them. Several core tools and techniques can be used to facilitate the interpretation of the new information including: cost/benefit matrix, root cause analysis, cost improvement plan, and cost opportunity improvement tracking form.

Cost/Benefit Matrix

A cost/benefit matrix helps management focus attention on the activities that fall under various headings, units, and responsibilities. Flexible in nature, this technique involves obtaining consensus on the value to be placed on each activity in relation to the strategic goals of the organization.

Management initially should focus on those *high-cost, low-value* activities that could be eliminated, reduced, improved, or automated to reduce the cost while increasing the value placed on the activity. *High-cost, high-benefit* activities also should be reviewed to identify ways in which costs can be reduced or improvements made in the efficiency and effectiveness of the activities.

Management should consider the *low-cost, high-benefit* activities that could be promoted, increased, or enhanced to increase their benefit to the organization. Finally, management may review the *low-cost, low-benefit* activities to determine whether improvements can be made.

Root Cause Analysis

Root cause analysis involves the identification of cost drivers and their relationships in determining what factors cause work and costs to occur. At a higher level, these relationships also are used as the basis for product and customer profitability analysis, activity-based budgeting, product and service line costing, and "what-if" scenario planning.

Root cause analysis is a popular brainstorming technique to analyze and understand what and where changes need to be made to existing processes to improve performance. Root cause analysis enables comparison of current processes against customer expectations. For example, at First Tennessee National Corporation, a regional bank-holding organization, cost management personnel who previously had applied ABCM to one operation at location A studied the same function at location B, interviewing the appropriate personnel to gain insight into the operation. Their analysis determined that processing efficiency in location B was lower than in location A.[5]

Cost Improvement Plan

Having more accurate process costs enables organizations to prioritize and set realistic cost goals for process reengineering efforts. Equally important is the ability to simulate and later track actual performance following process reengineering efforts.

Process Cost Opportunity Improvement Tracking Form

A key function is to document and monitor progress against the cost improvement plan. The process cost opportunity improvement tracking form is a tool that can be used in this effort. Generally used by department and process heads to document specific actions, a tracking form records progress in reducing specific process unit costs.

In addition to documenting the action plan designed to improve overall business process unit costs, other important aspects of the change plan need to be detailed, including quantification of expected benefits, responsibility for implementation, and the impact on other areas—both positive and negative.

7. Ensuring Ongoing System Requirements

The final step of a successful implementation is to determine how the ABCM system is to be maintained. Most ABCM implementations fail to place sufficient emphasis on installing the systems, procedures, and methods necessary to collect and report activity-based information on an ongoing basis. As a result, procedures and methods that are installed are often unresponsive to the needs of the users, difficult to update and maintain, and unreliable in the long term.

Like any information system, the ABCM information system must be updated and validated on an ongoing basis. Activities change over time. New activities are added. Drivers shift, or the measurements needed to capture them are modified over time. Improvement initiatives will likely lead to the elimination of non–value-added activities. Activity performance measures will improve and change over time. New products and services will be added; others will be discontinued. The key objectives for the maintenance phase of ABCM implementation include identifying areas for improvement to enhance the model and integrating them, establishing responsibility for ongoing model updates and maintenance, and establishing feedback on usage behavior.

To reach these objectives, a number of core tools and techniques can be deployed, including periodic systems assessments, update interviews and measurements checks, and establishing a permanent ABCM team.

Periodic Systems Assessments

Database systems constantly are being improved as computer technology and the software that drives it are changed to incorporate innovations. The result of these macrotrends is that installed systems, such as the ABCM system, need to be reassessed annually to determine if they are still the best fit for the organization.

New activities and a modified implementation plan will be generated by a decision to shift systems. In the end, the decision made at the end of the systems assessment will be based on the trade-offs between the cost to shift to an improved ABCM system vs. the benefits (i.e., improved speed, efficiency, capabilities, reduced update costs) that should ensue.

Update Interviews and Measurement Checks

Depending on the frequency of reporting, individual interviews and measurement checks should be updated. Some organizations have decided to let a year pass between reviews and updates, coupling the revision of the ABCM data to the budget process that is already part of the corporate activities. Others have created monthly or quarterly data collection efforts using tools, such as employee time reports to update the ABCM database constantly.

Update interviews and data from activity analysis need not be as exhaustive as the initial implementation interviews. The advantage of this targeted approach is that it increases the comparability of the data collected, reduces the time needed to validate the information, and identifies new activities or activities no longer performed efficiently.

ABCM Team

Once a satisfactory ABCM system is running and is being used on a regular basis by managers across the organization, the project team must continue to provide training for new employees, assess software or systems changes, and execute update initiatives. Maintaining the reliability and accuracy of the system requires ongoing review, analysis, and modification as organizational needs and realities change.

To ensure continuity in these core areas, at least two of the original ABCM core team members should remain actively involved on the permanent ABCM team. Having rotating members on the team has proven to be a successful approach for many companies because it results in increased awareness and interest in the system required to obtain and retain needed resources.

SUMMARY

While this chapter provides a basic summary of the core tools and techniques typically used to improve the ABCM implementation process, it should not be considered all inclusive. Every ABCM implementation is different, and the emphasis and elements to be covered are specific to the applications and the organization.

NOTES

1. Steve Player and David Keys, *Activity-Based Management: Arthur Andersen's Lessons from the ABM Battlefield,* 2nd ed. (New York: John Wiley & Sons, 1999).
2. *Ibid.*
3. *Ibid.*
4. The Process Classification Scheme was developed by Arthur Andersen, the International Benchmarking Clearinghouse and other leading companies.
5. Best Practices in Activity-Based Management; Phase I. Final Report (Houston: APQC, 1995).

ABOUT THE AUTHORS

Randolf Holst is the Research Director for Cost Management with Arthur Andersen. He is based in Dallas.

Robert J. Savage is a Senior Manager with Arthur Andersen's Advanced Cost Management Team. He is based in New Jersey.

2

BEST PRACTICES IN ACTIVITY-BASED MANAGEMENT

Matthew W. Kolb and Joseph P. Donnelly

In the last decade, organizations have increasingly recognized the value of activity-based management (ABM) and undertaken initiatives to implement ABM in their organizations. According to a survey completed by the Institute of Management Accountants in 1992, fewer than 100 ABM initiatives were under way in 1992. By the end of 1998, over 20,000 organizations are estimated to have initiated ABM implementations.

Since 1994, the American Productivity & Quality Center (APQC), Arthur Andersen and its research partners have collaborated to conduct and publish research on the best practices in the application, development, and use of activity-based management information systems and practices.

Since the first ABM Best Practice site visit in early 1995 (Current Inc. in Colorado Springs on February 15, 1995) until the most recent (Rocketdyne in Huntington Beach on November 6, 1998), a total of 45 site visits have been conducted with organizations that have achieved success with their ABM implementations. These 45 best practice partners have included distributors, manufacturing companies, service organizations, government agencies, utilities, retail sales organizations, telecommunications, financial institutions, and government contractors. Applications of ABM have ranged from product cost, updated annually, to full-scale enterprise-wide implementations covering the entire cost structure of an entire company, updated continuously. The base of knowledge is extensive.

While the focus of the site visits varied among the three completed ABM best practice studies and within each individual study, the process of collecting data and information for each study remained consistent. Survey questionnaires were designed to collect consistent quantitative and qualitative ABM survey data from each of the companies. In addition to collecting information about each specific area of study, site visits guidelines and questionnaires were designed to review and discuss key success factors, systems, and methods of reporting and general application and use. Each of the site visits made contributions to the ABM knowledge base that went well beyond the specific area of study and focus. Common themes and best practices have been apparent.

SEVEN COMMANDMENTS FOR ABM

Best practice companies emphasize similar requirements and experiences of success. Certain messages and best practices identified are so prevalent they have been identified as the Seven Commandments for a successful ABM initiative.

1. Management Commitment and Priority

Leadership commitment and support are critical success factors to an ABM implementation. Commitment and priority should not be stated only in words but also demonstrated through the commitment of resources and, more important, the commitment of time required to be involved in the ABM initiative. At best practice companies, management is deemed to include senior-level executives, operating and line managers, and cost center or department function managers.

For example, The Marmon Group, a $6 billion association of more than 65 service and manufacturing companies operating worldwide, has consistently outperformed the Fortune 500 averages with managers continuously striving for better ways to understand and improve their businesses. R. A. Pritzker, president of The Marmon Group, supports each company's objectives and the means to achieve those goals using ABM systems. Pritzker is a good example of a senior executive willing to commit personal time, effort, and knowledge to the ABM initiative. According to Pritzker, "ABM has done more in the past two years for the companies' understanding their costs than I have been able to achieve in the last 40 years."[1] Supportive top management includes not only top management of a company but also top management of the plant or facility in which ABM is implemented.

Management commitment and priority are visible and evidenced by the scope and breadth of training, level of ABM sponsorship, frequency of involvement by senior and operations managers, and percentage of total personnel involved in the implementation. Management commitment and priority are also evident in their involvement in the design of the information system, including the accuracy of information, level of detail and specificity, frequency of update, ease of access and use, flexibility, and relevance.

2. Priority, Application and Use

ABM initiatives are successful when they meet the business information needs of the organization. Information becomes valuable when it contributes to meeting the goals, objectives, and strategy of the organization. The failure to link the ABM system to what is important to the organizations is fatal. Build it and they will come is an oxymoron in the ABM world. The ABM system must be built to meet the specific needs and priorities of the organization. The purpose and expected results must be articulated, documented, and understood before an ABM initiative is undertaken.

ABM information must have wide use and applicability. It may be used to determine product or customer profitability, benchmark, measure performance, cut costs, increase revenue, budget, evaluate outsourcing alternatives, consolidate operations, price/bid products and services, and effect strategy deployment. Priorities, needs, and requirements at individual organizations are widespread and vary considerably over time. Best practice companies align the use and application of ABM information to meet a business need and to solve a business problem.

Best practice companies have learned single and limited use of ABM information fails to capture the full value and potential of the activity-based information. Therefore, they consistently seek new applications and uses of activity-based management information. This migration is important because the cost of maintaining ongoing systems must be balanced against the benefits provided.

Another perspective is expanding access to ABM information. Best practice companies understand the value of ABM information is created when people use the information to improve organizational performance. Many people acting on ABM information creates value. Therefore, focused efforts should be undertaken to increase the base of people who access and use ABM information.

3. Consistent Application of ABM Methodology

Best practice companies consistently apply generally accepted ABM methods, procedures, terms, techniques, and practices. Examples include consistent use of the CAM-I Cross (a graph outlining the relationship of activity-based costing [ABC] and ABM with an intersection at the activity level) (see Chapter 3 for greater detail), common activity dictionaries, and standard process classification frameworks. Best practice companies emphasize consistency and comparability in report design. Collection and analysis of cost from multiple units is done systematically. Investments made in common definitions, common coding, and consistent application of cost assignment methods help to ensure comparability.

Consistent application of ABM methodology also includes the consistent use of data collection techniques and methods. Best practice companies have used a variety of data collection methods including (1) manager interviews, (2) worker interviews, (3) questionnaires, (4) existing documentation, (5) observations, (6) group-based interviews, (7) work measurement, and (8) process mapping.

4. Cost Efficient and Reliable Reporting Systems

Best practice companies place significant emphasis on installing the systems, procedures, and methods necessary to collect and report activity-based information on a regular basis. The frequency of ABM reporting ranges from continuous real time to periodically. In general, those organizations using ABM information on a more tactical level, in such applications as process improvement, cost control, measuring performance, tend to report information more frequently and in more detail.

Best practice companies that use the information in more strategic applications, such as product cost and customer profitability, tend to report information less frequently but still on a regular basis. Either way, the systems, procedures, and methods installed must be responsive to the needs of the users, easy to update and maintain, reliable, and cost efficient.

Best practice companies place significant emphasis on systems and reporting for two reasons—cost and timeliness. First, ABM systems not integrated and linked to the existing financial and operations systems of the company can be difficult and expensive to operate and maintain. Second, linkage to and integration with existing systems ensures ABM reports are available at the same or nearly the same time as other financial and operating reports.

5. Link to Improvement Initiatives, Goals and Performance Measures, and the Operating Environment

ABM information provides value and benefit to the organization when it is used to make better decisions and to improve processes. ABM users are more likely to embrace tools that help them achieve their goals. Therefore, best practice companies recognize linking ABM information to goals and objectives and improvement initiatives is vital.

To support benchmarking and improvement initiatives, best practice companies design ABM systems so users can compare relevant internal cost and performance measures with externally driven targets. ABM systems can be designed to compare internal costs and measures with internal and external standards and requirements. Managers use comparative reports to set standards or highlight gaps for a particular activity or business process. System design specifications might take into account such techniques as benchmarking, best practices evaluation, and target costing.

6. Link to Incentives

Linkage to compensation is included as a best practice primarily because of its importance in achieving a successful ABM implementation. Best practice companies agree that compensation drives behavior in an organization and that linking information to compensation is powerful. While most of the best practice companies indicate this linkage as a priority for the future, few have linked ABM information to compensation in any kind of meaningful way. Examples are rare, and best practice in this area is just evolving and emerging.

When linked to compensation, activity-based management information systems are pay-for-performance models of compensation and reward. Activity costs and activity outputs, taken together, are a basic and fundamental measure of productivity and efficiency. In many respects, compensation has always been linked to activities. Perhaps the most obvious link is with the employee's paycheck. Paychecks are compensation to employees for performing business activities. Activities requiring significant skill levels or specialized knowledge always have been compensated at higher levels than activities requiring minimal knowledge or skill.

7. Training and Education

Training and education are critical factors for success because ABM information is of value only when people use the information to make better decisions and to improve processes and activities. Just as people are trained to use traditional financial information, people also must be trained in the application and use of ABM information. Best practice companies will use training and education to foster a cost management culture throughout the organization.

Best practice companies tend to be learning organizations that initiate extensive, broad-based, and multilevel training and cross-functional learning. Training beyond the traditional financial organization structure is required to enable people to apply activity management skills in their specific work situation. The commitment and emphasis on training and education is demonstrated in the wide use of ABM knowledge centers or centers of excellence.

The Defense Logistics Agency (DLA), a 55,000-person organization from the public sector (Department of Defense), demonstrates best practices in the area of training ABM implementation teams.[2] The activity-based project at DLA included all activities and processes associated with the supply operations, including procurement, contract management, and the distribution of over 4 million line items of supply to all four branches of the U.S. military. This agency-wide ABM initiative was staffed completely with internal personnel; therefore, knowledge transfer was critical.

The skill set and knowledge required to effectively implement ABM required that DLA develop training material to effectively transfer information and knowledge. The following are key elements of its ABM training:

- Commercially available, generic ABM training materials were purchased and customized to fit the agency's existing tools, techniques, methods and procedures.
- Examples and exercises were designed to contribute to understanding the existing work situation facing agency personnel.
- Over 90 percent of the training was delivered by a small group of instructors to ensure a consistent training message.
- The two-day ABM project team training was designed in a progressive manner with three modules that were attended only by those who wanted specific knowledge from each session.

Training delivered in this manner ensured all levels in the organization received a consistent but targeted message.

Interrelation of the Seven Commandments

The Seven Commandments are related and cannot exist independently of each other. Management commitment and involvement is conditioned by demonstrating value. Priority, application, and use of ABM information to meet a business need or solve a business problem are essential to demonstrate value. Consistent ABM methodology is a necessary and important part of making the ABM initiative successful. Systems and methods are required and necessary to report ABM information and make it available for people to use. Linking ABM to improvement initiatives, operating goals, and performance measures gives people a reason to use the information. Linkage to compensation gives them the incentive to use the information, and training and education provides the knowledge and skill to use the information effectively.

UNCOVERING BEST PRACTICES AND EMERGING TRENDS

Arthur Andersen and the APQC collaborated to conduct and publish a series of best practices research projects on ABM implementations. Key areas of focus include revenue enhancement, results and benefits, activity-based budgeting, systems, reporting, and transfer of ownership. Points from these studies follow.

Revenue Enhancement

- Customer profitability is the dominant first application.
- Improvement efforts are directed toward changing customer behaviors.
- Revenues are enhanced through alternative pricing models.
- ABM is used at both ends of the supply chain to enhance revenues.

As businesses gain control over their costs and the need for top-line revenue growth becomes a pressing issue for management, ABM has evolved into a powerful tool to help companies grow. Early indications have been very positive for companies taking this cost management approach to growing revenues. Previous ABM studies indicate that, in some cases, revenue increases have exceeded 700 percent. Revenue enhancement is driven by a company's ability to identify, create, and retain customers, segments, markets, or channels. To be successful, companies must focus on sustainable profitable revenue growth. ABM enables an understanding of what products and services profitably grow revenue.

Best practice companies are using ABM to understand selling activities and the associated cost to serve customer segments, to design menu pricing systems to bill for add-on products or services, and to analyze peaks and valleys in activity levels. They grow revenues by identifying logical follow-up sales opportunities or by designing their services to perform activities more efficiently than their customers, thus assuming added responsibility in the supply chain. Cost management is used as a key tool in explaining how their products and services provide higher value and lower total cost for customers.

Products and services are provided to markets and customers through various distribution channels or contractual relationships. Because products, services, and customers consume resources at different rates and require different levels of support, costs and profitability of different customers and markets segments must be determined accurately and understood. Customer profitability includes all of the costs to produce, design, support, distribute, and service after the sale. These costs are associated with individual customers, customer segments, customer groups, or distribution channels. This information is vital for selecting the individual and segmented markets where an organization competes and for pricing in those markets. Insights into significant "hidden" costs emerge from undertaking ABM-based customer profitability analyses.

For example, Owens & Minor, a Fortune 500 wholesaler-distributor of medical and surgical supplies, is attempting to follow patients as they migrate to surgery centers and outpatient clinics for services once performed in acute care hospitals. Owens & Minor attempts to maintain profitability in all cases by charging the appropriate service fees. Since some types of customers are more expensive to service, various pricing structures exist based on their activity expenses.

ABM forms the basis for Owens & Minor's activity-based pricing program called CostTrack[SM].[3] This is a program where customers choose from a menu of services to create a distribution program to meet their needs. The more efficient customers are able to enjoy lower distribution fees and the less efficient customers are given assistance to improve their efficiencies. Owens & Minor is now incorporating low-value activities into the menu of services and working with customers to eliminate any activity deemed not essential.

All prices for services are based on ABM. ABM studies are performed in all of its distribution centers to form the basis of the pricing. With ABM, the services are separated from product prices and an agreed-on profit is negotiated with the customers. Owens & Minor uses an open-book policy to share actual expense levels with customers. Owens & Minor therefore is able to offer competitive prices for their services.

Measuring Results and Benefits

- Measurement of results and benefits is application specific.
- Cost savings are identified and classified by type.
- Measuring the progress of the ABM initiative is becoming a priority.

Management expects to see benefits in return for its investments in information systems. Value is achieved when the users of the information are able to make better decisions and improve the effectiveness and efficiency of the organization's processes and activities. While organizations can articulate and define the resources and costs associated with implementing ABM, measuring enhanced value requires added discipline.

The value and benefit of ABM can be measured only by the decisions, actions taken based on the knowledge and information provided. Because ABM information is an enabler that drives and supports improvement initiatives and decision making, it can be difficult to measure and quantify its role separately. The result of some decisions can be quantified while the results of others cannot. ABM can measure the results of decisions and improvements, regardless of the improvement method or acronym that gets credit (i.e., TQM, Six Sigma). Most organizations view ABM as a tool and enabler to improvement and decision making.

The dollar quantification makes this information tool useful. Organizations and the people who manage them are bottom-line driven, and dollars are the language of business and the predominant measurement of choice. The dollar measurement seems to inspire people to action. The ABM information system tracks improvement and changes to judge the result of decisions and improvement efforts.

For example, Motorola calculates a return on investment to measure the overall performance of ABM.[4] Improvements in cycle time, equipment utilization, on-time delivery, and quality are linked to this dollar-based financial measure. Non–value-added activities are tracked in dollars using a simple pie chart. These costs are categorized according to activity area, such as setup, waiting time, inspection, and so on. A spreadsheet then is prepared to break down each category into specific activities. Beside each activity, the cost drivers are identified, along with actions to be taken to eliminate or reduce the cost.

Best practices for performing meaningful cost-benefit analyses are still emerging as quantifying the value of information can be difficult. Because activity-based management information drives and supports all improvement initiatives, regardless of acronym, it can play an important role as an improvement and decision-making tool. It can provide a way for organizations to develop procedures, practices, and methods for measuring and qualifying benefits from their financial and operating systems.

Activity-Based Budgeting

- Activity-based budgeting (ABB) is most commonly used to establish standards.
- Organizations align activities to strategic and operating plans.
- Accountability is at the process level.

Planning and budgeting have been viewed as key strategic areas where finance can add value within companies. Yet traditional budgeting processes often fail due to a focus on resources rather than on the activity these resources could produce. To compensate for the weaknesses in traditional systems, leading companies are expanding activity-based systems to include ABB. Specifically, ABB uses an activity-based management model as a framework to translate output demands and required activities. These activities also can be used to determine resource levels. In addition to more accurately forecasting nondirect overhead cost, activity-based management can be used to anticipate the impact of process improvement on resource utilization. Also, because it becomes a baseline for measuring change, ABB can be used to evaluate the impact of new investments.

Through ABB, the ABM system is linked to operations, giving managers the information necessary to determine supply and practical capacity in future periods. Budgetary planning and control is the most visible of accounting information in the management control process. By helping set standards of performance and providing feedback by means of variance reports, the accountant supplies much of the fundamental information required for overall planning and control.

An important feature of ABB is the strengthening of the interface between planning and budgeting. ABB allows the planning guideline to be broken down to the level of detail required to provide objectives for individual activities within the business.

Managers must have the right tools to help them to deploy increasingly scarce resources in today's rapidly changing business environment. The tools must not only help to allocate the optimum level of resources that the business needs to achieve its business vision, strategic goals, and objectives for the year ahead and beyond, but they must do so in a way that gains maximum management support.

By using ABB information, the user can arguably effect a change in the process before the process takes place. This is a very important concept because after the activity has been performed and the cost has been totaled, there is nothing that can be done to change the cost incurred; it is done. Taking a preemptive position with the activities and costs can result in a more favorable outcome.

Systems

- Companies are increasingly investing resources in systems integration and systems linkages.

- Data integrity is given high priority by best practice firms.
- Access to information is viewed as a key issue in the successful use of ABM information systems.
- The information system resource commitments made by best practice companies are appropriate to the decision applications.

ABM best practice companies place significant emphasis on installing systems, procedures, and methods to collect and report activity-based information on an ongoing basis. ABM systems that are not integrated and linked to the existing financial and operations systems of the company are difficult and expensive to update and maintain. Linkage and integration to existing systems ensures ABM reports are available near the same time as other financial and operating reports.

Systems integration can occur at different levels—across one organization (by functions, regions, processes, or the enterprise as a whole) or across multiple organizations. Efficient customer response (ECR) is a good example of systems integration across the value chain (suppliers, producers, distributors, retailers, etc.).

The Activity-Based Information System at BellSouth Telecommunications is an example of a large-scale fully integrated system. The basic system architecture is a database (Oracle/Visual Basic application running in a client/server environment) linked to and integrated with source financial (cost) transactions and operational information and transactions from existing information and reporting systems.[5]

Reporting

- Customization of reports is viewed as an ongoing part of systems development.
- There is greater recognition of the benefits of reports comparing costs (and other variables) across multiple units.
- Reports at best practice companies give high priority to value creation.
- Innovative data display/user interface is viewed as a high priority.

ABM information is communicated to the organization through reports, reporting capability, and access to information contained in databases. Organizations design and implement ABM reports and reporting capability to provide cost and performance information about significant activities, the cost of products, services, customers, distribution channels, and other organization-specific cost objectives. They also design reports and reporting capability to track the resource and activity drivers used to trace, assign, and allocate costs. Reports and reporting capability highlight the costs for non–value-added activities and identify opportunities.

At best practice companies, reports are designed so users can view information from many perspectives, in differing formats, and in relationship to other data. Many best practice organizations use flexible executive information systems (EIS) to generate reports and information on-line to users. Graphical and other innovative report displays are used to illustrate important aspects of reports.

For example, the reporting capability at Caterpillar provides both summarized reports of product cost by prime vehicle and drill-down capability to offer all the details of the components making up the vehicle at the various inventoried levels. Roll-up reports of prime product cost with supporting detail are available down to the lowest nut-and-bolt level.[6]

Transfer of Ownership

- Linking ABM information to operational goals/objectives and improvement initiatives is crucial for success.
- Successful pilot efforts prove the value of ABM initiatives through early wins.
- ABM implementations should be operationally funded and driven.
- Linking ABM information systems to compensation encourages operational and user ownership.

The real value and power of ABM comes from the knowledge and information leading to better decisions and improvements. If people in the organization do not use the information (regardless of their reason), the only results realized are the costs of development and implementation and the ongoing cost of maintaining the system until it is retired. Nothing may be more important to a successful ABM implementation than achieving ownership and accountability by the people who use ABM information to make decisions and effect changes in the organization. Likewise, nothing may be more difficult to achieve. People are comfortable with the systems they currently use; new systems and processes cause a feeling of discomfort and uncertainty until they are understood.

Many of the ABM best practices developed in leading-edge firms reflect the lessons learned from managing the ABM project through its stages and their pitfalls. For each of these organizations, the key has been continuing to strive for improvement in the quality, relevance, and action-ability of their ABM systems. Responding to user demands and seeking out the criticisms and concerns that can undermine the system leads to best practice performance for adopting organizations. Achieving ABM best practice is a journey, not a destination.

SUMMARY

After many years of experiments, successes, failures, and learning, ABM systems are proving they are here to stay. Much more than another form of accounting, ABM in best practice companies lies at the heart of the decision-support process. Integrating ABM within the total information and management control system of the organization can lead to quantum improvements as vital links between operations and strategy, processes and customers, value and cost are defined, measured, and understood.

Successful implementation of ABM will not look the same in every organization or follow the same path. Tailored to the unique strategy, structure, and capabilities and needs of the firm, ABM is a universal concept. ABM systems can take on a multitude of shapes and uses. ABM data should meet the needs of the company's decision makers and support their efforts to create value for stakeholders. An important measure of ABM success, then, is its use. ABM should drive measurable change across the organization as new opportunities and innovative solutions to problems are revealed.

As best practice companies have found, the ultimate payback for their ABM investment comes when the system achieves full integration with other information and management support systems and the process is fully embraced by the organization. Integration is not an end point, though. It is, rather, a significant milestone in the journey to create a dynamic and relevant knowledge base on which to build and support a sustainable competitive advantage. ABM is intricately linked to the growth and long-term health of the organization.

NOTES

1. Steve Player and David Keys. *Activity-Based Management: Arthur Andersen's Lessons from the ABM Battlefield,* 2nd ed. (New York: John Wiley & Sons, 1999).

2. Best Practices in Activity-Based Management: Phase I Final Report (Houston: APQC, 1995).

3. Steve Player and James W. Gibson. Winning the Profitability Battle: Activity-Based Management in Wholesale Distribution (Washington, DC: NAW, 1998).

4. Best Practices in ABM (see #2).

5. Best Practices in ABM: Phase II Final Report (Houston: Arthur Andersen and APQC, 1997).

6. *Ibid.*

ABOUT THE AUTHORS

Matthew W. Kolb is a Senior Manager with Arthur Andersen's Advanced Cost Management Team. He is based in Los Angeles.

Joseph P. Donnelly is a Senior Manager with Arthur Andersen's Advanced Cost Management Team. He is based in Detroit.

For those of you who would like full copies of the detailed ABM Best Practice Reports, please contact the American Productivity & Quality Center (APQC) in Houston, Texas.

3

CONVERGENCE OF ENTERPRISE SOFTWARE ON ACTIVITY-BASED COSTING

Steve Player and Charles A. Marx, Jr.

In researching the enterprise resource planning (ERP) software marketplace, *Information Week* recently noted that "now comes the next wave in ERP development as companies build out analysis, forecasting, and other adjunct systems to cut costs and improve customer service."[1] Recent developments regarding activity-based cost management (ABCM) clearly highlight this rapidly emerging trend.

Stephen R. Covey, author of *The Seven Habits of Highly Effective People* and *Principle-Centered Leadership,* helps explain why. Covey notes, "Those who look deeply into the process of activity-based management will find that it is an area of management that will empower them with the solid information about their organization that *enables* them to exercise leadership and wisdom in decision making."[2] Covey's words are important to those who doubt the applicability of activity-based management (ABM). He notes, "ABM is not just mere theory. It points with laser clarity to the practical. ABM gives you the operational guts to meet the leadership challenge and to see and seize your opportunities."[3]

As the market for enterprise application software shifts into the post–Year 2000 era, the focus moves beyond transactional processing to introduce higher value-added uses of information. A key target is the focus on analytical applications, such as activity-based cost and performance management. Currently, a number of PC-based tools inhabit these application spaces and have spurred developments over the last decade. This push for value-added information has created an unusual convergence on this activity-based costing application space by the enterprise software vendors, the PC-based tools and the on-line analytical processing (OLAP) tools.

Previously each of these vendors had executed its own strategy to achieve market dominance. The entry of powerful enterprise vendors, such as SAP, PeopleSoft, Oracle, J. D. Edwards, and Baan, have raised questions as to the long-term viability of the commercial best-of-breed cost management vendors. While these different forces have been drifting toward each other, the playing field changed dramatically on September 9, 1998, when SAP announced it had made a substantial equity investment in ABC Technologies to fund the joint development of ABCM solutions. That development ushered in an era of convergence. In this redefined market space, understanding customer needs may be as important as sheer size and financial resources.

This chapter examines this convergence of enterprise applications on the ABCM marketplace. It explains (1) the business reasons why companies are implementing ABCM, (2) why companies need multiple views of cost information, (3) the difference between strategic activity-based costing (ABC) and operational ABM, (4) the recent developments that have occurred to evidence this convergence, and (5) the factors that should be considered as companies launch ABCM initiatives.

WHY COMPANIES IMPLEMENT ABCM

Companies choose to implement ABCM for a number of reasons, ranging from strategic to operational in nature. (See Exhibit 3.1 for a listing of implementation reasons.) In essence, implementation efforts focus on increasing the value provided to shareholders by optimizing profitability.

In many cases chief executive officers review the size of the investments approved to implement ERP solutions and are shocked to find these systems merely provide the same basic cost management tools available since the 1960s. While advancements appear in areas such as supply chain management and sales force automation, most ERP systems have done little to improve the basic costing tools. Most top management teams expect leading vendors to provide state-of-art advanced cost management solutions, which clearly includes ABCM. In many cases, aggressive go-live schedules push functionalities such as advanced costing or ABCM to a next-phase activity.

Benefits of Using ABCM

As the magnitude of ABCM uses implies, there are many benefits to using this approach. These can be inferred from the list in Exhibit 3.1. Some warranting special mention are ABCM's use in growing revenues, providing multidimensional costing, scaleability, and use in benchmarking. In addition to Covey, its proponents include Michael Porter, Carla O'Dell, Tom Peters, and Peter Drucker. The dramatic benefits of using ABCM to enhance revenues is seen in two examples. Owens & Minor, a Fortune 500 distributor of medical sup-

EXHIBIT 3.1   Reasons Companies Implement Activity-Based Cost Management

Profitability/Pricing	**Attribute Analysis**
Product/service profitability analysis	Core, sustaining, and discretionary
Distribution channel profitability analysis	attributes
Customer profitability analysis	Four-quadrant analysis (important/
Market segment profitability analysis	urgent/not)
Product mix rationalization	Value-added (non–value-added) analysis
Estimating or bidding on customer work	Cost of quality
Supporting intercompany charge-outs on	Time variability analysis (fixed vs.
shared services	variable, input batch)
Pricing products	Primary vs. secondary activity analysis
	Mission-critical analysis
Process Improvement	
Business process modeling	**Strategic Decisions**
Supporting total quality initiatives	Strategic planning
Supporting, focusing, or quantifying	Strategy deployment
improvement initiatives	Consolidating operations analysis
Moving or replicating operations	Coordinating new product introductions
Defining accountability or responsibility	Acquisition analysis
for activities	Growing revenues
Cost Analysis	**Benchmarking**
Target costing	Internal benchmarking
Operational cost reduction	External benchmarking
Strategic cost reduction	Process-based costing
Understanding cost drivers	Activity-based performance measurement
Life-cycle costing	
Evaluating outsourcing	**Operations Analysis**
Cost driver analysis	What-if analysis
Inventory valuation	Project management
	Capacity management
Budgeting	Constraint analysis
Activity-based budgeting	
Capital justification	

Source: Adapted from John Miller's *ABM in Daily Operations* (John Wiley, 1996) and expanded by the CAM-I Enterprise-wide ABM Interest Group.

plies, successfully used cost management to win over $200 million in new revenue through the use of its CostTrack[SM] tool, an activity-based pricing tool for customers.[4] Electronics distributor TTI has grown its automatic replenishment program from $7 million to over $100 million using ABC to explain its value proposition to customers.[5]

ABCM can provide simultaneous customer, product, and process costing. It often forms the basis for shared service charge-outs and serves as a communication vehicle for what is being requested as well as what service levels are being provided. A powerful tool, ABCM can measure the benefits of savings identified as well as track to see that those savings actually are realized.

ABCM is scaleable for use at any level—from department to division to enterprise-wide. It has even been used to measure entire value chains, such as its use to measure the improvements from the Efficient Consumer Response (ECR) initiative throughout the grocery industry including manufacturers, distributors, and retailers. ABCM enables companies to speak a common language and, thus, ensures benchmarking efforts yield appropriate measures. It serves as a powerful what-if tool for strategic analysis and a multidimensional lens to examine costs under a myriad of attributes including value-added, cost of quality, time variability, and mission critical.

As expected, with this power ABCM has many proponents. Harvard professor and noted strategist Michael Porter said, "Activities are the atoms of strategic advantage."[6] The current demand for ABCM systems seeks to view those atoms to assure proper alignment in achieving strategic aims.

Carla O'Dell, president of the American Productivity & Quality Center (APQC) and co-author of *American Business: A Two-Minute Warning,*[7] comments that "When ABM was first introduced, many people thought that it was a passing fancy that would not last. Yet ten years have seen the use of ABM grow and expand. Results of Best Practice Studies, sponsored by Arthur Andersen and the APQC show that organizations across industries are implementing ABM in record numbers, and moving aggressively toward enterprise-wide implementations." O'Dell also states, "ABM has spread from the backroom to the boardroom. It is being used to improve companies around the globe."[8]

Even the dean of management thinking, Peter Drucker, agrees. In his 1954 classic *The Practice of Management,* Drucker noted "Questions can only be answered by analyzing the activities that are needed to attain objectives."[9] He continues to support ABM, noting in *Managing for the Future* that ABM "has already unleashed an intellectual revolution. The most exciting and innovative work in management today is found in accounting theory with new concepts, new methodology—even what might be called new economic philosophy—rapidly taking shape."[10]

While ABCM is a powerful toolset, a great deal of confusion still exists. This is caused not only by the multitude of uses for activity-based costing information (as noted in Exhibit 3.1) but also by the fact that three fundamentally different views of cost information exist. Understanding these multiple views is the key to harnessing the power of ABCM.

WHY DO COMPANIES NEED MULTIPLE VIEWS OF COST INFORMATION?

One of the hardest questions for cost management is to articulate which of the three views of cost a company is trying to address. Often managers confuse these three views, thereby dramatically complicating the potential solution they seek. As Exhibit 3.2 shows, the financial, operational, and strategic views of cost focus on different variables including the time frame; users and uses of cost information; levels of aggregation; reporting frequencies; and types of measurements.

Financial View

The financial view of cost can be compared to a person facing backward, because of its adherence to the historical cost concept. The financial controller, tax manager, and treasury department use this cost information to value inventory and report to shareholders, lenders, and tax authorities. The level of information and aggregation required under this view of cost is high and often company-wide. Public reporting requirements and the need to adhere to generally accepted accounting principles (GAAP) drive the financial view, which corresponds to the reporting system most companies use. The reporting frequency is often monthly, but can be quarterly or annually. The type of measures used are almost exclusively financial.

Although this view receives the most attention, it is usually ineffective for operational and strategic uses.

Operational View

The operational view of cost focuses on the information needed for day-to-day management. Line managers, process improvement teams, quality teams, and day-to-day managers use operational cost information as an indicator of performance and to determine if activities are adding value. By understanding the root causes of problems, managers use this type of costing to identify where improvements can be made.

Since operational managers direct only finite portions of the total operation, cost information needs to be finite. Detailed data focused on a concentrated area allows managers to determine the root cause of problems. Since it is used on a frequent basis, this information must be delivered in a timely fashion. Traditional month-end reporting is not useful for this purpose, as operational managers need immediate feedback (e.g., weekly, daily, or—as in a cellular manufacturing environment—minute by minute). If a process drifts out of control, the manager must know instantly in order to take corrective action.

Interestingly, operational managers are most comfortable with, and often use, physical rather than financial measures. Examples of physical measures include number of units produced, first-pass quality, or temperature of each batch. These measures can easily be quantified in cost terms, but the operat-

EXHIBIT 3.2 Three Views of Cost

Areas of Difference	Financial	Operational	Strategic
Time Frame	**Yesterday**	**Today**	**Tomorrow**
Users of Information	Financial controllers Tax managers Treasury Tax authorities	Front-line managers Process improvement teams Quality teams	Business/strategic planners Sourcing groups Capital budgeting Cost engineers
Uses	Shareholder reporting Inventory valuation Preparation of tax reports Lenders monitoring condition	Key performance information Value/non–value-added indentifiers Manage daily activity	Activity-based product costing Target costing Make/buy analysis Investment justification Life-cycle costing
Level of Aggregation	High Often company-wide data May be on a legal entity basis	Very detailed Work unit level	Product-line aggregation Information detail based on type of decision
Reporting Frequency	Periodic, usually monthly Probably quarterly or annually if other needs were met	Immediate Possibly hourly or daily	Ad hoc, as needed Usually a special study
Types of Measures	Mostly financial	Mostly physical	Combination of physical & financial

Source: This concept was originally developed by Steve Hronec, Arthur Andersen LLP, for an internal training course entitled, "Cost Accounting in the Reinvented Factory of the Future," presented in December 1983. It was first used in this form by Steve Player on an engagement for Nordic Track, October 1993.

ing manager really does not manage the dollars. Instead he or she manages physical activities.

Strategic View

The strategic view of cost differs from the financial and operational views in that it is the forward-looking view of cost. Users are concerned with improving tomorrow's results; yesterday and today are important only in how they help explain how to improve tomorrow. Investment justification, target costing, life-cycle costing and make vs. buy decisions benefit from the strategic view. The strategic planner, cost engineer, and people doing product sourcing use this view to determine how to change future costs and improve profitability.

The level of aggregation in this view is solely dependent on the specific issue being addressed. It could be a very short-term decision with a low level of aggregation (e.g., such as whether to outsource a specific item) or a long-term, highly aggregated decision (e.g., whether to buy a business, open a new plant, or launch a new product line).

In the strategic view, both physical and financial measures play important (and interrelated) roles in planning for the future.

DIFFERENCES BETWEEN STRATEGIC ABC AND OPERATIONAL ABM

ABCM systems focus on either the strategic view of cost with a strategic ABC approach or the operational view of cost with an operational ABM approach. While an activity-based approach is used for both strategic and operational needs, it is used in differing ways.

Strategic ABC

ABC, the cost assignment view, focuses on the strategic view of cost. Strategic ABC provides information such as product costing, customer costing, and distribution channel costing. Strategic ABC answers the question "What do things cost?"

ABC can be illustrated by the Consortium for Advanced Manufacturing-International (CAM-I) expanded ABC model also known as the CAM-I Cross. (See Exhibit 3.3.) As noted in the vertical bar, the assignment of costs is achieved by a two-stage driver model that moves from resources to activities (stage 1) and then from activities to cost objects (stage 2).

Resource drivers measure the quantity of resources consumed by an activity. Activity drivers measure the frequency and intensity of the demand

EXHIBIT 3.3   CAM-I Cross

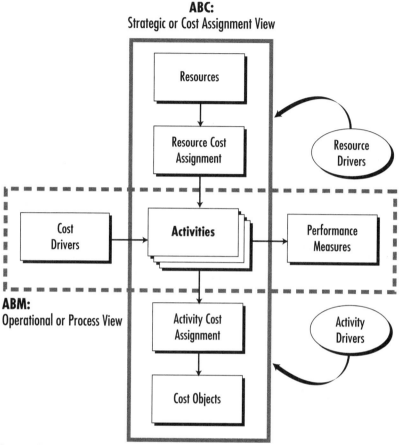

Source: CAM-I

placed on activities by cost objects. Examples of activity drivers include number of part numbers, customer orders, lines purchased, and shipments. As a result of these assignments, an activity driver typically represents a line item on the bill of activities for a particular cost object (e.g., a product, customer, or distribution channel). A bill of activities lists each activity, activity drivers, number of units, unit cost per driver, and extended cost, which, taken together, compose the total for any particular cost object. Resource drivers and activity drivers, as typically used, are single-factor methods of allocation (i.e., one resource driver per resource, one activity driver per activity).

Operational ABM

Operational ABM, which is often called the process view, focuses on the operational view of costs. It provides information such as activity attributes for cost reduction opportunities, cost-of-quality statements, and performance improvement ideas. Operational ABM answers the question "What causes cost to occur?"

The CAM-I Cross illustrates operational ABM, which shifts to a focus on cost drivers instead of activity drivers. (See Exhibit 3.3.) A cost driver is defined as "any factor that causes a change in the cost of an activity. While activity drivers are *single* factors, an activity often has *multiple* cost drivers associated with it."[11]

Combining these views provides a conceptual linkage between the strategic ABC and operational ABM at the intersection of activities. While conceptually powerful, this depiction contributes to why people confuse strategic ABC and operational ABM.

While the two views intersect at activities, the level of activity definition required is widely different. Strategic ABC can use a very high-level activity definition. For example, work can be defined as the shipping activity, because the entire cost will be assigned based on the number of shipments.

However, operational ABM often requires a closer view of the work. To understand what causes cost to occur in shipping, much greater activity detail is required. Thus, the activity of shipping could be split into a lower level of activities including:

- Receive shipping notice
- Locate finished goods
- Pick up finished goods
- Pack shipping boxes
- Label boxes
- Arrange trucks
- Load trucks
- Recount shipment

This greater detail provides insight into how work occurs. A three-dimensional view of the CAM-I Cross depicts this depth (as shown in Exhibit 3.4). In addition to the level of activity definition, strategic ABC and operational ABM also differ in the way drivers are analyzed. Exhibit 3.5 outlines how Hewlett-Packard North American Distribution Organization identified driver differences for strategic and operational needs.

Strategic ABC can operate effectively using a system with relatively few activities. For example, the ABC models used for the Efficient Consumer Response (ECR) initiative in the grocery industry consist of 17 primary activities and 70 supporting activities. ECR illustrates how a high level of activity definition can be strategically used across the entire industry's value chain.

EXHIBIT 3.4   Two Different Levels of Activity Definition

Strategic ABM
Activities defined at a
strategic level for
cost assignment to
cost objects

Operational ABM
Activities defined at an
operational level for
process improvement

Source: Steve Player first developed this concept for an article, "The Difference Between ABC and ABM," which appeared in the Cost Management Insider's Report, July 1995.

For operational ABM, the level of detail is often much greater. It is similar to placing a microscope on various parts of a company's operations. Today real-time enterprise systems now have the power to capture actual information about both financial and physical measures. Operating managers can harness the power to provide ongoing operational control. This control is key to improving real-time decision making.

However, managers should be cautious to avoid trying to use this fluctuating daily operational information instead of the longer-term strategic ABC costs. Doing so runs the risks of confusing operating fluctuations with ongoing strategic costs.[12]

Impact on the Financial View

Since the financial view of cost remains the most aggregated view, it receives little impact from the additional activity-based analysis. In some cases, companies are beginning to use strategic ABC to provide inventory valuation. Most of these moves are driven by the desire to minimize accounting support costs. This is achieved by eliminating the duplicate costing system for financial reporting.

But care must be taken in this approach. Some items that should be included in strategic ABC costs (i.e., distribution and selling costs) are not allowed as product costs under generally accepted accounting principles. Further, allocation of cost-of-capital charges might be included in strategic ABC but not under the financial view.

EXHIBIT 3.5   Example of the Differences in the Use of Drivers at Hewlett-Packard

An example from the ABCM implementation at Hewlett-Packard's North American Distribution Organization (HP-NADO) helps explain how strategic ABC and operational ABC use differing levels of detail. To illustrate the differences in the definition of activities and drivers, the implementation team was asked to consider the following example of the purchasing department's activities.

Strategic ABC would assign the resources cost of the purchasing department (i.e. salaries, facility costs, and supplies) to activities based on resources drivers (i.e. percent of time spent by activity). The activity costs would then be assigned to the cost objects (i.e. products or customers) based on an activity driver (i.e. number of purchase orders issued).

This approach is efficient in gathering driver data and reasonably accurate in associating those drivers with the end-use cost objects. It provides a reasonable answer to the question, "What do things cost?" However, if the question is "What causes cost to occur?" then the use of these resource and activity drivers is not detailed enough and in many cases inappropriate.

A purchasing manager trying to understand what causes departmental cost to occur finds that strategic ABC does not provide enough detail to answer questions. If the strategic ABC system indicates that the number of lines purchased is a key activity driver, the purchasing manager who uses this information may produce disastrous results. Often an operating manager will mistakenly begin to manage the activity driver instead of the activity; in this case managing the number of purchase orders issued instead of purchasing department activities and true cost drivers. Reducing the number of purchase orders may result in efforts to buy in larger quantities. While this reduces the number of purchase orders issued, it has the opposite of the desired effect, resulting in an increase in the company's overall costs.

For the purchasing manager to understand what causes costs to occur, he must focus on a multitude of true cost drivers. The number of purchase orders issued could be one driver, but more likely drivers include:

- Number of vendors used
- Location of vendors compared to company facilities
- Number of vendor audits or evaluations performed
- Quality of each vendor
- Number of operating locations supported
- Type of goods purchased (commodity or specialized items)
- Paperwork used to process purchases
- Computer system used
- Complexity of the purchasing process
- Internal controls required
- Policies regarding who can approve purchases
- Number of expedited purchases.

All these factors cause cost to occur in the purchasing activities. An understanding of each provides the basis for cost reduction and operating improvements. However, any attempts to use this level of detail in a strategic ABC system would take a series of super-computers to process the detail for a single activity.

With this understanding, the HP-NADO team confirmed the project focus as strategic ABC. The key business issues were product and customer profitability. The team went on to successfully install a strategic ABC system for product and customer costing.

RECENT DEVELOPMENTS IN THE ERA OF CONVERGENCE

While there have been many signals of a convergence, a press release issued on September 9, 1998, provided clear evidence that the era of convergence had begun: "Enterprise application market leader SAP AG announces an equity investment in ABC Technologies, Inc., the market leader in stand-alone activity-based costing software."[13] This event changed the focus of the industry by confirming the era of convergence and accelerating the pace of development as well as launching a highly competitive effort in which market leadership will be hotly contested. Exhibit 3.6 provides an overview of the key developments leading to convergence in cost management.

Historically, costing has long been an element within enterprise applications. The functionality centered on an ability to calculate and maintain standard costs. As activity-based costing's acceptance grew in the late 1980s and early 1990s, companies increasingly requested this functionality. In many cases these requests were fueled by the growing industry of ABCM implementers, which were supported by research groups such as CAM-I, leading academics, consulting firms, and niche software houses.

EXHIBIT 3.6   Developments Leading to Convergence in ABCM

96	April 15:	Lawson Software releases an *activity management* application to integrate business planning, operations, and financial management.
97	Sept. 9:	PeopleSoft, KPMG Peat Marwick, and leading academics join to produce performance management software with OLAP capabilities.
	Sept. 15:	SAP releases CO-ABC module as part of R/3 Version 3.Oe.
98	May 20:	Oracle acquires ACTIVA ABC software from Price Waterhouse.
	Sept. 9:	SAP AG and ABC Technologies begin to jointly develop and market cost management software. SAP makes equity investment in ABC Technologies.
	Sept. 30:	Sapling and Hyperion team up to integrate the Essbase OLAP server with modeling and performance measurement software.
99	June 7:	J. D. Edwards signs strategic alliance to link its One World System with Armstrong Laing's Metify
	May 18:	Hyperion acquires Sapling Corporation

PC-Based Software Solutions

The initial software approaches focused on ABCM were mainly PC-based tools built either by consulting firms or niche software vendors. For the niche firms, the primary, if not the only, product was focused on supporting ABCM implementations. Over time the consulting firms abandoned this market to focus on their core business of integration consulting. This left a group of independent niche firms.

Since 1990 this group of vendors has grown dramatically. Competition has greatly advanced the capabilities these tools can provide, including the importing of data, multidimensional cost allocations, and user-defined reporting of output. In addition to providing technical support, the PC-based vendors have provided a host of support tools focused on growing this industry. Numerous educational materials and change management tools exist to aid implementations. These support services include basic and software-related training classes, rapid prototyping and other development tools, industry and functional specific case studies, and web-based support tools. These extended product offerings have enhanced the number of and percentage of successful ABCM projects.

Today there has been a marked increase in the size and scope of ABCM implementations. ABC Technologies, Armstrong Laing Group, and Sapling Corporation are the top three PC vendors based on 1998 revenue. Each has focused on enterprise-wide ABCM solutions. Their targeted sales approach is based on an intimate knowledge of what the users of ABCM systems seek to achieve with enterprise-wide systems. Armstrong Laing recently received an infusion of venture capital funding to pursue these larger scale systems as well as launched an alliance with J. D. Edwards. Sapling was acquired by Hyperion to enhance the functionality of Hyperion Enterprise Performance Management. ABC Technologies has received an equity investment from SAP that provides for joint development.

Armstrong Laing has used its venture funding to rewrite its product offering into the recently released Metify product line, which is targeted at enterprise-wide users. In addition, Armstrong Laing and J. D. Edwards formed a Products Alliance partnership to deliver integrated value-based management analytical solutions. It has also increased its U.S. marketing and sales forces. Its marketing campaign centers around an educational message of helping users understand the success companies have with enterprise-wide ABCM systems and how the Metify system can enable this development.[14]

In May 1999, Sapling Corporation was acquired by Hyperion Corporation. This announcement follows the news of a global reseller and co-development agreement with Sapling and the introduction of Hyperion Enterprise Performance Management in April 1999. Two new products have emerged from the acquisition: Hyperion Activity-Based Management, formerly Sapling NetProphet, and Hyperion Performance Measurement, formerly Sapling NetScore. Prior to the acquisition, Sapling's products were integrated with Hyperion Essbase OLAP Server and Hyperion's analytic solutions platform for enterprise-wide information delivery.

ABC Technologies chose to forgo venture funding but now finds it is flush with development and marketing funds provided by the SAP investment. ABC Technologies' short-term plans are to use this funding for codevelopment of a bridge that will link its Oros® software to SAP's CO-ABC™ system. Users will prototype in Oros for strategic analytical applications while seamlessly transferring to CO-ABC to perform ABC on an embedded basis as part of the full R/3™ system. In the longer term, ABC Technologies plans to further integrate its Oros software with SAP while continuing to also sell it on a stand-alone basis. It is felt that this alliance has the potential to be very significant and could redefine the ABC market. In some ways it has already begun to achieve this by accelerating the pace of development. The combination of these two market leaders gives this alliance breakaway potential.

Enterprise Application Vendors

Enterprise applications are also converging rapidly. The early leaders appeared to be Lawson Software and SAP. Lawson launched its Activity Management module in 1996. It followed this release with a strong marketing focus on the healthcare industry. Lawson also gained direct experience with ABCM as Arthur Andersen helped pilot ABC within Lawson itself in 1997. Upon success, Lawson expanded the pilot to a company-wide deployment of ABCM in mid–1998.

As part of version 3.0 of the R/3 system, SAP introduced some ABC capabilities with the CO-ABC module in 1996. However, the company has been somewhat frustrated by the lack of module adoption, particularly in the United States. In some cases this has been due to customer prioritization of development efforts. Many customers have focused on implementing the basic R/3 modules first for financial accounting and to meet Year 2000 deadlines, leaving ABCM for a later date.

In addition to its investment in ABC Technologies, SAP is also continuing to enhance the functionality of its CO-ABC tool to provide robust ABC fully embedded within the power of enterprise software. This two-pronged approach indicates SAP's commitment to market leadership in the area of cost management.

PeopleSoft began its aggressive convergence on the analytical applications market by teaming with Harvard academics Robert Kaplan and Robin Cooper as well as KPMG. On September 9, 1997, PeopleSoft announced a joint development project to produce an ABC module that is scheduled for release in late 1999.

In May 1998, Oracle moved to provide ABC capability by acquiring the ACTIVA ABC software from Price Waterhouse. It is continuing to sell ACTIVA while in the process of rewriting it to better fit with the Oracle suite.

In May 1999, J. D. Edwards launched a partnership with Armstrong Laing to deliver value-based management analytical solutions. Armstrong Laing's Metify ABM Solution will be used to transform J. D. Edwards' transaction data into process and activity-based insight. It will form a key component of the value based management suite and ActivEra™ Knowledge Management Solution.

On-line Analytical Processing (OLAP) Vendors

The historical owners of the analytical applications space also have launched enterprise efforts. With the merger of Arbor Software and Hyperion to create Hyperion Solutions, the dominant OLAP players have been visibly involved in this convergence into the ABCM space. In addition to acquiring Sapling, Hyperion has relationships with ABC Technologies and Armstrong Laing due to the prior strategic relationship each of those vendors had with Arbor's Essbase tool. The Essbase functionality historically has been an approach PC-based tools have used to overcome concerns regarding the ability to handle large volumes. The continued linkage and future developments between these companies remain to be clarified.

The release of version 5.0 greatly enhanced Essbase's calculational capability. This has further added to the convergence, causing some companies to consider using Essbase as an ABCM tool on a stand-alone basis. Many of the enterprise applications, such as Lawson, Baan, and J. D. Edwards, also have strategic relationships with both predecessors' companies: Hyperion and Arbor. There still remains considerable sorting out in regard to who is aligned with whom and what functionality exists now—and in the future.

CONSIDERATIONS COMPANIES SHOULD MAKE IN MOVING FORWARD

The current convergence leaves many companies concerned as to what path they should take to move forward. The various system options can seem overwhelming. When viewed solely as a system choice, the selection can be challenging. However, focusing solely on system selection misses a key point: Successful ABCM implementations begin with a clear management understanding of business objectives. As noted, the approach taken and related level of detail varies widely depending on the expected business uses of the system.

Implementing ABCM is far different from converting from one general ledger or manufacturing resource planning (MRP) package to another. In many cases the basic activity data have not yet been produced. A tremendous amount of model design, data collection, and cost analysis is needed before input into any system can occur.

The critical first steps are to define which business uses will be addressed and in what priority. While ABCM can meet many needs, the system design varies across the different views of costs and uses. Implementation teams must understand what is required to respond to management's key business needs. Trying to implement both strategic ABC and operational ABM simultaneously is often a prescription for disaster. This issue is a recurring one as Tom Johnson, Tom Vance, and Steve Player warned users against the pitfalls of using ABC drivers for operational purposes in an article written in 1991.[15]

Cooper and Slagmulder note that these two uses "demand very different types of cost information. Unfortunately, many firms try to use only one system to perform both tasks. Such single systems are doomed to perform poorly."[16] Cooper and Kaplan echo this thought, noting "Managers must be aware that the two managerial cost systems are so different in requirements for accuracy, timeliness and aggregation that no single approach can possibly be adequate for both purposes."[17] While separate systems are required, there exists a need for these systems to interact with each other (including with the costs reported under the financial view of cost). Care should be taken to appropriately integrate these multiple views of cost information.

Key Points When Getting Started

Companies considering the implementation of ABCM should keep the following seven points in mind.

1. Begin with a clear articulation of the business needs that management expects to meet through implementation of ABCM. These statements will:
   a. Provide a clear case for the cost/benefit justification needed for implementation to proceed
   b. Focus on which of the three views of cost—strategic, operational, or financial—need to be addressed
   c. Maintain a clear direction for "the end in mind" as to what the completed system will provide
2. Identify the activity information needs and related data collection required to support the use selected. In many cases this information will have yet to be defined and collected. It must be gathered to feed into any system selected.

3. As part of the ABCM conceptual design, the interfaces between the different views of cost should be considered. The degree and frequency of integration must be planned.

4. The strategic ABC system should:
   a. Be separate from the on-line operational system for use in analytical analysis
   b. Provide an easy-to-use, flexible modeling environment
   c. Feed activity and process templates for the operational system to provide a common costing framework
   d. Provide activity rates to serve as performance targets for monitoring within the operational system

5. The operational ABC system should:
   a. Be used to monitor ongoing performance as compared to targets
   b. Provide updates on practical capacity to the strategic ABC system
   c. Consolidate driver data to feed the strategic ABC system periodically

6. The financial view of cost should:
   a. State overall expense information allowing it to reconcile to the operational ABM system
   b. Be fed cost-object values from the strategic ABC system as the base from which overall adjustments can be made for differences required by financial accounting

7. Companies should move forward with implementing ABCM rather than using the current convergence as an excuse to delay implementation. There is ample evidence that ABCM systems can and will yield substantial benefits. Any delays will result in permanently lost savings. All signs indicate that the convergence in supporting technologies is resulting in continued improvements in the functionality and ability to support enterprise-wide ABCM solutions. Such improvements will serve only to enhance and expand a robust collection of already established ABCM enablers and proven solutions available currently.

NOTES

1. Bruce Caldwell, "Beyond ERP," *Information Week,* November 30, 1998.

2. Stephen R. Covey, "Foreword," *Activity Based Management: Arthur Andersen's Lessons from the ABM Battlefield,* 2nd ed. (New York: John Wiley & Sons, 1999): xi.

3. Ibid.

4. Michael Stefanic, Presentation to the National Association of Wholesaler-Distributors, February 3, 1998.

5. Steve Player and James W. Gibson, Jr., *Activity-Based Management in Wholesale Distribution: Winning the Profitability Battle* (Washington, D.C.: DREF/NAW Publications, 1997), pp. 136–137.

6. Michael Porter, "Linking Strategy to Activities," Keynote address, ABC Technologies User Conference, October 1997.

7. Carla O'Dell and C. Jackson Grayson, Jr., *American Business: A Two Minute Warning: Ten Changes Managers Must Make to Survive into the 21st Century* (New York: The Free Press, 1988).

8. Steve Player and Carol Cobble, "Foreword by Carla O'Dell," *Cornerstones of Decision Making: Profiles of Enterprise ABM* (Greensboro, NC: Oakhill Press, 1999): vii.

9. Peter Drucker, *The Practice of Management* (New York: Harper & Row, 1954).

10. Peter Drucker, *Managing for the Future* (New York: Truman Talley Books/Dutton, 1992).

11. This definition is from Norm Raffish and Peter B. B. Turney, eds., *CAM-I Glossary of Terms* (Arlington, TX: CAM-I, 1991), Document R–91-CMS–06. These terms are included in the Glossary at the end of the book.

12. For more information on this problem, see Robin Cooper and Robert S. Kaplan, "The Promise—and Peril—of Integrated Cost Systems," *Harvard Business Review* (July–August 1998): 109–119.

13. "SAP AG Makes Substantial Investment in ABC Technologies" Press Release ABC Technologies Inc. and SAPAG, AP Wire, September 9, 1998.

14. For more information, see Steve Player and Carol Cobble, *Cornerstones of Decision Making: Profiles of Enterprise ABM* (Greensboro, NC: Oakhill Press, 1999).

15. H. Thomas Johnson, Thomas P. Vance, and R. Steven Player, "Pitfalls of Using ABC Cost Driver Information for Operating Decisions," *Corporate Controller* (January–February 1991).

16. Robin Cooper and Regine Slagmulder, "Strategic Cost Management," *Management Accounting* (September 1998): 12.

17. Cooper and Kaplan, "The Promise—and Peril—of Integrated Cost Systems," p. 110.

ABOUT THE AUTHORS

Steve Player is Managing Partner for Cost Management with Arthur Andersen. He is based in Dallas, Texas.

Charles A. Marx, Jr. is a Partner with Arthur Andersen's Business Consulting Practice. He is based in Chicago, Illinois.

4

DEVELOPING CORPORATE REPORTING SOLUTIONS

Dennis Sparacino, Heidi A. Labritz, and Sanjay K. Upmanyu

Many organizations face an information deficit while experiencing a data surplus. The information needed for strategic decision making is not available in a timely manner for the appropriate people. It is not uncommon for an information technology (IT) analyst to have more information concerning product and service sales, cost, or profitability than the vice president of sales. This chapter examines the fundamental framework necessary for developing corporate reporting solutions with a focus on on-line analytical processing (OLAP) technology.

First, it is important to understand how this information deficit arose. Databases were originally developed for the purpose of transaction processing. These systems were designed for data input and referred to as on-line transaction processing (OLTP) systems. In other words, users enter or electronically capture transaction data and the transaction is processed by the system, which produces some type of invoice or standard billing. These systems typically produce a standard suite of reports for management. However, these are often inadequate for strategic decision making.

These OLTP systems evolved into huge databases storing vast amounts of corporate data. As the competitive environment became fierce, companies demanded access to this data to develop strategic plans. IT departments had to query and report from these large databases. Information belonged to IT and not the decision makers.

Since these databases were designed for transaction input, it was difficult to extract the data quickly and in a usable format. This often led to outdated reports and useless analyses. By the time the report was delivered to the appropriate personnel, it often had little value.

Information is time-critical. When information is requested its value is high, but as time passes its value diminishes greatly. In the current business environment, the information is often rekeyed into spreadsheets for further analysis and presentations.

In developing corporate reporting solutions, these issues can be overcome by remembering these guiding principles:

- Information is time critical.
- Information belongs with the decision maker, not IT.
- Information needs to be usable and accessible.

First, organizations must have the ability to produce information quickly. When a customer or supplier has a question, organizations must have the capability to answer promptly.

Information belongs in the hands of the decision maker, not IT. It does not make sense for an IT department to hire a team of reporting specialists to develop reports based on requests. It does, however, make sense for an IT department to develop a system that allows the decision maker to produce reports quickly.

Information must be usable and accessible. It must be in a format that is easily understood, allows efficient access, and supports further manipulation without IT involvement.

To develop a comprehensive corporate reporting and analysis system, three different types of data or information storage mechanisms are available. These mechanisms are: (1) OLTP or operational databases, (2) relational data warehouses, and (3) multidimensional databases/OLAP systems. See Exhibit 4.1 for an illustration of the interrelation of these systems.

EXHIBIT 4.1   Information Storage Mechanisms

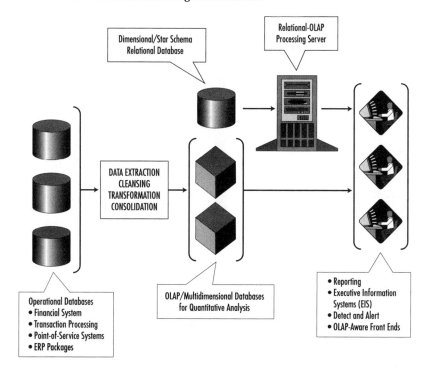

INFORMATION STORAGE MECHANISMS

Operational Databases

Operational databases are the mission-critical systems of the corporation and support the corporation on a day-to-day basis. If these systems are not running on a 24-hour per day, 7-day-per-week basis, a corporation often cannot run its business. These systems typically have the following characteristics:

- Read and write
- Singular updates
- Mutually exclusive purpose
- Complex data models

The systems read and write data. The databases process transactions and allow for limited look-up and basic reporting. These systems usually support only singular updates, such as customer records or billing items that are modified one at a time. Additionally, these systems have a mutually exclusive purpose. Several will exist across and support one area of the organization. Since these systems were originally designed for efficient data input, the data models are often complex and difficult to understand.

Relational Data Warehouses

Relational data warehouses support the decision making of an organization. The databases often contain information from several operational systems. These databases typically have the following characteristics:

- Read only
- Analytical
- Batch updates
- Combined data models
- Discrete data fields
- Simplified data model

Data warehouses are typically read only and do not process transactions. They often are updated in batch or bulk; in other words, records are added to the database at once. A data warehouse should combine simplified data models from several different operational systems. For example, the combination of cost and revenue data generates profitability information; however, the source data may originate in separate systems. Data warehouses store data in discrete data fields. In other databases, the data must be queried on a selection of fields based on specified criteria to produce information. Data warehouses are huge storage facilities that contain data, not information.

OLAP/Multidimensional Database Systems

OLAP, or multidimensional database system, is a key technology involved in deploying a corporate reporting solution. As presented in Exhibit 4.2, OLAP turns data into information by organizing data in the form of dimensions, levels, and members. A dimension usually reflects the way a business is categorized or understood. Levels and members comprise the hierarchy of the dimension. By using dimensions, levels, and members, organizations can build a customized model of their business to be used as a framework for analysis. OLAP systems or multidimensional databases have the following key characteristics:

- Data are stored as a multidimensional model/outline.
- The data model represents a model of the organization's business.
- Data are typically summarized.

EXHIBIT 4.2   Sample Multidimensional Database/OLAP Outline

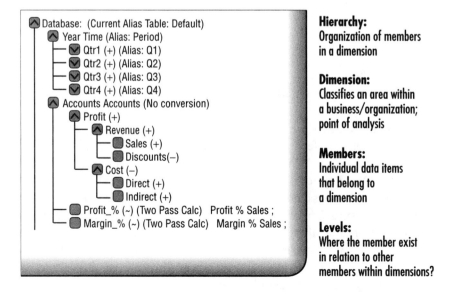

- Data are typically quantitative vs. qualitative.
- There is a quick response time.

By contrast, in a relational database, data are stored in fields within tables with relationships between the tables based on certain key fields. To navigate the relational database, the user must have some basic understanding of Structured Query Language (SQL). Whereas tools (i.e., SQL Generator or QBE) are provided to construct SQL statements in the background, there is always some risk as to the level of understanding among user, SQL generator, and data. With a multidimensional database, users simply select a combination of members from the outline to perform analysis.

OLAP FUNCTIONALITY

OLAP is a key piece of technology necessary for the successful implementation of a corporate reporting solution. OLAP offers several key advantages over relational databases and allows an organization to develop not just reporting and analysis systems but also analytical business solutions to automate key business processes.

Key Advantages

OLAP offers key advantages in the following areas:

- Usability
- Functionality
- Deployment
- Integration with Cost Management Systems

OLAP systems are easy for decision makers to use. The decision maker is not typically a systems professional but rather a business professional. These decision makers require the ability to analyze corporate information and manipulate data quickly. OLAP systems meet this need by prepackaging data in well-defined and understood business models. OLAP systems are designed so information is returned quickly in a format that can be readily understood and further manipulated by a business analyst, middle management, or senior management.

In the daily work environment, OLAP systems are also extremely functional and easy to use. Frequently during implementations, the seamless integration of a solution into people's daily work routines is often overlooked.

The analysis of information should not be a lengthy process. OLAP accomplishes this by delivering information to the desktop within seconds. By using OLAP systems, organizations can move from generic reporting to exception reporting, retrieving information based on certain predefined criteria. The information that needs to be analyzed is brought to the forefront, eliminating the need to sift through data in problem areas. Additionally, complex reports and analyses can be created by simply pointing and clicking on members in the multidimensional database.

OLAP systems are typically easy to deploy and offer out-of-the-box connectivity to a number of reporting and analysis systems. Access to the system is very easy to set up, usually by installing a simple connection protocol on the user's PC. These protocols do not require complex log-in parameters or special database configurations. Since the OLAP server contains preprocessed, highly indexed data, the PCs do not require added capacity or customization.

With the popularity of the Internet and corporate intranet sites in today's environment, web-deployable solutions are becoming a necessity. OLAP systems are readily deployable, providing users with easy access to valuable information through a desktop browser. One example is depicted in Exhibit 4.3.

EXHIBIT 4.3   OLAP with Web-Enabled Front End

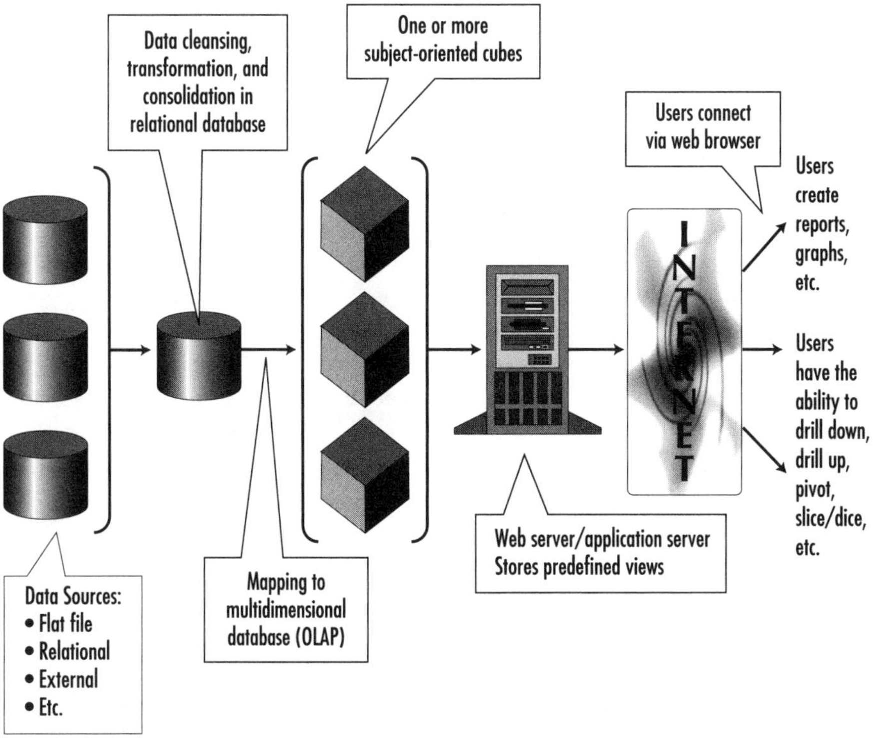

Several software products are currently available that interface with OLAP servers to deploy solutions to organizations based on web browser technology. By using web browser technology, user installations require only a browser and appropriate network connections. Implementing this type of solution would require the addition of an Internet server connecting to an OLAP server.

Today the market for OLAP or analytical business applications is at an all-time high. The acceptance of OLAP over the past few years has led leading software organizations and other third-party organizations to integrate OLAP into existing applications across a broad spectrum.

For example, Hyperion Essbase integrates with or links to software applications in the areas of cost management, enterprise resource planning (ERP), risk management, performance management, financial management, and many others.

International Data Corporation (IDC), an analyst research organization, forecasts the market for analytic applications to grow from over $600 million in 1996 to over $2.6 billion by 2001. This represents a compound annual growth rate of 35 percent over the five-year period.[1]

FOCUS ON COST MANAGEMENT

OLAP has revolutionized the analysis of cost management information. The recent convergence of OLAP software in the cost management arena has enabled the delivery of cost information across the enterprise. In fact, the combination of ERP and OLAP vendors incorporating cost management software tools has further validated that cost management, specifically activity-based costing, is becoming more mainstream than ever before.

Henry Morris of IDC notes: "A new market for analytical applications is emerging, and activity-based management will be incorporated into a range of systems, from budgeting and planning to sales and profitability analysis and optimization."[2]

The flexibility of using OLAP technology in the delivery of a cost management solution can be broken into several different categories. The following discussion focuses on three approaches to deliver an OLAP cost management solution, highlighting the pros and cons of each. This comparison provides organizations with the ability to differentiate between the various approaches. The approaches include off-the-shelf, hybrid, and ERP linkages.

Off-the-Shelf Cost Management Vendors

Three main activity-based costing software package vendors—NetProphet (Sapling), Metify (Armstrong Laing), and Oros (ABC Technologies)—have linkages to Hyperion Essbase. In May 1999, Hyperion acquired Sapling Corporation and its related products. In addition, Metify and Oros have linkages to

Cognos PowerPlay, a desktop OLAP tool. The attractiveness of using Hyperion Essbase is having the cost management information available on an enterprise-wide basis. Hyperion Essbase is a client-server application that enables the information, or cube, to be stored centrally. Obviously, the deployment of cost management information using Essbase is an investment in both money and skill level; however, the potential benefit is enormous. Gigabytes of information can be queried and filtered in seconds. The added ability to create ad hoc reports or query the database can alleviate work from the IT department. In essence, OLAP technology delivers unlimited analytical capability to the end user.

The actual linkages of the software packages to Essbase are similar, but differ in terms of execution and output. The actual generation of the Essbase cube from one of the cost management solutions is executed through a Wizard module. The information contained within a model is pregenerated and exported to an Essbase cube. All of the packages have different options as to what is actually generated, but more important, there is little customization beyond that point. Given the lack of customization of output with this direct approach, sufficient planning must go into the model design, as this will ultimately impact the presentation of data in Essbase. Exhibit 4.4 illustrates the

EXHIBIT 4.4 Hyperion Essbase–Generated Outline

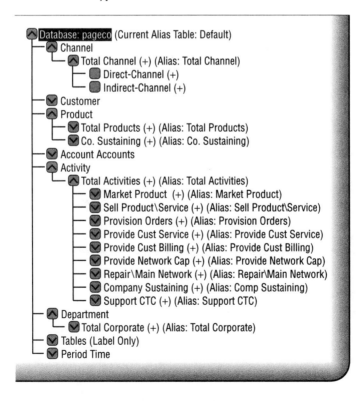

type of analysis that can be obtained using a direct link. The example highlights a Hyperion Essbase-generated cube with eight dimensions. The outline represents a fictitious telecommunications paging company that wants to understand profitability by geography, channel, and product. The other five dimensions represented are: (1) account, (2) tables (cost), (3) period, (4) department, and (5) activity.

Once the cube has been generated, users can build reports or just view the data in an ad hoc fashion. Hyperion Essbase has a series of tools, ranging from Microsoft Excel to Active X components, that enhance the data presentation layer. For example, a process-centered income statement created in Microsoft Excel is shown in Exhibit 4.5. This report highlights the process contribution by channel segmentation. The information shown was created by simply double-clicking and formatting the various dimensions in Excel.

EXHIBIT 4.5   Process-Centered Income Statement

	Direct	%	Indirect	%	Total	%
Revenue	$186,015,403	100%	$49,337,296	100%	$235,352,699	100%
Less: Rsv for Uncollect.	($15,168,956)	–8%	($1,162,044)	–2%	($16,331,000)	–7%
Cost of Operations						
Market Product	$12,610,332	7%	$12,425,218	25%	$25,035,550	11%
Sell Product/Service	$84,958,549	46%	$12,324,000	25%	$97,282,549	41%
Provision Orders	$16,587,668	9%	$19,310,377	39%	$35,898,044	15%
Provide Cust Service	$7,775,512	4%	$1,034,786	2%	$8,810,298	4%
Provide Cust Billing	$2,185,036	1%	$800,665	2%	$2,985,701	1%
Provide Network Cap	$25,384,870	14%	$7,135,187	14%	$32,520,057	14%
Repair/Maintain Network	$1,602,358	1%	$1,326,042	3%	$2,928,399	1%
Total Cost of Operations	$151,104,324	81%	$54,356,275	110%	$205,460,599	87%
Operations Margin	$19,742,123	11%	($6,181,022)	–27%	$13,561,100	6%
Co. Sustaining					$48,816,847	21%
NOPBIT	$19,742,123	11%	($6,181,022)	–13%	$13,561,100	6%
Units In Service	1,516,928		871,402		$2,388,330	

Exhibit 4.6 illustrates an ad hoc report that segments resources by sensitivity (fixed, variable, step-variable). The flexibility and ease of use of reporting extensions such as Excel is suited for power users, making all information fair game. The term "power user" may be a bit overstated, but the point is that these types of users must have some familiarity with the data and the business

EXHIBIT 4.6   Ad Hoc Report: Segmenting Resources by Sensitivity

Resources:	Fixed:	Variable:	Step Variable:
Advertising/Promotion	2,384,000		
Commissions/Bonuses			5,634,400
Depreciation	16,400,000	14,000,000	
Network Operation	1,802,480		
Occupancy	3,462,600		
Other	5,536,000		
Pager Cost of Goods			11,200,000
Pager Repairs		4,551,600	
Personnel	22,050,321	20,459,771	
Reseller			10,696,000
Site Rentals	4,180,000		
Supportive Outsourcing	11,334,400	688,000	
Telephone	12,798,360		
Vehicles—All Technicians	216,000		
Total	$80,164,161	$39,699,371	$27,530,400

outline. Users will quickly understand information overload by double-clicking a few times on a multidimensional database with gigabytes of data.

A more formal decision-support tool such as Wired for OLAP can be built for management, as shown in Exhibit 4.7. This tool provides more control over which data are presented and is geared for the non–power user. Unlike prior decision-support tools, users can still dynamically drill down on data; however, this presentation layer sets the boundaries on which data are available. The illustration highlights an activity contribution report by product.

The following list highlights the pros and cons of using the vendor-provided link to an OLAP reporting engine.

Pros

- Simple
- Fast implementation
- Low cost

Cons

- Minimal or no customization
- Information limited by data in ABC model
- Limited to ABC vendor-provided OLAP tool

EXHIBIT 4.7 Sample WIRED for OLAP Report

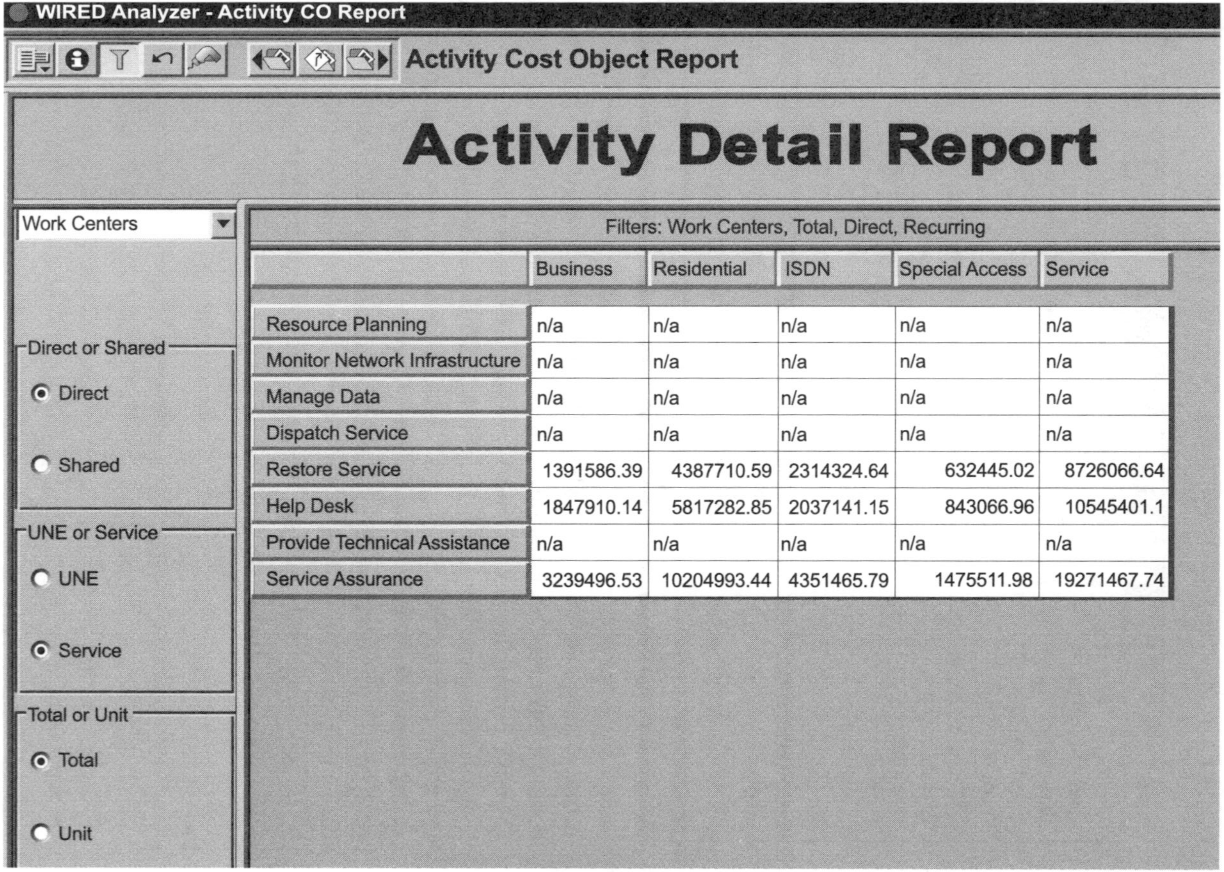

WIRED Analyzer - Activity CO Report

Activity Cost Object Report

Activity Detail Report

Filters: Work Centers, Total, Direct, Recurring

	Business	Residential	ISDN	Special Access	Service
Resource Planning	n/a	n/a	n/a	n/a	n/a
Monitor Network Infrastructure	n/a	n/a	n/a	n/a	n/a
Manage Data	n/a	n/a	n/a	n/a	n/a
Dispatch Service	n/a	n/a	n/a	n/a	n/a
Restore Service	1391586.39	4387710.59	2314324.64	632445.02	8726066.64
Help Desk	1847910.14	5817282.85	2037141.15	843066.96	10545401.1
Provide Technical Assistance	n/a	n/a	n/a	n/a	n/a
Service Assurance	3239496.53	10204993.44	4351465.79	1475511.98	19271467.74

Work Centers

Direct or Shared
- Direct
- Shared

UNE or Service
- UNE
- Service

Total or Unit
- Total
- Unit

EXHIBIT 4.8   Microsoft OLAP Cube Browser (Cost Cube)

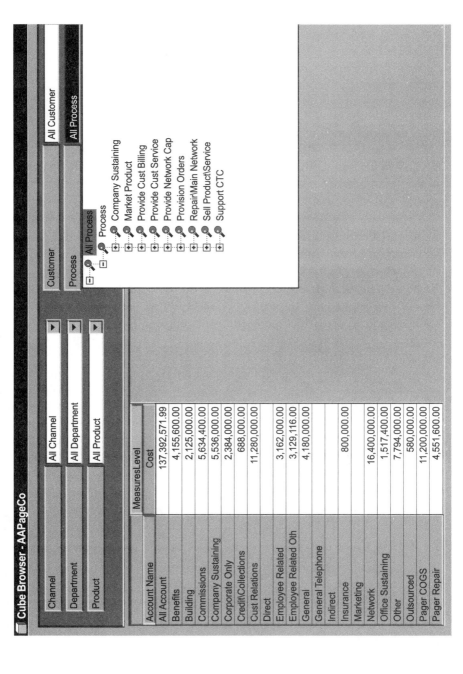

Hybrid Approach

The second approach is a combination of the off-the-shelf packages with some customization. One of the limiting factors in going with the vendor-provided link, using an off-the-shelf package, is the lack of customization. The hybrid approach would be appropriate in the situation when the company uses the modeling tool but wants more control over what appears in the OLAP cube. (See Exhibit 4.8.) OLAP vendors such as Hyperion, Oracle, and Microsoft have tools that integrate data sources such as OLTP, data warehouses, and activity-based systems to create the metadata layer needed to process OLAP cubes.

These data can be merged to provide financial and nonfinancial information in the multidimensional cube. For example, a telecommunications company may want information on department utilization, performance measures, or regulatory information that is not contained in the activity-based model. While companies may begin using the first approach to report results, sooner or later the value of activity-based information is realized when combined with other application-rich information.

Exhibit 4.9 combines a cost and performance view for the Southeast region for all digital pagers in service. This report shows activity cost; performance benchmark activity costs; performance achievement percentage; and utilization by geography, product, department, and attribute (volume-sensitive variable). Additionally, alarms (shaded area) can be set for activity information that falls out of a certain criteria range, in this case 65 percent or below for performance achievement.

EXHIBIT 4.9   Example of the Hybrid Approach

Volume Sensitive Resource Performance and Utilization (Digital)—Southeast Region							
Period	Department	Activity	Total Activity Cost	Activity Unit Cost	Benchmark Unit Cost	% Achievement	Labor Utilization
Jan. '98	Technicians	Receive/Log Excep	39,084.04	18.66	14.85	0.80	67%
Jan. '98	Technicians	Receive/Log Prevent	54,717.66	12.25	11.50	0.94	67%
Jan. '98	Technicians	Execute Work Ord	88,168.08	88.61	57.85	0.65	67%
Jan. '98	Inventory Management	Program/Test Pagers	13,506.56	7.27	7.50	1.03	73%
Jan. '98	Inventory Management	Process Changeouts	7,506.56	9.09	9.00	0.99	
Jan. '98	Customer Service	Resolve Prog Issues	45,106.12	4.89	5.00	1.02	64%
Jan. '98	Customer Service	Resolve Billing Inq	59,127.36	8.65	8.50	0.98	64%
Jan. '98	Customer Service	Process Disconnect\Cancel	38,904.77	5.67	5.80	1.02	64%

Companies are realizing that various systems must be integrated to deliver information, and using a vendor-provided link limits the availability of products. Microsoft has just recently released its OLAP services, which are bundled with SQL Server 7.0. Given the marketing and ease of use, Microsoft OLAP services are an option that should receive serious consideration when the hybrid approach is selected. Exhibit 4.10 illustrates the built-in Cube browser that ships with Microsoft OLAP services.

In many instances companies may have strict IT standards, existing tools (Oracle or Microsoft), or a desire for customization. No matter what the reasons are for migration to the hybrid approach, many companies are integrating existing production systems with these best-of-breed OLAP and ABC systems. The result is the capability to design and implement a company-specific cube that contains operational and strategic information.

The following list highlights the pros and cons of using a hybrid approach.

Pros

- Customized views
- Ability to integrate with other data sources
- Ability to deliver data from any area of the model

Cons

- Cost
- Complexity; need for IT infrastructure development
- Need for technically skilled resources

ERP Linkages

The last approach is ERP software. Many of the ERP packages not only have cost management modules but also offer links to Hyperion Essbase. Specifically, Hyperion Essbase integrates with PeopleSoft, Lawson, SAP, Baan, J. D. Edwards, and Oracle Financials. The advantages here are obvious for an organization if it already has ERP software and if the ABC module meets its requirements.

SUMMARY

OLAP servers/multidimensional databases have distinct advantages in disseminating information throughout an organization. OLAP turns data into

EXHIBIT 4.10 Cost Cube Browser

Cube Browser - AAPageCo

Channel	Indirect	▶		Customer		All Customer
Department	All Department	▶		Process		Digital
Account	All Account	▶				

- Parent	- Activity Parent Name	Activity Name	Measures\Level Cost
All Process	All Process Total		17,472,628.00
	Process Total		17,472,628.00
	+ Company Sustaining	Company Sustaining Total	
	+ Market Product Total	Market Product Total	944,821.24
	+ Provide Cust Billing	Provide Cust Billing Total	800,665.49
	+ Provide Cust Service	Provide Cust Service Total	996,483.14
	+ Provide Network Cap	Provide Network Cap Total	7,135,186.57
	+ Provision Orders	Provision Orders Total	5,428,041.44
- Process		Repair\Main Network Total	326,041.19
		Execute Work Ord	151,914.49
		Obtain Software Upgr	3,271.41
	- Repair\Main Network	Pre\Dist Network Rep	
		Rec Corrective Act	41,933.28
		Receive\Log Excep	46,096.16
		Receive\Log Prevent	58,290.31
		Sched\Dist Work Ord	24,535.54
	+ Sell Product\Service	Sell Product\Service Total	1,841,388.93
	+ Support CTC	Support CTC Total	

information and delivers that information to the decision makers' desktops. OLAP has the following key advantages over relational database technology in the realm of reporting and analysis:

- Usability
- Functionality
- Deployment
- Integration with cost management systems

These key advantages have moved OLAP into the IT mainstream.

As OLAP has moved from the exception to the rule, vendors of cost and performance management software have seen the ability to expand their reporting and analysis across an organization through linking their products to OLAP servers. While organizations have been utilizing OLAP to report and analyze information from their transaction processing system, they now can collect information from their cost management systems to perform sophisticated cost analysis, cost benchmark analysis, performance analysis, and profitability analysis.

NOTES

1. Henry Morris, "ABC Technologies: A Business Methodology Foundation for Analytic Applications," White Paper #16838, Framingham, MA: International Data Corporation, May 1998.

2. *Ibid.*

ABOUT THE AUTHORS

Dennis Sparacino is a Senior Manager with Arthur Andersen's Advanced Cost Management Team. He is based in Chicago, Illinois.

Heidi A. Labritz is a Senior Manager with Arthur Andersen's Business Consulting Practice. She is based in Dallas, Texas.

Sanjay K. Upmanyu is a Manager with Arthur Andersen's Advanced Cost Management Team. He is based in Houston, Texas.

PART TWO

Global Case Studies

5

IDENTIFYING THE COST OF SERVICES AND DETERMINING CUSTOMER PROFITABILITY USING ACTIVITY-BASED MANAGEMENT

Juarez Lopes de Araújo, Clodomarcio Tosi,
and Roberto Lacerda
Arthur Andersen, São Paulo, Brazil

CASE STUDY: Banco Real, São Paulo, Brazil

SUMMARY

Business Issue

With the opening of the banking sector to external capital providers, Banco Real faced a fall in the interest rate spread it could charge as well as a simultaneous increase in competition. To respond, an accurate understanding of costs was needed to facilitate strategic decision making. With many costs not tied directly to a specific product or service, the company needed a quantitative means to measure the total cost of services. It also needed a tool to help evaluate various operating models.

How ABM Was Used

Initially ABM was introduced as an information tool to better identify and track customer profitability. The bank was able to modify and increase profitability across products and services as well as customer and distribution channels. ABM also allowed Banco Real to address budgetary impacts of key issues such as tariff decisions and changes in various performance measures.

Banco Real's Results

Cost management enabled Banco Real to improve cost traceability by addressing over 44 percent of indirect costs in general management that previously were treated as overhead. In addition, service costs were mapped to evaluate the profitability of financial transactions as well as customers and bank branches. With the revised costing information and decision support tools, the company was able to disseminate a budgetary framework and culture throughout all levels and departments.

BACKGROUND

The expanding use of activity-based costing (ABC) among service companies in Brazil is demolishing the myth that a refined view of costs is of interest only to the industrial or manufacturing sector.

Initially ABC was successful in the manufacturing industry. This responded to the need of those industries to better understand their costs, increase operational efficiency, reduce or promote changes in product offerings, and offer more competitive prices. From an accounting point of view, the purpose was to accurately cost goods produced. In the financial services industry, physical goods are nonexistent. In services businesses, all costs are treated as expenses which are included directly in the period costs of operations. Assessing physical stock is not necessary.

In times of high inflation, the Brazilian financial system did not develop a culture of costs. Costs did not represent a problem because the profit spreads or margins were comfortable. But in a low-inflation scenario, knowing costs in the banking area is vital for business. Greater competition also increases the need for better cost information. The Brazilian banking market has become far more competitive due to the opening of the banking sector to external capital, resulting in a fall in spreads, due to increased competition. To meet these challenges, banks must make key strategic decisions. An accurate understanding of costs facilitates these strategic decisions, such as defining what tariffs to charge, understanding new products to launch, determining where to open new bank branches, and redefining the impact of differing points of sales.

Moreover, today it is clear that cost does not center only in the bank's physical facilities or branches. Until recently bank branches performed economic feasibility studies focusing on their "contribution margin," which considered operating costs simply as those connected to the bank's structure. However, information systems, personnel in general, juridical, and product development expenses were not considered. Nor were expenses involved with operations of automatic teller machines (ATMs), telephone services, telemarketing initiatives, and other corporate structures that provide sales services.

Since not everything spent by the branch was directly related to a product, discovering total costs became a major concern when financial gains decreased due to a fall in the rate of inflation. The current atmosphere of economic stabilization brought to the Brazilian financial institutions the need for knowledge, control, and effective management of costs. With the advent of increased competition, banks need to have competitive costs when compared to services provided. For example, if tariffs are determined by the market, banks need to know whether they are profitable or not when operating at those market-controlled prices.

BUSINESS ISSUES

Banco Real, the fourth largest bank in the country, consists of close to 1,650 branches or sales points, 14,000 employees, 200 cost centers, and 800 transactions or types of services. Concerns with costs initially were focused on quality improvement decisions, information access and accuracy, and the need to modernize the cost system. In gauging profitability per product, portfolio, customer, and branch, the previously used methods required frequent operational and systemic conceptual updates. Due to its countless deficiencies, it could not be used as an effective management tool. Problems included the following:

- The mapping of branch activities considered only direct costs (tellers, services and support).
- The system showed opportunities for improvement in the way costs were allocated to the products. This was a result of use of distributed approaches that were incompatible when compared with the expended effort.
- The indirect costs of the general administration represented 19 percent of the total costs. Yet these costs were classified as "overhead" and were not allocated to products or activities.
- The adopted cost criteria were different from the operational reality of the branches.
- A lack of formally defined criteria prevented the standardization of cost centers.
- Conceptual differences between the pro rata system, used for profitability calculations, and the cost system led to confusion.
- Visions of how cost information could be used differed.

Once these distortions were identified, Banco Real decided to implement an innovative cost system in the national financial atmosphere—activity-based costing. The project began, using bank personnel, in June 1997. The first phase of the project, which was internally known as Project Cost 10—Heading for Modernity, was completed in December of the same year.

The main objective was to improve the existing methodology, which was strongly dependent upon the mainframe computer. The system, which was slow to update, did not fully meet the bank's internal demands and was not flexible enough to provide answers concerning the costs of products and services. In addition, cost components for the internal area of costs could not be explained or detailed. A new, more transparent tool was needed, one that could cover all bank operations and allow faster updates.

A critical objective was to identify and create a system people fully trusted so that, once implemented, it ceased being a system proprietary to the accounting or financial area. Ownership and responsibility was removed from a single area and disseminated to all departments. After all, cost is spread throughout the bank. As a result of this knowledge and subsequent ABC implementation, employees began to believe more in the information, which, in the end, facilitated the decision-making process.

HOW ABC WAS USED

Before beginning the project, Arthur Andersen set up a case to illustrate how the new model/vision would function. Primary changes and considerations included the following:

- Global revision of the cost system and structuring of a conceptual model based on the ABC costing methodology
- Implementation of a cost-per-activity model linked to the products and services offered by Banco Real as cost objects
- Activity cost per transaction used to calculate the profitability of products for margin follow-ups, and in feasibility studies for new products
- Use of integrated software, featuring simplified operations and simulation capacity to make activities interactive and more autonomous in relation to developments in the information system area
- Total integration of the activity cost with the input systems, accounting, and output systems, and in calculating the effective result per customer or segment
- Reduction in the rounding-up and calculation of a cost period
- Possibility of monthly calculation of effective results per customer or segment with calculation base cost in relation to the previous month
- Centralization of registry base of the products and services Banco Real offered to internal and external customers
- Identification, analysis, and segregation of corporate expenses, information systems, and service channels
- Change in the criteria for allocation allowing for decentralization
- Segregation of costs related to products and services of the bank and of other companies of the group
- Calculation of direct labor idleness costs of work in branch transactions and internal banking branches using the concept of effective capacity
- Individualized financing of several steps in the banking process or ac-

tivity so that the cost of a certain transaction becomes understood as the sum of the resources used by that item

- Creation of a cost system, characterized by openness and great stimulation capacity, as a basic tool for analysis of bank operations and results

ABC was first used as an information tool by crossing it with the previously developed profitability system. Once costs for each transaction and the number of customer transactions and activities were available, the bank calculated the spread and the profitability per branch and per customer. Using the information, the bank was able to modify and increase profitability for the units/companies, processes, products, customers, and distribution channels. In addition, managers could carry out all budgetary aspects to support pricing and manage performance measures. Managers also may set up a more developed information system for the management of processes and profitability analysis in various decisions, such as point of sales, processes, portfolios, customers, and segments.

RESULTS

Among the initial results, Banco Real identified the opportunity for improvement in cost allocations. ABC allowed Banco Real to allocate 70 percent of costs more accurately. Not less than 44 percent of the costs of indirect areas of general management were treated as overhead and, therefore, not allocated to products or activities.

Of the bank's general cost, about 38 percent referred to corporate costs (i.e., administrative support, human resources, and management structure) and 15 percent were related to costs of information systems. Prior to this, the costs related to information systems were not allocated directly to the product. Information systems costs were broken into almost 200 system applications and applied directly to the product using the specific applications.

One project advantage was to facilitate a vision of costs per product or financial transaction and per distribution channel. This made it possible to obtain a statement on transactions in a checking account at the branch itself, via modem, computer, ATM machines, or 24-hour offices. The costs of these services were mapped to evaluate the profitability of financial transactions. A cost mapping was then carried out involving all branches. This verified how much of the corporate structure was allocated to each operation and the cost of each transaction. Such information, whether profitable or not, allows for more knowledgeable and secure strategic decisions. The project managed to debug the information and motivate managers to use ABC as a decision-making mechanism. Prior to ABC, managers made cost-based decisions more on the basis of personal experience and intuition. ABC facilitated the precise knowledge about which products were viable for certain channels.

With ABC, information reliability increased, which is important with the ever-changing structure of a bank. An accurate and unbiased contrast between revenue and cost improved managers' abilities to act on decisions rather than using the old system that did not cover all the details of cost.

ABC was undertaken to disseminate a budgetary culture throughout the bank. Prior to the ABC project, all areas were not involved with or participated effectively in deciding what would be spent. ABC enabled Banco Real to design and implement a new budget process that crossed all departments and functions.

LESSONS LEARNED

In the case of financial institutions, with a great volume of operations, products, and services, possessing precise knowledge of the financial variables already in place at the beginning of a project is vital. Having a complete list of transactions performed by the bank, to facilitate mapping and correct measurement of operations, is also important. Generally customers do not know or have control over all products. Managers often do not know how many transactions are performed in a given time period or the number performed per product. Lack of these facts greatly hinder the measurement of these processes. The banking activity is very dynamic and products change rapidly. Banco Real listed more than 800 types of transactions—services and products—in the beginning of this project.

It is necessary to involve the right people from the start to help ensure a project's success. When implementing ABC at major banks, which are supported by mainframes, it is critical to include key professionals belonging to the technical areas of the financial institutions. These professionals should bear the administrative and operational vision as well as a wide knowledge of operations. In this case, the project involved 12 complementary financial companies with very different products and characteristics. As such it is important to have technical personnel with expertise in details of the operations. They should master personal computers, in order to download data from the mainframe to tabulate the information.

Prior to structuring the project, it is very important to set up a conceptual model, which should be discussed and validated with operating management.

It is not necessary to spend time and resources to assess costs in detail, even with complex structures such as those of a major bank. It is possible to select a consistent database and cover the essentials of the general expenses. Before beginning a project, the degree of detail desired must be defined. In this case, 108 of the company's 200 cost centers were in the corporate area, but only 46 were necessary for mapping, as they accounted for approximately 92 percent of costs. This sample was sufficient for the correct measurement of data. To assess data correctly, it is enough to define, with criteria, the grounds for the mapping, such as relevance, proximity of the product, and specific characteristics. It is possible to work with samples for very similar structures. From the total 33 CPDs, a systems structure decentralized for processing data and transactions, only three were needed for mapping. In addition, mapping should be done only after the conceptual cost models and transactions are defined.

The decision to review costs and redefine expenses provides for other initiatives. For example, with standardization, the bank began to better control some initiatives for opening or closing a cost center as well as for the creation of products. The project created a mechanism for beginning and finalizing each product.

Since a project of this scope demands a long time from start to finish—around six months in this example—controls should be in place for the constant updating of information throughout the project. Communication or monitoring changes in product and service lines ensure accuracy and faster validation of the model. Model validation also requires the most current expense structure.

Upper management must always be involved in the process. Banco Real had major differences in structures, so each change in the cost system involved certain gains and losses as costs were distributed differently. Thus it is important for everyone to participate in the validation of the information. In this way the final result, based on the new concepts and established criteria, is unquestionable. The validation process must involve product managers and process areas; the process must be formalized, and the analysis requires a review period following the model's implementation.

ABOUT THE AUTHORS

Roberto Lacerda is a Partner with Arthur Andersen in São Paulo and is responsible for the project's quality control.

Juarez Lopes de Araújo is a Partner with Arthur Andersen in São Paulo and is responsible for the project.

Clodomarcio Tosi is a Manager with Arthur Andersen in São Paulo and is the coordinator of the project.

6

TELECOMMUNICATIONS— FACING THE CHALLENGES OF COMPETITION WITH ACTIVITY- BASED COSTING

Carlos Eduardo Rocha and Arthur Azevedo
Arthur Andersen, São Paulo, Brazil

Jóse Luiz Santos Azevedo Filho
Arthur Andersen, Belo Horizonte, Brazil

CASE STUDY: CTBC Telecom, Uberlândia, Brazil

SUMMARY

Business Issue
Facing increased competition as a result of deregulation of the telecommunications industry in Brazil, CTBC Telecom understood the need to obtain better and more accurate costing information in order to compete successfully. The company needed to identify the nature of costs as well as map costs to segments, activities, and products.

How ABC Was Used
The company developed a cost management model to provide accurate product costs and to support cost reduction and continuous improvement efforts. The project spanned 18 departments and five regional offices. In addition, CTBC employed its Oracle Financial System to extract much of the data for processing the ABC model.

CTBC Telecom's Results
Upon understanding the total cost, the project revealed cost results for existing operations as well as justifications for future investments. Product and segment profitability allowed CTBC Telecom to support decisions on where to focus resources. Also, critical findings were identified related to the cost of new technologies, which drive constant change and competition throughout the industry.

The deregulation of the telecommunications industry in Brazil has had a major impact on the country's economy. As state monopolies are privatized and competition increases, the surviving entities must rely on new managerial weapons to face the challenges of a competitive environment. No industry—including telecommunications—is immune to this reality.

COMPANY BACKGROUND

CTBC Telecom is the only private organization operating on both fixed and cellular telecommunications in Brazil. The company is controlled by one of Brazil's largest conglomerates, the Grupo Algar. The company's head office is located in the city of Uberlândia, in the state of Minas Gerais. CTBC Telecom reported revenues of US$270 million in 1997, representing approximately 5 percent of the local telecommunications market. Service covers areas within the four states of Minas Gerais, São Paulo, Mato Grosso do Sul, and Goiás.

BUSINESS ISSUE

In 1996 discussion about the privatization of the Brazilian telecommunications system began. At that same time, the management of CTBC Telecom concluded that the company would, very soon, be operating in a competitive environment. In order to compete successfully, the company would need to make a number of internal changes. As a result of these discussions, a modernization project was initiated.

The first step was to send managers and directors abroad to visit several telecommunications companies. They studied specific issues for improvement at CTBC Telecom, such as the quality of the information regarding cost of products, services, and result centers. After assessing several existing management information systems both in and out of the telecommunications industry, technical visits began. One such visit was to major telecommunications companies in Chile, where information about the cost system in place was collected. According to its research and later confirmation by Chilean companies, the team concluded the most appropriate methodology to be used at CTBC Telecom would be activity-based costing (ABC).

Brazilian telecommunications companies lagged behind their international peers in the area of cost management. CTBC Telecom's executives believed they could not access critical costing information. There were also issues as to the accuracy of the cost information. As a result, it was difficult for management to make informed decisions.

Important data were not readily available. For example, existing cost information could not provide the cost of a wireless user in transit, customer invoicing, or changing a phone address. Management did not understand costs associated with specific customer segments, products, and activities. In addition to identifying the nature of costs, the company also needed to be able to map those costs to each segment, activity, and product. According to Marineide da Silva Peres, CTBC Telecom's chief financial officer, "The telecommunications sector in Brazil will not be the same after deregulation and privatization. Its future configuration cannot be precisely predicted. However, we expect strong competition from some of the largest companies in the world. Consequently, understanding our true costs and margins and knowing their drivers will be critical to be one step ahead of other players."

HOW ABC WAS USED

Once ABC was chosen as the costing methodology, CTBC Telecom executives decided on the following criteria to guide the design of the costing model. The model should be able to:

- Demonstrate profitability of products and markets
- Simulate cost related impacts of strategic decisions
- Enhance cost reduction and continuous improvement efforts
- Measure the relationship between internal customers and suppliers
- Improve the analysis of investments in new products and services
- Support pricing analysis and decision

The project's objective was to develop a cost management model that would improve the precision and accuracy of product costing while also supporting efforts to reduce costs and to implement continuous improvement. The scope of the ABC project at CTBC Telecom covered:

- All cost centers at the central and regional offices
- All categories of expenses
- All products and markets

In many ways, the success and continuity of any project of this nature related directly to the dissemination of the cost management concepts, particularly the ABC approach, throughout the organization. This acceptance and success can be achieved only through effective participation of the employees. At CTBC Telecom the project task force was a joint team of company employees and consultants from Arthur Andersen. This group was joined by approximately 25 employees selected to represent all result centers. The result center employees were designated team leaders and received training on the methodology so they could actively participate in the design of the conceptual model. This group was also responsible for the dissemination of the project concept throughout the organization. Presentations were made over the course of the project for both management and coordinators, in order to obtain the commitment and buy-in of these top executives.

From December 1996 to the end of April 1997, the implementation project covered the entire organization—18 departments and five regional offices. A pilot project, which began by mapping the activities of the central office and of one regional office, preceded implementation. The model later was replicated to the other regions.

The first phase involved training the team. This step was to facilitate the complete transfer of the ABC methodology. The second phase was to identify the products. The third consisted of identification of the activities.

During the second step, the project team faced its first major challenge: identifying products for costing purposes within a service company. In the manufacturing industry, most products are quite obvious and readily identifiable. However, the process becomes quite a bit more complex when examining telecommunications services. Exhibit 6.1 provides an example of the

EXHIBIT 6.1   Example of Product Structure

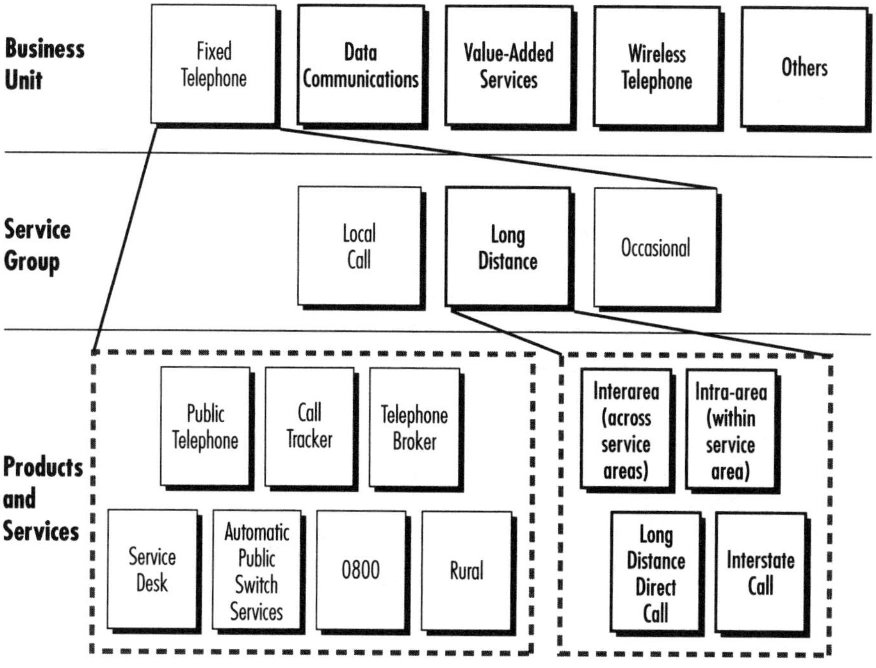

structure of the products identified. According to Wellington Miranda, cost analyst of CTBC Telecom and full-time member of the project team, "Existing methodologies were not able to handle the complexity of today's telecommunications network, where new value-added services, such as data transmission, integrated services, voice and video conferencing, are provided together with traditional local and long-distance calls."

After identifying the product structure, the project team mapped the activities of all 18 departments. This resulted in the design of the conceptual model and contained all resources, activities, and products. Salaries, benefits, depreciation, and taxes are some of the resources mapped and allocated to the activities performed, according to distinct resource drivers. For example, salaries and benefits were allocated to each activity based on the "number of employees" or "dedication percentage," which is the estimated percent of time spent on each activity. Depreciation was directly assigned according to the dedication of each piece of equipment. After building the model in Oros software by ABC Technologies, the resulting cost model structure was approved by each department manager. The overall prototype was then developed with the assistance of the Information Systems Division. All necessary data was provided in electronic file format.

The next step was to run the system and process the costs per department, activities, and products. After verification of the numbers, an implementation plan was generated, allowing the ABC system to be processed in a recurrent, automated manner.

CTBC Telecom's goal was to apply all prior experience in activity mapping of telecommunications companies when defining the company's activities and processes. The objective was to provide a horizontal view of the organization in addition to the vertical view already provided by existing functional cost centers. The project team also applied a structure of processes suggested by Arthur Andersen's Global Best Practices℠, a worldwide knowledge base. The Global Best Practices knowledge base has many industry-specific process maps, including one specific to telecommunications companies. An extract of this structure can be seen in Exhibit 6.2. The company believed that applying the format contained in the Global Best Practices would allow for benchmarking as other companies begin to adopt similar models.

One concern was to optimize investments already made by the company in information systems. CTBC Telecom used the Oracle Financial Corporate System, which provided most of the data used for processing the ABC model. ABC Technologies' Oros software was selected and used to gather important characteristics due to its ease of integration, applicability to the specific needs of the industry, and better support of the expectations of CTBC Telecom's executives.

EXHIBIT 6.2   Example of CTBC Telecom Processes

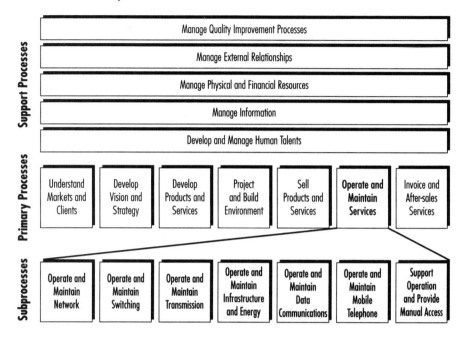

RESULTS

Since the previous cost control system was weak, one of the biggest surprises of the project was learning actual costs. Surprised reactions, such as "this figure must be wrong"—common in ABC projects—were also prevalent at CTBC Telecom. This was exactly what happened when the Finance Department had its costs compared to other companies by benchmarking against comparative finance cost data also obtained from Arthur Andersen's Global Best Practices knowledge base. Work groups were established to suggest cost reduction measures. For example, the Accounts Payable Programming activity was simplified by having CTBC Telecom employees switch to using corporate credit cards to pay travel expenses. In other cases more complex solutions, such as contracting out, are being studied.

Among the important discoveries, this ABC project showed a certain service demanded more cost than expected. As a result a greater number of users were necessary to justify new investments in this segment. The company already had spent a significant amount of time and effort in marketing a service to customers. This service also requires large investments to maintain. However, this service's users do not use the service very often. ABC provided the elements for CTBC Telecom to better judge whether it should stimulate sales of this service or discontinue it. These profitability analyses allow the company to evaluate changes in the strategic direction of the business based on the profitability of all products and services. In reviewing the strategic uses of ABC, Jacimara A. B. S. Crozara, coordinator of the Control Division, says: "Activity-based costing information has already supported us in determining price for interconnection agreements with other telecommunication companies. Under the concept of incremental cost, we have used it to study the feasibility of new technologies and network expansion."

In the telecommunications industry, several distinct technologies make certain types of service available. Some of these technologies are subject to more interesting tariffs or pricing. Such services include data transmission and value-added services like voice mail, telephone directory assistance, and Brazil's emergency, toll-free, and paid numbers (i.e., 112, 130, 0800, and 0900 numbers). These are more intelligent services using modern technologies, and therefore, they justify differentiated tariffs and represent the highest value and most profitable means of using the installed plant.

Before ABC, CTBC Telecom's executives did not have precise information to support business decisions, such as the development of a new product. In observed practical examples, the company verified that the demand for certain services did not provide enough revenue to cover associated costs. Marketing efforts then could be addressed to those niches shown to be profitable. Miranda says: "In the Marketing Division, the breakdown of product costs and margins showed the cost carried by recently launched products tends to reduce as they move forward in their life cycle."

LESSONS LEARNED

When applicable, use the advantages of benchmarking to facilitate the project team's efforts. In the case of CTBC Telecom, Arthur Andersen already had implemented similar projects in Portugal (see Portugal Telecom in Chapter 14) and in Spain (Telefónica Movile). It was very important for the project team to observe similar systems already in place to better understand what should be done. Technical visits were important for defining the extent of the project in advance. Benchmarking also helped locate those with experience in the implementation of ABC integrated with the Oracle platform. CTBC Telecom discovered a similar integration in Spain, carried out by Arthur Andersen at Telefónica Movile, and replicated the same experience in Brazil.

Another lesson was the scope of the pilot. The strategy at CTBC Telecom was to build a prototype that did not cover the whole company, but only the central office and the regional one at Uberlândia. This made the initial project leaner and faster to complete.

It is essential not to neglect the importance of establishing a partnership between the company and the consultant. In this case, CTBC Telecom's involvement and interest in knowledge transfer reached such an extent that the number of analysts understanding ABC exceeded that of the consultant's team. Part of the project involved training the client's team to work with the new tools. There was, therefore, a high degree of client participation in the development and implementation of the project. This permitted the consultants to act more in the role of coordinator and coach and allowed the project team from within the company to complete the actual implementation of the model. This transfer of knowledge enabled CTBC Telecom to continue to advance the ABC system after the consulting support was gone.

ABOUT THE AUTHORS AND TEAM MEMBERS

Carlos Eduardo Rocha is a Partner with Arthur Andersen in São Paulo.

Arthur Azevedo is a Manager with Arthur Andersen in São Paulo.

Jóse Luiz Santos Azevedo Filho is a Manager with Arthur Andersen in Belo Horizonte.

Mariniede da Silva Peres is the chief financial officer of CTBC Telecom.

Jacimara A. B. S. Crozara is the coordinator of CTBC Telecom's Control Division.

Éder Novais Arantes is the technical specialist of CTBC Telecom's Control Division in charge of the implementation team.

Wellington Miranda, Fernando Ribeiro Faria, and Nádia Regina de Oliveira are the analysts who have set up the ABC implementation team for CTBC Telecom.

7

ACHIEVING STRATEGIC AND OPERATIONAL EXCELLENCE WITH ACTIVITY-BASED COSTING

Roberto Lacerda and Arthur Azevedo
Arthur Andersen, São Paulo, Brazil

with

Ruy de Campos Filho, João Carlos Brega, Victor Gilman, and Pedro Alba Bayarri
Multibrás São Paulo, Brazil

CASE STUDY: Multibrás Electrodomésticos, São Paulo, Brazil

SUMMARY

Business Issue
In view of the growing international interest, Multibrás decided to strengthen its competitive capability through a focus on reduction of expenses combined with improvements in productivity and quality. Even amid a sales boom in the appliance industry, new competition squeezed profit margins for the company.

How ABC Was Used
Multibrás introduced activity-based costing (ABC) methodology to provide strategic information such as profitability analysis along a multidimensional framework. These analyses were used to achieve favorable product mix strategies. ABC also was used to determine operational information, such as cost per activity and process, which was then used to identify cost reduction opportunities.

Multibrás's Results
From the analysis, the company identified and analyzed profitability by unit, by product, by market, by distribution channel, and by customer. In the product profitability area, Multibrás found high volume items were subsidizing items of low volume, larger production runs subsidized the smaller runs, and a correlation existed between the unproductive time in factory units and the operation time of the machines.

Multibrás, a Brazilian company recognized for the excellence of its products, manufactures household appliances including refrigerators, freezers, dishwashers, air conditioners, washing machines, stoves, and microwave ovens.

Even with the sales explosion in appliances, Multibrás has never rested in its position of leadership. In fact, the entry of new consumers in the market resulting from earnings generated by the Real Plan spurred the company to enhance competitive weapons. The Real Plan, named after the Brazilian currency, is an economic stabilization program launched by the government in 1994, which resulted in significant reduction in inflation and improvement in the purchasing power of Brazilian consumers, especially those in the lowest economic levels. As a result, a large portion of the population who previously did not have access to home appliance goods started to generate an important market demand for those products.

Amid the sales boom, the company adopted activity-based costing (ABC) as part of its efforts to be more competitive and to position itself better in view of the market entry of international competitors who also have been attracted to the vigorous growth in the Brazilian home appliances sector. The advent of this new competition exerted heavy pressure on profit margins. Thus Multibrás had to prepare itself for the new times while making use of a current favorable market position compared to much of its competition.

Major foreign investors are attracted to this marketplace due to the industry's growth potential. In view of the modest penetration of appliances in Brazilian homes, major world manufacturers—which in the United States and Europe face a low-growth, saturated market—believe that companies with the fastest response to an emerging economy will receive better profit margins.

Multibrás Electrodomésticos, the leader in the electrical and electronics industry, offers consumers a complete range of appliances, including Brastemp and Consul brands. Revenue in 1997 was approximately $1.7 billion, and profits were in the order of $129 million. Controlled by the North American Whirlpool Corporation, a traditional home appliance manufacturer with strong penetration in major world markets, Multibrás employs 9,000 people in six industrial units and one administrative center, which is located in São Paulo. The six industrial units are spread throughout Brazil with each manufacturing certain products. For example, facilities in São Paulo and Recife manufacture stoves while the facility in São Bernardo do Campo produces refrigerators and distributes spare parts. Some facilities manufacture multiple products; for example, Manaus produces microwave ovens and air conditioners, and Rio Claro manufactures washers and dishwashers. The industrial unit in Joinville has the most diverse mix of product lines: refrigerators, freezers, dryers, and air conditioners.

BUSINESS ISSUES

In view of the growing international interest, Multibrás's reaction had to be immediate. The company decided to strengthen its competitive capacity by means of classic measures, such as reducing expenses and making productivity and quality improvements. In addition, the company added a powerful weapon to its arsenal: ABC, an innovative support tool for decision making. In this context, the introduction of the new costing methodology had the following objectives:

- To support the strategic administration by generating profitability analyses per product, business, customer, distribution channel, and market
- To support the operational administration by assessing and disclosing cost per activity and process
- To aid the identification of cost reduction opportunities in the scope of an existing reengineering initiative
- To redefine product and customer mixes to obtain improvement of profitability per product and per customer; it was also necessary to identify which customers and products were unprofitable and generated losses
- To rationalize the activities

The first two objectives were related directly to the structuring of an information base supporting the administration of business. In effect, the existing cost management model no longer met the executives' growing needs because they depended excessively on pro-rata allocation approaches based on volume. Raw materials and direct labor were easy to appropriate directly to products using standards. However, the use of cost sharing based on direct costs for general fabrication expenses was more problematic. Such general expenses include: indirect labor, benefits, training, maintenance, trips, services, leases, storage, commissions, advertising, and guarantees.

From the analysis, it was concluded that 29 percent of cost allocations were based in the arbitrary criteria that did not guarantee precise information in connection with cost and profitability per product. In view of the complexity of the operation, the previous method (allocation of indirect costs based on volume) did not meet many of the organization's essential needs. According to João Carlos Brega, Multibrás's general manager of control, "We need to be certain about the costs and margins of each product in order to make accurate decisions. This was our greatest motivation when we selected activity-based costing as our costing methodology."

One of the most common distortions was that indirect costs were distributed in indiscriminately. As a result, products considered highly profitable actually were way over the budget. For example, the company produced a line of high-end refrigerators and stoves. All of these products were manufactured in small lots and considered to be generally higher value added. However, despite expectations, these products were not very profitable. The activity mapping detected that costs were very high when machinery was calibrated or set up to produce a small lot. The work of engineering alone to complete product drawings and efforts to maintain the product line, divided by the actual number of units produced, resulted in huge costs. Having these new figures, the company was able to rethink the best strategy for the most sophisticated and less profitable products. Prior to this analysis, the commercial area received inducements to increase sales efforts for products with low returns.

Other surprises came with the revised distribution of the corporate or administrative center cost. With the new model, costs that previously were divided according to revenue or variable cost criteria were now attributed based on the services performed for the units. Once this older distortion was corrected, initially perceived lower profitability products became more lucrative. According to Ruy de Campos Filho, chief financial officer of Multibrás: "The actual effort of the administrative center bears no relation to the amount of variable costs incurred in a certain plant. ABC was effective in correcting this situation." Potential impacts are illustrated in Exhibit 7.1. For example, Exhibit 7.1 shows product line F was believed to have a margin of 11 percent, according to the previously used methodology. However, after the implementation of ABC, margin actually could range from –9 percent to 13 percent, suggesting radically different courses of action.

EXHIBIT 7.1   Potential Impacts on Profitability

Description	Result			Potential Impacts		
	Income	Cost	Margin	Potential Fluctuation (1)	Minimum Margin	Maximum Margin
Line A	100	83	17	10	7	27
Line B	100	91	9	11	(2)	20
Line C	100	84	16	10	6	26
Line D	100	74	26	9	17	35
Line E	100	139	(39)	16	(55)	(23)
Line F	100	98	2	11	–9	13
Line G	100	88	12	10	2	22
Line H	100	72	28	8	20	36
Line I	100	89	11	10	1	21
Line J	100	91	9	11	(2)	20
Line K	100	72	28	8	20	36

(1) Maximum 40% variation considered on the cost portion subject to imprecise allocations: 29%

Shaded lines indicate that the impact of imprecise allocations can distort managerial messages contained therein, suggesting actions or strategies with undesired final effect.

Traditional methodology hindered appropriate managerial actions because from the strategic point of view, it did not illustrate the real margins per product and line of business. As such, it did not contemplate the market vision and customers. And from an operational aspect, it did not provide enough detail for understanding the origins and reasons for costs.

HOW ABC WAS USED

Multibrás management introduced ABC methodology for cost assessment with multiple views. This multidimensional approach provided the ability for the company to "slice and dice" the data to analyze results along lines of business, process, and market. The business view allowed the company to drill down into unit and product analysis. Process views included subprocesses as well as activities. A robust view of market findings enabled the company to analyze profitability by region, sales channel, and even individual client. Prior to implementing ABC, the company employed a bi-dimensional model, which documented the nature of expenses with the business.

The first ABC project, which lasted four months, involved several steps: (1) planning the project, (2) mapping activities, (3) generating a database/matrix for processes reengineering, (4) designing the model in the software, (5) feeding the model with actual data, (6) validating the information, and (7) implementing the model. The model's efficiency was proven in the factory in São Paulo and the administrative center, which is responsible for the conglomerate's main activities. The first model was then expanded to other factories.

Project Roll-out

The strategy was to set up a model allowing the multiple views of costs and profitability. This would satisfy the needs of the major groups of users: marketing, sales, manufacturing, and control. Due to the size of the company, an implementation with a project scope involving all the industrial units would take too long to generate results. Consequently, the adopted strategy was to implement the methodology on a pilot basis in the industrial unit of São Paulo and in the administrative center of Multibrás. Soon after, the units of São Bernardo do Campo, Joinville, and Rio Claro and the spare parts distribution center were targeted. The phased approach is illustrated in Exhibit 7.2.

The company eventually determined that the creation of a consolidated model (corporate) would allow a group vision for all the factories. At this point, Arthur Andersen became involved with the project, which included

EXHIBIT 7.2   ABC Implementation Strategy

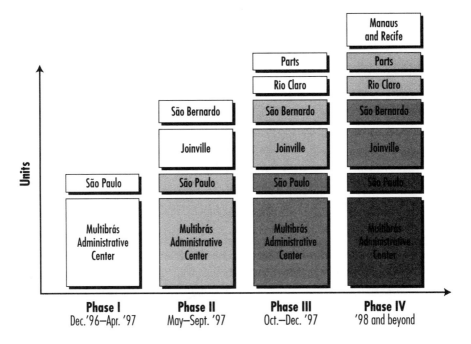

several factories located in different areas as well as six models working simultaneously. Pedro Alba Bayarri, coordinator of the ABC team at Multibrás, states: "Multiple sites running independent models simultaneously to generate a consolidated report of the company's results proved challenging to be completed in a reasonable amount of time. As such, this characteristic made the ABC project unique in Brazil."

To guarantee uniformity and means of comparison, a single model of activities was developed, including both production and support for each industrial unit. The activities and efforts for each factory and/or customer were mapped at the administrative center of Multibrás. A summary of the Multibrás model is presented in the illustration (Exhibit 7.3).

The market vision was one of the strong points of the conceptual model of Multibrás. In each sales region, distribution channels were mapped and main customers were selected inside each channel. (See Exhibit 7.4.)

In addition, profitability for each customer was assessed, starting with the cost of serving a given customer and the cost of producing a certain product. Other visions then were easily generated through the aggregation of this information by distribution channel, regional market, brands, product line, business, and unit.

The technical platform was Oros ABC software manufactured by ABC

EXHIBIT 7.3   Summary of the Multibrás Model

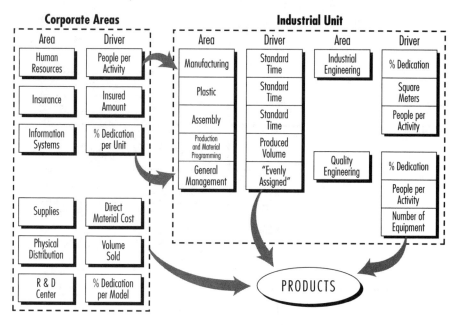

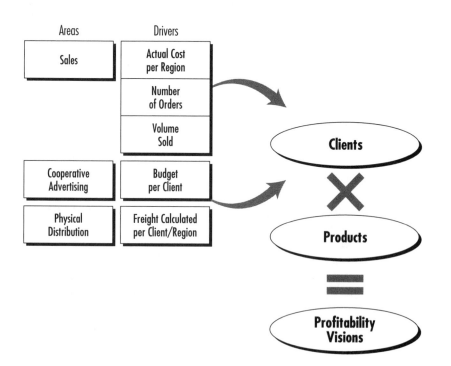

EXHIBIT 7.4   Market Vision

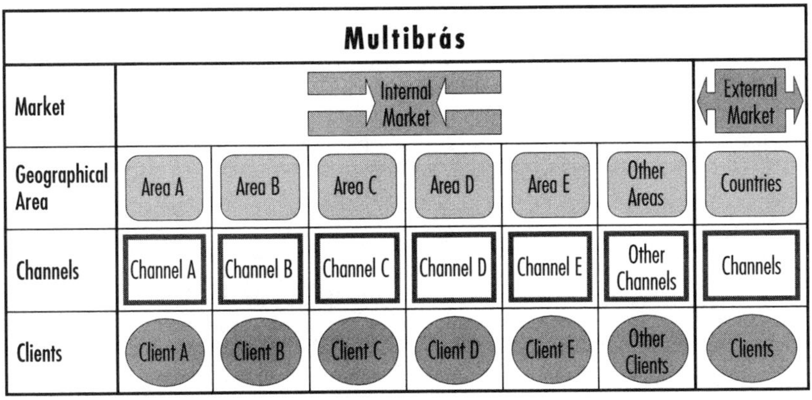

Multibrás							
Market		Internal Market					External Market
Geographical Area	Area A	Area B	Area C	Area D	Area E	Other Areas	Countries
Channels	Channel A	Channel B	Channel C	Channel D	Channel E	Other Channels	Channels
Clients	Client A	Client B	Client C	Client D	Client E	Other Clients	Clients

Technologies, which was capable of assessing costs. Multibrás used Microsoft Access to generate reports and analyses. A specific model was developed and copies of the programs were installed for each unit. In addition, local teams were trained to manage the system and use its results in each location. On a monthly basis, information from the mainframe updates the Oros model using specially designed interfaces. Decentralizing the processing as well as the knowledge acquired during the project provided better support to plant managers. Exhibit 7.5 shows the configuration of the processing model.

RESULTS

Among the main results obtained, profitability can be highlighted in three areas.

Profitability per Unit

The arbitrary criteria for cost allocation of Multibrás's administrative center for the units was replaced by real information obtained by measuring the cost drivers of each mapped activity. In one certain plant where, comparatively, the number of employees was high due to manual operations and the product manufactured required a lower level of variable costs, the amount of costs transferred from the Human Resource Department (administrative center) was adjusted using the driver "number of employees." Exhibit 7.6 shows the changes observed in the total cost and margin of each industrial unit after Multibrás implemented the ABC methodology.

EXHIBIT 7.5 Processing Model

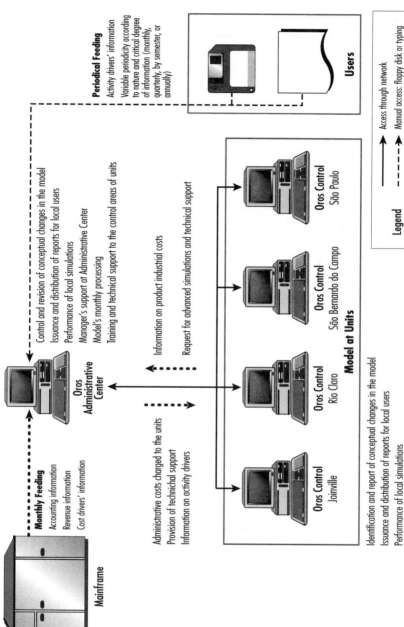

EXHIBIT 7.6   Comparison of Profitability per Unit

Amounts in percentage

Unit	Income	Traditional		ABC	
		Cost	Result	Cost	Result
Unit A	100	92	8	85	15
Unit B	100	93	7	89	11
Unit C	100	93	7	74	26
Unit D	100	108	(8)	111	(11)
Unit E	100	108	(8)	96	4
Unit F	100	109	(9)	100	0

Profitability per Product

When the real production effort and support to products in line, and the expenses in connection with warranties and advertising were mapped, managers were surprised to note the profitability—or lack thereof—of items. Areas of primary concern included:

- Items of high volume were subsidizing items of low volume
- Products that were lower value added were subsidized by products of higher value added
- Big production runs or lots subsidized the loss evoked by smaller lots
- Unproductive time in factories was significant in relation to the operation time of the machines

Exhibit 7.7 highlights profitability by product under both a traditional method and an ABC method. For example, before implementing ABC, some higher-value-added products of brand A received more costs than they should have due to allocation criteria based on variable costs. According to Victor Gilman, manager of Costs and Economic Studies of Multibrás: "The effort of the Engineering team to maintain any model in the production line is the same. It does not matter whether the product is a luxury or a popular model and carries more or less variable costs; therefore, all the models must receive the same amount of cost."

Deficit products were analyzed in two ways:

1. From a strategic point of view, the product's importance in the portfolio was related to obtaining market share and providing a complete line

EXHIBIT 7.7   Comparison of Profitability per Product

Product	Income	Traditional		ABC (%)	
		Cost	Result	Cost	Result
Brand A	100	101	(1)	91	9
Product 1	100	106	(6)	101	(1)
Product 2	100	98	2	81	19
Product 3	100	103	(3)	97	3
Product 4	100	99	1	75	25
Others Brand A	100	96	4	111	(11)
Brand B	100	131	(31)	142	(42)
Product 1	100	146	(46)	142	(42)
Product 2	100	125	(25)	123	(23)
Product 3	100	103	(3)	129	(29)
Product 4	100	92	8	124	(24)
Others Brand B	100	108	(8)	163	(63)
Others	100	119	(19)	271	(171)

of products embracing several segments of prices available to the market.

2. From an operational point of view, detailed composition of efforts and production costs provided a basis for the value-added analysis of each activity used by the product.

Discontinuation of a product involves a complex decision process and should be preceded by margin recovery efforts through revision of the value added by the composing activities. In this regard, Exhibit 7.8 highlights how the cost of a certain product can be detailed and understood using the reports generated by the ABC system. From this example, Engineering could drill to the level of activity where the cost of every activity used to manufacture a product can be identified and compared to the value added.

Profitability per Market/Channel/Customer

The main costs of serving were identified and associated to major customers and presented together with the result of the mix of sold products. The result represents each customer's contribution individually for the global result of the company.

EXHIBIT 7.8   Product Cost Composition

TRADITIONAL		ABC		
Price		Price		
Material		Material		
Direct Labor		Fabrication		
General Fabrication Expense		Finishing		
		Assembly		
		Industrial Support		
		Idleness		
Total Industrial Cost		Total Industrial Cost		
Expenses		Corporate Cost		
Guarantee		Warranty		
Other Expenses		Marketing		
		Sale and Distribution		
Expenses		Expenses		
Total Cost		Total Cost		
Result		Result		

LESSONS LEARNED

Four major lessons were learned from the project.

- The ABC tool, if well used, is capable of unmasking inaccuracies and revealing the true total cost. Products or factories considered profitable and efficient can be revealed to be exactly the opposite.
- During the initial phases of the project, the work team should concentrate its attention on the quality of the basic data, especially in the production patterns or standards (operations and times). Engineering involvement is fundamental for revising and maintaining the patterns and to carry out the mapping follow-up of productive activities. Critical information includes:
    —control of stock for finished products
    —production patterns
    —machine efficiency and productivity
    —production capacity
    —structures of products to be mapped
    —accounting cost per cost center
    —prices and discounts

- The technology information area should cosponsor any ABC project and dedicate a professional for the design and operation of the interfaces. During the tests and in the first months of processing, special attention should be given to the fast execution of file adjustments.
- Control devices on the critical information should be put in practice, in order to prevent changes on the source database without the knowledge of the ABC team. The following actions are critical and must be authorized by the ABC team: introduction of new cost centers, modification of existing cost centers, introduction of new work centers in the engineering system, and substitution of existing work centers. In addition, modification of the products or clients identification codes, review of products material structures and production standards, and introduction or discontinuance of products should also be approved.

ABOUT THE AUTHORS AND TEAM MEMBERS

Pedro Alba Bayarri is an ABC coordinator of Multibrás.

Arthur Azevedo is a Manager with Arthur Andersen in São Paulo, Brazil, and is the coordinator for the project.

João Carlos Brega is the general manager of control at Multibrás.

Ruy de Campos Filho is the chief financial officer of Multibrás.

Roberto S. De Lacerda is a Partner with Arthur Andersen in São Paulo, Brazil, and is responsible for the project.

Victor Gilman is the manager of cost and economic studies of Multibrás.

8

MODELING FOR ANSWERS WITH ACTIVITY-BASED COSTING

Michel Maisonneuve and Stephane Mercier
Arthur Andersen, Montrèal, Canada

CASE STUDY: Alcan Smelters and Chemicals, Montrèal, Canada

SUMMARY

Business Issues

As a 90-year-old company that has seen much growth and expansion over the years, Alcan Smelters and Chemicals (AS&C) did a thorough market analysis to explore activity-based costing (ABC) and to see how other businesses were using ABC internally. The company found that ABC would integrate its finance area with the overall business. Fulfilling that need was crucial for AS&C because its continual growth needed to be matched with continual building of knowledge in financial software applications and problem-solving approaches and techniques.

How ABC Was Used

AS&C piloted the project in one of its smelting plants in Quebec, Canada. ABC was implemented to enhance decision making, continuous improvement, and performance tracking. In the area of decision making, the company concentrated on investment justification, costs estimates, pricing, target costing, and cost accounting. The continuous improvement effort included cost reduction, downsizing, process reengineering, and benchmarking. In the last area, performance tracking, the company's endeavors included budget follow-up, activity performance measures, inventory valuation, and capacity usage.

AS&C's Results

ABC was able to evaluate the real or true cost of products and customers by establishing which methods could better serve AS&C for certain decisions.

AS&C is a member of Alcan Aluminum Limited, a Canadian corporation. Alcan is the parent company of a multinational industrial group engaged in all aspects of the aluminum business. Through subsidiaries and related companies around the world, the activities of the Alcan Group include bauxite mining, aluminum refining, aluminum smelting, manufacturing, sales, and re-cycling. Over 35,000 people are directly employed by the Alcan Group, with thousands more employed in related companies.

The history of Alcan can be characterized by growth over a period of more than 90 years. Based initially on ownership of hydroelectric power in Canada, Alcan has grown into an integrated aluminum enterprise extending to other countries and other continents. Alcan has become one of the largest aluminum companies in the world. Alcan Smelters and Chemicals (AS&C) is the Canadian division that operates major activities in the aluminum smelting sector. This chapter describes AS&C's experience with activity-based costing using the experience of one of the smelting plants, Shawinigan Works, in the province of Quebec, Canada.

BEFORE IMPLEMENTING: A MARKET ANALYSIS OF ABC SYSTEMS

In early 1990s, activity-based costing was seen as the way to go; it was considered cutting-edge technology for many companies—an answer to every costing question. But ABC can be a complex concept with myriad approaches and a like number of software systems to offer support. In light of such a wealth of information, AS&C undertook a market analysis to study and understand what others were doing in the area of ABC and why.

AS&C's research found:

- ABC was promoted mostly by the finance functions, primarily accounting.
- Most companies implemented a pilot or trial stage first, then progressed to full deployment.
- Organizations offered company-wide information about ABC systems, but its actual use was often limited to finance.
- ABC often ended with the production of additional accounting or finance reports, but with no real penetration in the world of operations and key decision making.

Still, ABC was an approach that made good business sense. And the AS&C finance area needed to become more closely involved in the overall business. Considering the size of the company and the actions that needed to be undertaken to improve the finance competency profile, the company sought to implement ABC through a series of pilot projects. These implementation projects were used to build knowledge about ABC approaches and software applications.

In preparing for these pilots, AS&C made other discoveries regarding ABC during the market analysis. These findings included:

- There is no uniform, standard, or ready-to-use approach to ABC. The approach depends on the goal being pursued. Software and technology are only enablers; the focus must be on training, and there must be sufficient time for knowledge building.

- Any ABC initiative must be sponsored by operations people, with support provided by finance. This new role is indeed in line with the new Finance competency profile requiring finance people to become coaches for nonfinance employees. The goal is to integrate financial aspects in all areas of decision making related to operations.

- An operational approach to ABC is preferable to a financial approach, which means the approach should be based on operational mapping and operational data. Dollars should be mapped only at the end of the process, as part of a final overall reconciliation with general ledger figures. This way results are based on operational data that correspond with financial measures; otherwise the model would be out of balance.

- The market has little experience with an operational approach. Very few companies have adopted it. Some cases have been handled manually using the storyboarding approach, but when the approach is being loaded into an ABC system, it is transformed to a general ledger decomposition approach.

- Buy-in to ABC grows very quickly when properly targeted. It pulls accounting and finance into a new world, a new way at looking at business. It becomes a day-to-day exercise when operational personnel require more data and use it to identify value-adding options for the business.

HOW ABC IS USED

At AS&C, the ABC project approach is driven by operations while being supported by the finance function. Several pilot experiences led to a global as well as tailored internal methodology to answer the demand for improved decision making, performance tracking, and continuous improvement. ABC is not a top-down exercise led by corporate management but rather must answer business needs at the plant level. For that reason, the project team reports to a project board consisting of one director from operations and one finance director from corporate. A typical project team has one operations representative, one management accountant, one internal consultant, and one external consultant in ABC. Every initiative is also monitored by the AS&C-ABC Interest Group, which is composed of members who have participated in past projects or show buy-in for the approach.

AS&C approached ABC by focusing on decision making, continuous improvement, and performance tracking. In the area of decision making, the company concentrated on investment justification, costs estimates, pricing, target costing, and cost accounting. The continuous improvement effort included cost reduction, downsizing, process reengineering, and benchmarking. In the last area, performance tracking, the company's endeavors included budget follow-up, activity performance measures, inventory valuation, and capacity usage.

When planning the initiative for Shawinigan Works, the project team found "ABC Readiness" was there. There was a general sense that traditional costing reports were inaccurate. There were many project requests from aluminum casting managers. Overall there was a willingness to provide operations and plant accounting employees to participate. These factors provided strong support to initiate a pilot.

Shawinigan's approach to ABC included the following steps: (1) mapping of floor processes, (2) interviews, (3) group sessions, (4) general ledger mapping, (5) results analysis and (6) support after implementation. Because AS&C operates about 10 other smelting and casting plants in North America, ABC implementation took into consideration the need for a common foundation for the activity dictionary, software and interfaces, and global architecture. This commonality is achieved through an ABC User Group that maintains the activity dictionary, validates the global architecture, maintains the business relationship with the software provider, and communicates results and achievements.

The objectives at Shawinigan Works were to better understand the behavior of costs and to improve profitability information by product and by customer. An operational model, which was built in approximately three months, closely linked the different process issues and considered many of the operational drivers. The production environment is complex and interrelates. There are many different links between the operational activities, such as which activities impact the time used of other activities, the overall process constraints, and the different equipment setup scenarios.

The model is used in the casting process, whereby molten aluminum is received and is transformed into value-added ingots. These ingots are produced in different diameters, different alloys, and different lengths. Ingots are sold as raw material to produce aluminum tubes and forms, building products such as windows, doors, and other finished goods. Operating at full capacity, Shawinigan can produce over 400 different types of ingots.

The activity model has approximately 20 different activities and related drivers. Examples of activities include preparing the furnaces, casting, sawing, wrapping, handling, and shipping. Examples of drivers are numbers of setups, number of interdrops, and hours of maintenance.

The first phase was recently completed and considered successful.

In completing the model, the project team identified three additional issues that help improve the modeling of capital intensive process-oriented business. They are as follows:

1. Cost of capital should be included in profitability analysis. With its inclusion, the profitability analysis provided by the model integrates well with the economic value-added (EVA) concept. However, questions arose regarding which capital costs were relevant for profitability analysis, including market value of the fixed assets as compared to the net book value. Cost of capital was separated and traced depending on the different types of assets. Carrying costs such as inventory related costs were traced to work-in-process and finished goods; receivables were traced to customers; and fixed assets were traced to different activities.

2. Economic opportunity costs will arise with the plant at full capacity. As such, cost-modeling efforts should include the opportunity costs of actions such as scrapping products. If a plant is at full capacity and just ready to ship a product when the product is scrapped, you lose its margin forever. This technique may be difficult to implement because these costs are not in the general ledger. It may also be difficult to quantify because the company must estimate the value of the margin lost, which requires estimating a net sales price. Yet this type of economic modeling is critical to evaluating production improvement efforts, capital investment decisions and understanding the magnitude of lost profits.

3. The cost of idle capacity should not be traced to the products or customers unless those products or customers are the cause of the idle capacity. If idle capacity is included, the cost models should try to isolate it or at least identify its magnitude so that it does not lead to erroneous decisions.

The AS&C model was developed using ABC Management Budget Software from Decimal Technology. The model explores four different views to trace costs:

First was labeled as "Pure ABC," which calculated the activity rate based on the practical capacity. Then costs were traced to the products based on the per-unit usage of the activity driver.[1] Once the model was complete, there were capacity costs not allocated to products. Even though the process is in full capacity, some operations may not be.

Second was "ABC high rate," which was also called ABC modified. The modification consists of using an activity rate was calculated based on the actual capacity used. As a result the modified rates will be higher reflecting the inefficiency between actual production and practical capacity.

The third method calculates process costs under a Theory of Constraint (TOC) approach. Under this approach fixed costs were allocated to the products based on the constraint in the process. Rate calculations were based on the total fixed costs divided by the total constraint hours. The rate then was applied to the products based on the unit-based demand of the constraint hour.

Finally, a hybrid method was developed using the Pure ABC approach with allocation of the excess capacity costs to products through the TOC approach.

More Insight on the Process and Structure

The results, outlined in Exhibit 8.1, illustrate significant differences in the product costs.

With four views, the dilemma became how to determine the best one to meet AS&C's primary needs. Different groups continue to have a variety of opinions; however, there is agreement that different views of product profitability should be available, based on the type of decision to be made.

AS&C believes either the ABC Modified or Hybrid figures are closer to "real costs" than the other two methods for margins analysis while TOC figures are more appropriate for process improvements. More cost behavior analysis and knowledge experience is now required to right-size the new information. Michel Boyer, Coordinator Finance Systems and Processes, explains: "Today there is a general feeling we are closer to real numbers. We can raise all kinds of questions and work to find the answers."

This ABC information and supporting tools enable simulation, what-if scenarios, and access to different sets of reports. In general, different ques-

EXHIBIT 8.1   Understanding Product Cost Differences

			Views of Fixed Costs Per Unit			
	Net	Variables	Pure ABC	ABC Modified	TOC	Hybrid
	Price	Costs	Variable Margin	Variable Margin	Variable Margin	Variable Margin
Product A	130	30	100	75	50	65
Product B	130	30	100	85	50	90
Product C	160	30	130	120	220	180

tions should be answered before establishing which method is better for certain decisions. Questions might include:

- Is this a short-term or long-term decision?
- Is the plant at full capacity?
- Are there many bottlenecks (constraints) or just one in the process?
- Can the capacity at the constraints be increased?
- Can the constraints be managed independently and, in so doing, can the process be optimized?
- Is it possible there will be new constraints in the process in the near future?
- Which costs will vary with the level of production over the long term?

Current thinking is that it may be dangerous to use the TOC methodology for some decisions, such as pricing.[2]

If constraints move from one place to another, will managers send memos to customers, advising of a price that is now double what it was one year ago? For example, product A and B had the same usage of the constraint, but product B was consuming more of the other activities. Should the costs be the same for these two products? Also, the definition of the fixed costs is less true when examining decisions impacting an organization on a long-term perspective. According to authors Robert S. Kaplan and Robin Cooper, "If managers fail to follow up, any reductions in the demands on organizational resources or process improvements will create excess capacity, not increase profit. . . .The expenses were fixed, however, only because managers did not take the actions required to make them variable."[3]

When there are multiple constraints in the process (as in the AS&C model), optimizing the process may provide a better result than the information provided by TOC. If the market value of the cost of capital is included with the costs of activities in the model, and the ABC system shows a profitable product, it could indicate a need for investment and an increase in capacity to make more money.

RESULTS

Actual internal demand at AS&C is heavily driven by plant operations and sales. It is possible to understand cost behaviors by using ABC to simulate situations and model different business scenarios. ABC also is used as a costing tool to evaluate the real cost of products and customers and to make pricing decisions.

The project at AS&C is still in process (not considering the various completed pilots). One plant of the ten in the group is now fully implemented and four are in the implementation process. Every ABC cost report is matched with cost reports under other approaches (like TOC) in order to understand differences and to make proper decisions. The value of better pricing decisions quickly appears as a change in product mix can generate substantial increases in net revenues.

LESSONS LEARNED

Other considerations for ABC implementation at AS&C include:

- Using a stand-alone implementation with a common foundation to allow comparisons and benchmarking with other plants.
- Avoiding any complex software solution. This avoids diverting your ABC knowledge building project into an information technology project.

ABOUT THE AUTHORS

Michel Maisonneuve is a Partner with Arthur Andersen in Montrèal, Canada.
Stephane Mercier is a Manager with Arthur Andersen in Montrèal, Canada.

NOTES

1. While the first method was labeled as "pure ABC," it used practical capacity in setting unit activity rates. While many would agree with this definition, some would argue that the use of theoretical capacity would be more "pure." Our objective does not lie in arguing definitions. Therefore, we limit our discussion to reporting what was actually done.

2. For greater discussion of the theory of constraints, see Eliyahu M. Goldratt and Jeff Cox, *The Goal: A Process of Ongoing Improvement* 2ed. (North River PR, 1992).

3. Robert S. Kaplan and Robin Cooper, "Profit Priorities from Activity-Based Costing," *Harvard Business Review* (May–June 1991): 135.

IMPROVING PROFITABILITY THROUGH BETTER DECISION MAKING

Alan Peretz
Arthur Andersen, Edmonton, Alberta, Canada

John Anderlic
Arthur Andersen, Vancouver, British Columbia, Canada

CASE STUDY: Finning International, Inc., Edmonton, Alberta, Canada

SUMMARY

Business Issue
Finning (Canada) sought to review the distribution and sales aspects of the company's Parts Business in Canada. The goal was to develop a strategic tool to improve efficiency and profitability of the business while maintaining a high level of customer service.

How ABC Was Used
An activity-based costing (ABC) model was introduced to analyze the indirect costs related to the Parts Business. To understand the total cost involved in delivering a part to a customer, the company conducted a comprehensive analysis including customer, branch, part category, and process views of the business.

Finning's Results
After implementation, Finning obtained a clear understanding of the true costs of distributing and selling parts in its business. The information resulted in strategic and operational improvements based on a breakdown of process costs. The model validated expenses for the organization's transportation and distribution-center costing. In addition, the company found the sales process to be more time-consuming and costly than originally perceived and that the size of a branch directly related to the cost of processing a part.

Finning International Inc., a heavy-equipment dealer, sells, finances, and services Caterpillar and other complementary equipment. With over 5,000 employees worldwide, the company serves its principal markets in western Canada, the United Kingdom, and Chile.

In 1997 the Parts Business of Finning (Canada) exceeded US$200 million in revenue. The Parts Business employs 600 people working through a network of 50 sales branches in British Columbia and Alberta. Sales orders are forwarded from the branch locations to two centralized distribution warehouses for fulfillment.

The Parts Business stocks hundreds of thousands of different parts from a large number of suppliers. Although Caterpillar parts are greater than 90 percent of sales, Finning also spends significant effort stocking other parts considered complementary to its business, such as hydraulic hoses and motor oil.

Finning's existing costing systems provided only limited data, which did not supply management with sufficient information for decision-making purposes concerning the actual total cost of delivering a part to a customer.

BUSINESS ISSUES

Finning embarked on a Parts Strategy Project to review distribution and sales aspects of the company's Parts Business in Canada. The goal of the project was to develop a strategic tool to improve the efficiency and profitability of the Parts Business while maintaining a high level of customer service.

HOW ABC WAS USED

Arthur Andersen assisted Finning in the development of an ABC model to analyze the indirect costs related to the Parts Business. The goal was to obtain a clear understanding of the total costs involved in delivering a part to the customer. The analysis included costing information at the business process level as well as cost and profitability data for customers, branches, and part categories.

The ABC project team was comprised of three dedicated Finning personnel and four external consultants from Arthur Andersen's Vancouver office. The company personnel were selected for their expertise in the Parts Business, in distribution and logistics, and in the accounting and information systems of the company. The ABC team leader was also the project manager who had responsibility for formulating the Parts Strategy. This role was critical to completing the project successfully and within the original time frame. The project sponsor was the general manager of customer service. His support was also very important to ensure the project received cooperation from the branches as well as the appropriate level of internal support from senior management.

The ABC project was kicked off with a two-day Rapid Application Prototyping (RAP) session, where the joint Finning/Arthur Andersen ABC team mapped out the initial development of the ABC model. The objective of the session was for Finning's management to gain understanding and comfort that the ABC model would provide the expected benefits and information useful in operating the business. The RAP session was successful, as it obtained buy-in for the project from Finning senior management.

One of the key items developed during the RAP session was the parts value chain, which, is depicted in Exhibit 9.1. This session output provided a summary of the significant processes of the organization. The parts value chain identified the key cross-functional business processes and high-level activities, which formed the basis for the branch interviews. The initial computer-based model developed during the RAP session remained intact and proved to be a good framework as the project progressed.

EXHIBIT 9.1   Parts Value Chain

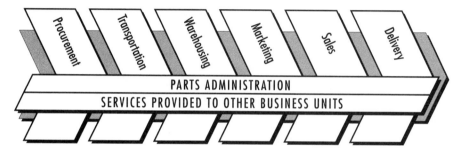

Project Approach

The next step was a four-day planning session during which the ABC team developed the workplan. The objectives achieved included:

1. Facilitating knowledge transfer to the Finning team concerning ABC concepts
2. Developing a clearer understanding of the work steps ahead, resource requirements, and key project deadlines
3. Ensuring that Arthur Andersen team members obtained a clear understanding of the complexities of the Parts Business

Key deliverables included:

- Project time line and high-level work plan
- Discussion and development of the costing philosophy for the ABC model (i.e., fully allocated, incremental, hybrid approach)
- Branch visit schedule including a representative sampling of branches to ensure the ABC team visited locations of various sizes (large, medium,

and small) as well as branches in various geographic locations serving
different industries (i.e., forestry, mining, construction, and petroleum)

- Scheduled head office interviews to capture activities and services pro-
  vided for the Parts Business
- Preliminary activity dictionary
- Data collection templates for large, medium, and small branches
- Clearly defined cost objects and ABC costing hierarchy (see Exhibit 9.2),
  which formed the basis for the ABC model

EXHIBIT 9.2   ABC Cost Hierarchy

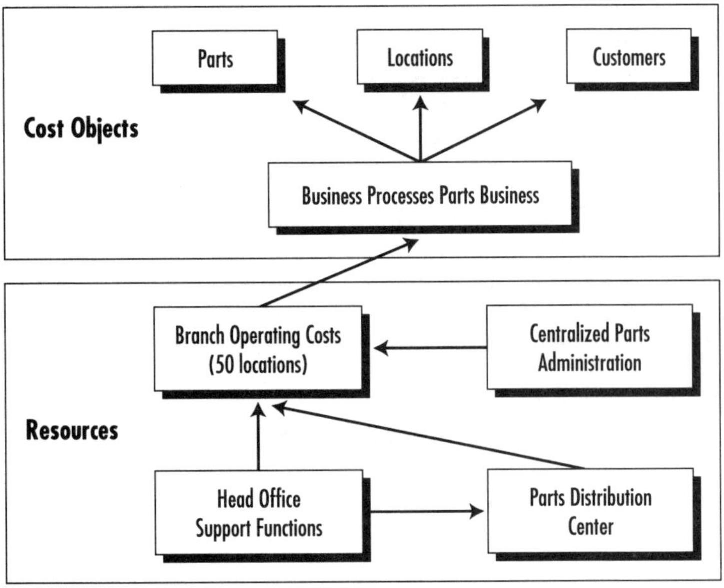

Branch Visits and Head Office Interviews

The ABC team embarked on four weeks of branch visits and head office interviews. Due to time and resource constraints, the team was not able to visit all 50
branches. Therefore, the approach taken included a sampling of a number of
branches that provided a good cross-section of the business. Data collection
templates and telephone interviews were used to collect activity and cost-driver
information from branches not directly visited by the team. Interviews were
held directly with parts supervisors who take and fill customer orders and
handle inquiries, warehouse personnel, and branch management. By interviewing personnel directly involved in serving customers, the team was able to get a
clear understanding of the level of effort and time spent related to each activity.

As a result of the data collected from the branches and the head office interviews, the team was able to determine process costs for the Parts Business. Exhibit 9.3 provides a percentage breakdown of the total cost of operating the Parts Business as well as the process view of costs.

EXHIBIT 9.3   Parts Business: Process Costs

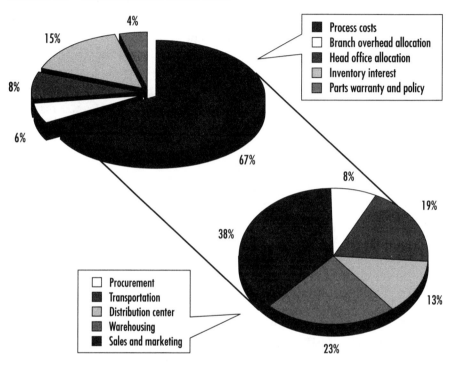

The process view of cost provided some surprising results for management, such as:

1. Distribution Center costs are reasonable as compared to other distribution and warehousing alternatives. Mauk Breukels, Finning's project manager, noted: "The activities conducted by our Distribution Center cannot be assumed by the branches for a lower corporate cost. Specialization and size result in efficiencies."

2. The sales process proved to be far more time-consuming and costly than previously thought. The sales process is a critical component of the business as it can help differentiate Finning from its competitors. The ABC team also learned that the level of effort spent on the sales process varies significantly from branch to branch depending on the customer profile and geographic location. Given the costs related to the sales

process, Finning plans to examine the process carefully in order to identify opportunities including alternative sales methods.

3. The ABC model confirmed that the size (revenue) of a branch has a direct impact on the cost of processing a part. (Economies of scale are achieved.) Although Finning was not really surprised at this result, the key is to determine at what point economies of scale apply in practice. This information can be very important in determining the optimum size for a branch to ensure maximum profitability.

4. On the surface transportation costs appeared high; however, in comparison to alternative third-party carriers, the Finning Freight Parts Express (FPE) system is very cost effective, given the large number of geographically dispersed branches. The ABC information confirmed management's belief that FPE provides Finning with a competitive advantage over smaller competitors.

Project Benefits

The objectives and approach just described made it clear that Finning had both short- and long-term benefits in undertaking this project. The short-term benefits were:

- To act as a pilot to determine whether more advanced costing information would be helpful in the decision-making process for the Parts Business and other business units at Finning
- To gain an understanding of the cost of obtaining such information as compared to the benefits received from the information
- To provide information to develop a strategy for the Parts Business and to assist in an immediate decision regarding warehousing logistics
- To act as an ongoing management tool and, potentially, a basis for performance measurement.

The end product was successful in helping Finning to achieve each of these objectives.

In building the ABC model, the team found that the information was extremely difficult to obtain from existing systems. This was heavily influenced by a major systems-conversion process that was occurring at the same time as the ABC project. In addition, one of the key drivers for the new information systems was the need for better and more complete costing information, which is now being provided by the ABC model. Therefore, in the future the information will not be nearly as difficult to obtain.

At present, this information is needed only periodically and not on a real-time basis. Obtaining this information on a real-time basis would involve a significant cost and require additional effort. However, the cost of obtaining the information on a periodic basis—such as semiannually or annually—is easily justified by the benefits the information provides. As such, Finning concluded that the information provided benefits well in excess of the cost to deliver it on a periodic basis.

From a long-term perspective, Finning intends to use this advanced costing information as a strategic asset with which to make such decisions as:

- Optimum branch size
- Parts pricing
- Benchmarking and, therefore, identification of opportunities for improvement
- Pricing of distribution services provided to third parties
- New business opportunity analysis
- Other strategic decisions yet to be identified

The information will require input to update and be available as a stand-alone system.

FINNING'S RESULTS

The ABC model helped Finning to obtain a comprehensive understanding of the true costs of distributing and selling parts in its business. The results of the model were used directly to assist with parts-strategy decisions concerning the distribution and warehousing activities. The model also identified many future opportunities for management to explore further, which could allow Finning to operate the business more efficiently and cost effectively.

The information provided valuable insights into Finning's short-term decisions on restructuring logistics of the Parts Business and specifically the logistics related to the central warehousing function. The costing information provided by the ABC model allowed management to consider various alternatives to determine the most cost-effective method of distribution and logistics for the Parts Business.

Overall, from this pilot project, Finning concluded that advanced cost management information would be a strategic tool and provide a competitive advantage.

Finning plans to review activity-based information now being provided for the Parts Business to determine its applicability to other aspects of the integrated service delivery offered. The pilot project in the Parts Business, although undertaken partially for short-term benefits, likely will lead to a culture of more detailed, advanced costing information throughout the business including new and used equipment sales, service, and the Parts Business. Finning also may use this information as the foundation for a performance management system in assisting with identifying drivers of the business and key areas for measurement.

LESSONS LEARNED

Some of the lessons learned by Finning are:

- The initial RAP session with senior management was important in crystallizing the benefits and expected ABC output prior to the project beginning.
- Senior management from Finning was directly involved in collecting these data, which significantly improved the timeliness and accuracy of the information. The project had strong leadership from company management. This commitment is an essential element to a successful ABC implementation.
- Time did not permit the ABC team to visit each of the branch locations. In this case, sampling can provide a good cross-section that is representative of the business. Customized data collection templates can be used to obtain activity and cost-driver data from the medium-size and small branches that could not be visited by a member of the project team.
- Initially the team did not plan to visit all of the larger branches due to time constraints. However, they found that it was difficult to use data templates for the larger, complex branches without actually visiting the location in person.
- An "owner" of the project and modeling "tool" was not available to assist as the project progressed. This made the transition of the project ownership and understanding of the details of the tool difficult. Having this individual involved from the beginning and throughout the project is critical.

ABOUT THE AUTHORS

Alan Peretz is a Partner with Arthur Andersen in Vancouver, British Columbia, Canada.

John Anderlic is a Senior Manager with Arthur Andersen in Edmonton, Alberta, Canada.

10

UTILIZING ACTIVITY-BASED MANAGEMENT FOR SHARED SERVICES' CHARGEBACKS

Mitch Max
Arthur Andersen, Toronto, Canada

Carol Cobble
Armstrong Laing, Atlanta, Georgia

CASE STUDY: Clarica (Formerly The Mutual Group), Waterloo, Canada

SUMMARY

Business Issues

As with many organizations, Clarica sought to reduce the cost of corporate support functions by establishing a shared services organization—the Corporate Services (CS) Division. Initially CS was perceived as an overhead organization that added little value. By using activity-based management (ABM), CS sought to be viewed as a business partner critical to the success of the business units and entire organization.

How ABM Is Used

Clarica used ABM to manage expenses as well as change the way the business units viewed the CS Division. ABM was used to identify costs that could be eliminated or reduced, to provide a mechanism to accurately charge costs to business units based on their consumption of the shared services, to provide cost information to support pricing decisions and profitability analysis, and to provide a means for comparing internal costs to outside service providers to evaluate outsourcing decisions.

Clarica's Results

The business units now have a clearer understanding of the costs assigned to internal products and services and, thus, are better able to manage those costs. ABM helped focus the company on the need to understand service levels and enabled the use of service-level agreements, which have greatly enhanced accountability and communications. CS created an expense management framework, which places accountability for volumes at the business unit level, while shared services are held accountable for rates and service levels. This approach facilitates monitoring of performance measurements and the use of benchmarking to drive opportunities for process improvement.

Many organizations have reduced the cost of corporate support functions by establishing shared services organizations. In doing so, they often find that it takes more than simply consolidating service functions to truly optimize costs. If all support services are pushed together, how can they be held accountable to the business units they are designed to support? How do the shared services organizations justify the prices they charge to the organizations they support?

Business units, in many companies, demand lower charges for shared services, but how can a company determine if those demands are reasonable? What should these services cost? If third-party providers quote lower prices, how can the company evaluate if they offer the same service levels? For that matter, how can any company analyze service levels in relation to the costs it takes to provide the services?

To answer these questions, many companies now implementing shared services are also implementing activity-based management (ABM). Used together, these two techniques can help reduce the cost of shared services, provide a reasonable basis for billing out service charges, and also provide the means of communicating the impact of varying service levels. This chapter illustrates how Clarica, a Canadian financial services company, successfully dealt with these issues.

BUSINESS ISSUES

In 1993 Clarica began to implement shared services for its various business units. It did so by forming the Corporate Services (CS) Division, which was composed of five main areas:

- Information Systems
- Finance
- Corporate Affairs
- Strategic Planning
- Shared Business Services (which included Human Resources, Administrative Services, and Legal)

At the time, CS employed 800 people and had a cost base of over C$100 million dollars, which was one-third of the company's total non–sales-related expenses.

The business units initially viewed CS as an overhead function that added little value, so they placed tremendous pressure on CS to cut expenses quickly.

The business units also requested improved cost information to support their pricing decisions. Many of the business units believed that the cost system used by CS was inaccurate—and that, in some cases, it actually motivated the wrong behavior.

Because of these concerns, CS sought to use ABM to address the following business needs:

- To identify costs that could be eliminated or reduced
- To provide a mechanism to charge costs to business units accurately based on their consumption of the shared services
- To provide accurate cost information to support pricing decisions and profitability analysis
- To communicate the service levels provided and the cost of varying levels so that users could help determine the most cost-effective level
- To provide a means for comparing internal costs to the costs of outside service providers for evaluating outsourcing decisions
- To provide a better tool for facilitating budgeting by internal services and products

Clarica used ABM not only to manage expenses but also to change the way the business units viewed them. CS soon evolved from being perceived as an overhead organization that added little value to being perceived as a business partner that was critical to the success of the business units and of the organization as a whole.

BACKGROUND

Clarica, which has helped Canadians secure their financial future for over 120 years, provides life insurance, healthcare insurance, corporate loans, commercial and residential mortgages, financial planning, and other related services. The company has C$38 billion of assets under management.

Tracing its roots back to 1870 as Ontario Mutual, Clarica is Canada's first and oldest mutual life insurance company. With over C$280 billion of insurance in force, Clarica is one of Canada's largest financial organizations and the fourth largest life insurance company in the country. It recently acquired the Canadian Operations of Metropolitan Life. The company has more than 7,000 employees and agents to serve its customers.

EXISTING SYSTEMS

When the CS Division was founded, the chargeback and allocation systems were fairly simplistic. Half the costs were charged back using very few drivers for large bundles of costs, while the remainder was allocated as general overhead. The largest chargeback was for Information Systems (IS), which accounted for about 40 percent of the entire CS division.

Hourly rates across varying job classifications were established to charge the business units for internal consulting and programming services as well as for a couple of other major business processes. Other IS costs were mostly charged out based on utilization of computer time, but this created a highly inflated cost for mainframe computer time because of the other costs that were combined with the computer costs. After the ABM system had been implemented, the mainframe rate was cut by 60 percent. "Large-bucket" costing methods such as these often raise concerns among the business units that receive the charges.

The charge-back system at CS used various allocation bases or arbitrary drivers. Because services were bundled together for allocations, the resulting charges were rarely based on the customer's actual consumption of the services. Business units felt hampered in their efforts to influence spending because they had no influence on the allocation bases used.

Several issues arose because of CS's cost system, including:

- A critical need to understand and manage expenses because of a rapidly changing business environment
- A belief that the cost system provided inconsistent views of expenses and inadequate tools for managing
- Some dysfunctional behavior because of the way costs were charged back to the business units
- Skepticism about chargebacks
- Weakness in identifying opportunities for cost reductions
- An inability to link expense budgets for CS to the volume requirements of business units

Many companies have found that simplistic cost allocations of support services create a "buffet pricing mentality." When everyone is charged the same average price, regardless of their actual usage, the incentive is for everyone to use more than the average. Think, for example, of an all-you-can-eat buffet that charges a single price: Everyone tries to get his money's worth by eating as much as possible.

This mentality creates a particularly troubling situation for managers of support departments. Top management pressures them to reduce overall costs while demand for their services is surging. Cutting back on costs is often impossible except in an arbitrary fashion, which causes general frustration and conflict between the users and providers of the service.

The key to breaking the buffet-pricing, all-you-can-eat mentality is to use ABM to charge users only for what they consume and to communicate clearly what it costs to provide varying services. This gives consumers the ultimate choice. It also makes possible the comparison of costs and service levels of the internal provider to those of outside providers. This was the path Clarica eventually took, but it took a while for the company to get there.

PRELIMINARY COST REDUCTION INITIATIVES

When the CS Division was formed, the business units immediately pressed to reduce expenses by 20 percent. Andrew Beacom, manager of ABM, says that there was "intense pressure on the organization to reduce costs—and to reduce them in a rather dramatic fashion." Rather than just cutting costs across the board, CS's management decided to look closely at its business processes by costing out the activities and business processes performed.

But CS went one step further. Instead of just determining process costs at current service levels, CS's management also wanted to give the business units cost information to show what costs would be at different service levels. According to Beacom, the goal was to be able to tell the business units "this is what we perform, this is what it currently costs, and in addition, these are what the costs would be at alternative service levels."

Explaining different service levels and the related cost differences required some analysis, Beacom says: "The persons involved in this exercise were challenged to come up with levels of service that were, say, 50 percent of the current amounts. Therefore, we would be able to say 'This is what I can provide you for 50 percent of the current cost—and, oh, by the way, if you want current-plus service levels, I can provide you these services for 125 percent of current costs.'"

The business units were asked to rank CS's processes in the order of importance. The business units also were asked to rate whether existing levels of service should stay the same, be increased, or be decreased. The units also determined which processes should be eliminated.

"We asked them to go back, look at all the bundles of services, and then rank them in terms of relative priority and contribution to their own business objectives," notes Beacom. This ranking allowed the business units to "draw an affordability line" and to identify services that they did not see as adding value. Many of these were eliminated. For example, some public relations functions were eliminated while others, such as graphic services, were replaced with lower levels of service combined with outsourced solutions. Additionally, service levels of certain processes were increased because the business units sought—and were willing to pay for—improved services.

This rating of CS's processes was considered successful, because it made the cost of support processes clear to the business units. It also gave the business units a mechanism for choosing the services they wanted given their affordability and value. But this exercise was a one-time initiative. Beacom explains that CS still had "no system that could track cost on an activity basis. We couldn't prove to the business units that we were actually going to deliver the savings that we promised."

As a one-time effort the project did not create a mind-set of cost management. It lacked the permanence needed to change the corporate culture. It also failed to highlight how these support processes add value to Clarica's customers. Yet the need for improved information and more accurate chargeback grew out of this initiative and ultimately led to the implementation of ABM.

ABM ROLLOUT

CS focused its efforts on reviewing the expense-management needs of key users in both corporate services and business units. As a result, the ABM project was launched in June 1995. The goal of the ABM project was to redesign the existing shared services cost system and thus to provide a better framework for managing costs.

Clarica needed an ongoing system that could accurately cost out CS's products and services and relate those costs to the levels of service provided. The system was to be used for:

- Charging out costs on a monthly basis
- Monitoring overall cost reductions on both a unit cost and total cost basis
- Ultimately converting to budgeting on an activity basis

The ABM team consisted of a six-person core team supported by another six cross-functional members from CS and three consultants from Arthur Andersen. Arthur Andersen provided training, ABM experience, help with project management, and active participation on the ABM team when needed. The ABM team had a strong change management role, which focused on managing expectations, changing behaviors and accountability, training users, and providing overall support.

The ABM implementation was completed in six months and included the following steps:

- Defining the resources to be included
- Using interviews to define activities
- Validating the resulting activity definitions
- Developing resource and activity drivers
- Mapping the costs through activities to the services provided and then to the business units
- Building the costing model using *Hyper*ABC software from Armstrong Laing

Exhibit 10.1 shows an overview of the shared services costing model.

EXHIBIT 10.1   Overview of Shared Services Costing Model

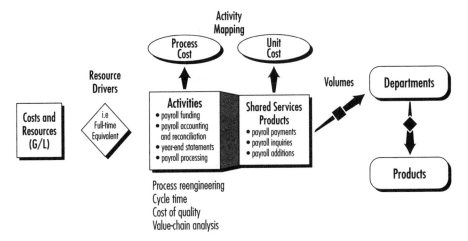

The ABM team used a steering committee of senior managers drawn from the different functions and business units. This committee met every two weeks to update status and to resolve problems that arose.

The project also included an extra step to define the shared services products, which determined how activities were bundled. Beacom explains that this exercise focused on "how the business units wanted CS to configure activities for the bill-out purposes." Different business units might want to view chargebacks differently.

For example, the health claims operation wanted to understand all the systems costs associated with performing an on-line dental claim assessment or processing a batch of dental claims. Therefore, this department wanted to know the bundled price for all the activities that supported its own business unit's products. It did not want all the detail about costs of the central processing unit or about tape storage costs in its chargebacks. It also did not need detail about each activity included in this bundle.

As Beacom notes, "We bundled these activities up into products that were meaningful to the business units and billed them back on that basis." The business units found this to be more useful for them in their efforts to understand, control, and directly influence costs. It also speeded the rollout of ABM to areas such as group health claims processing, because part of the work had already been completed.

In addition to the original five areas, new shared services are added to the ABM model as they are identified. These include various IS areas previously contained in the business units and, more recently, a marketing area that supports part of the retail business unit.

ONGOING ABM RESPONSIBILITIES

After completion of the initial model, the ABM team became a smaller team whose purpose was to support users. This central ABM team is part of the financial management area of the Canadian Customer Business Unit (into which most of CS was merged because of a recent reorganization).

The central ABM team, which has four full-time equivalent team members, is responsible for maintaining the ABM model and the related reporting tools, including updating the data and producing the overall reporting. As Beacom notes, "The central team's role is to manage the infrastructure, facilitate analysis, and provide training and education." The team also coordinates activity-based budgeting (ABB) and helps with ABM implementations in other parts of the company.

Data used in the model belong to the shared service that provides the data. Each shared services activity or product has an associated product manager who is accountable for the management and analysis of the shared services product. In addition to the central team, analytical support also comes from the financial management area of the IS group and the Shared Business Services Group.

The ABM team provides ongoing training, including a "training blitz" on ABB before the budgeting season, because nearly everyone needs a refresher.

The team also offers refresher courses on ABM, the data collection tools used in ABB, and the reporting tool used (Cognos PowerPlay).

The team uses "drop-in sessions" to train employees. Specifically, experts in particular areas set aside time when users can drop in and ask questions, review models, or seek in-depth help about problems.

BUILDING THE USER BASE

Despite the support available from the central team, Beacom notes, there is "an ongoing challenge in getting people to focus on the information, getting people to use it, and getting people to incorporate it into their day-to-day living." This challenge exists even when using a user-friendly visual tool like PowerPlay.

In early ABM reporting, Beacom recalls:

> We gave product managers views of the data and said, "Okay, here—slice and dice and drill and change dimensions and so on." We thought it was great, and they were all just sitting there with glassy eyes. To overcome this problem, we have simplified the number of reports and are moving to categorizing users into two groups—simple users and power users. Many product managers may not be adept at slicing, dicing, and drilling down, so we are giving them simplified reports that provide a pictorial view of their results for the month. They can do the drill-downs that they need and also some rudimentary analysis. If they get stuck they've always got someone to call on for help.

Power users understand the data flow from beginning to end; they also know how to use the tools. While there may be fewer of them, the ABM team recognized that "you can't turn everyone into a cost accountant." The broader issue is to find ways to embed this information into the regular business processes and decision-making frameworks.

Another advanced aspect of this implementation is that all reports are on-line—hard copies are not even distributed. The company's planned shift to Web PowerPlay for reporting will make it even easier to access data and to present the results in a user-friendly manner.

ACTIVITY-BASED BUDGETING

In rolling out ABB, the ABM team developed intuitive, user-friendly tools. When users go on-line to use these tools, the software lists all the products consumed last year. It also provides a completed budget projection based on current annualized consumption, as adjusted for expected volume changes. Internal customers then adjust these amounts to set their plans.

Internal customers' demands for activities are then pushed back to the shared services areas to reconcile demand with capacity and budgets for shared services resources. Most of the activity budgets for the shared services affect each other, so a reiterative process of allocation and reallocation among the shared services must occur before budgets are finalized. For example, Human Resources consumes IS activities, and IS consumes Human Resources activities.

The relative stability of the company's business over the last two years has made using this ABB process easier. When the business experiences major changes, such as a major acquisition or divestiture, ABB will be much more challenging.

RESULTS

Clarica built an ABM model that included all shared services activities and services. With ABM, both CS and the business units now have a better understanding of the costs that are assigned to the internal products and services. CS can now identify and bill consumers of the products and services it provides based on actual consumption. And because CS now understands the drivers of its costs, it can better manage those costs.

ABM has helped focus the company on the need to understand service levels. These have been captured in service-level agreements that define:

- The scope of shared services products being provided
- The term of the agreement
- The agreed-upon levels of service and related performance standards
- The agreed-upon unit price and volume-commitment range
- The feedback mechanisms that will be used for ensuring quality service

These service-level agreements have greatly enhanced accountability and communications.

The ABM project developed a new framework for expense management that is illustrated in Exhibit 10.2. The framework was designed to provide accountability for cost, time, and quality of services provided by CS and to support the "product" volumes consumed by the business units.

This framework places accountability for volumes at the business-unit

EXHIBIT 10.2   Expense Management Framework

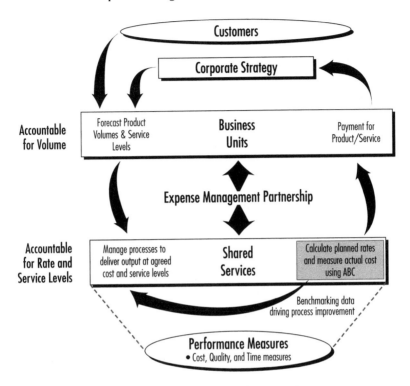

level, while shared services are held accountable for rates and service levels. Monthly billings are processed on this basis. This approach also facilitates monitoring of performance measurements and the use of benchmarking to drive opportunities for process improvement.

Overall, management at Clarica has been pleased with the ABM system, because it provides much better information for decision making.

FUTURE PLANS

Clarica also plans to use ABM in other ways. The team is working on specific business unit applications.

The ABM team has identified the need to use ABM to provide a better understanding of individual and collective customer costs. ABM also may be used to help managers better understand sales channel and product costs.

LESSONS LEARNED

The following lessons were learned.

- *Customize support to the type of user.* The ABM team identified many users who needed ABM information but had neither the time nor the interest to become power users. Making ABM reports easy to understand increased their usage.

- *Sponsorship is critical to project implementation and ongoing success.* Link the goals and objectives of operational owners to the model and involve operations in the implementation. Also link the ABM project to other improvement initiatives and key business decisions. ABM must become integrated into the financial management framework.

- *Provide user-friendly reports.* Develop simplified, high-level reports that address the needs of most users. Give them the information they need to manage, but do not overload them with information. Provide detailed reporting only to those power users who ask for it. Also, provide reports only as often as needed to address business needs. Switching to on-line reporting facilitates this by the elimination of monthly paper reports.

- *Review reporting and report customization needs on an ongoing basis.* Report development should be an evolutionary process. Continue to consult with the users to obtain their feedback and clarification of their business needs. Also, continually review technological advancements in reporting software.

- *Eliminate complexity to keep the model simple as possible.* It is easy to define activities in too much detail, but this will cause headaches later. Keep the number of activities and cost objects to a minimum. Some accuracy may be lost in the model, but it makes life a lot easier when training users about reporting and analysis of the ABM information.

- *Teach people how to use the data.* Shared services and business unit users need to be trained and educated on how to read ABM reports. Do not expect them to understand the information unless it is explained to them. Remember that the company *wants* them to use the data. A lot of time has been spent collecting and producing the information, so the company should make sure people are taught how to use it and how it can help them in their work.

- *Consider the project a change management exercise, not an accounting exercise.* With ABM, deeply ingrained behaviors and accountabilities are being changed. Results happen when employees change their behavior. All the accounting efforts are merely steps along the way so that these changes can occur. Behavioral changes occur faster when the ABM team continually focuses on change.

ABOUT THE AUTHORS

Mitch Max is a Senior Manager with Arthur Andersen in Toronto, Canada. Carol Cobble is Vice President of Client Services for Armstrong Laing in Atlanta.

Note: This case originally appeared in *Cornerstones of Decision Making: Profiles of Enterprise ABM* by Steve Player and Carol Cobble (Greensboro, NC: Oakhill Press, 1999).

11

IMPROVING PROFITABILITY WITH ACTIVITY-BASED MANAGEMENT

Isabelle Lacombe and Henri Tcheng
Arthur Andersen, Paris, France

Carol Cobble
Armstrong Laing, Atlanta, Georgia

CASE STUDY: AscoForge Safe, Paris, France

SUMMARY

Business Issues

AscoForge Safe lacked true product cost information and information to prepare accurate price estimates for new business proposals. In fact, only 2 percent of estimates resulted in orders. AscoForge Safe sought a costing system to provide insight into margins for products and customers. The company wanted to manage costs.

How ABM Is Used

AscoForge Safe conducted a detailed analysis of its activities using activity-based management (ABM) to address both strategic and operational needs. The ABM system provided a more accurate understanding of product costs, refined controls over indirect costs, enabled product and customer profitability analysis, and supported process improvement initiatives.

AscoForge Safe's Results

The ABM system maps over 75 percent of the company's indirect costs to products. Asco-Forge Safe learned 23 percent of its products were actually unprofitable; as a result, the company was better able to price products and services as well as reduce product offerings where necessary. ABM identified customer profitability differences by assigning the cost of quality assessment based on end-customer requirements. And prices are set according to the policy with requirements of each customer to simultaneously enhance profitability and customer service.

As manufacturing companies around the world have discovered, traditional cost accounting systems do not always provide accurate information about product costs. As companies become more technologically advanced, their overhead increases and their direct labor costs decrease. This change in a company's cost structure can cause overhead to be misallocated if traditional allocation bases (such as a percentage of direct labor or direct labor hours) are used.

Typically, high-volume products are "overcosted" (assigned excess overhead), while low-volume specialty products are "undercosted" (assigned too little overhead). This chapter illustrates how costs were misallocated at AscoForge Safe, a French manufacturing company. It shows how management took the steps necessary to cost products correctly by implementing activity-based management (ABM).

BUSINESS ISSUES

Managers at AscoForge Safe found that inaccurate product costs were causing the company to lose potential customers. Salespeople did not have the information they needed to prepare accurate price estimates to compete for new customers or to win repeat business from existing customers. Concern intensified as AscoForge Safe realized that only 2 percent of all the estimates the company provided led to orders. The business was barely breaking even, and losses began to loom on the horizon.

Finally AscoForge Safe appointed a new financial director, who immediately began to assess the situation. Daniel Souloumiac, the new financial director, recalls: "When I arrived, I immediately noticed the lack of cost control and the production of inaccurate product cost information. Indirect costs represented one-quarter of the total cost whenever direct costs represented the other three-quarters. Indirect costs were being allocated on an equal proportion as well." This practice produced inaccurate product costs, because each product requires a different amount of effort for indirect costs, such as design, preparation, production, and quality assurance.

As Souloumiac says, "We didn't have a clear assessment of our margins for our products and customers. Therefore, we urgently needed to take steps to manage costs and institute methods for seeking out opportunities to increase our productivity."

AscoForge Safe's management decided to launch an ABM initiative to address the following business issues:

- Inaccurate product costs
- A lack of confidence in the company's cost system
- The need to improve controls over indirect costs
- The need to increase product and customer profitability
- The need for process improvement initiatives

BACKGROUND

AscoForge Safe is headquartered in Paris and its 1997 revenues exceeded 600 million francs (US$100 million). The company has 500 employees, including 30 engineers.

As a subsidiary of Usinor, AscoForge Safe manufactures products for the automotive industry, including parts for gearboxes, differentials, axles, and transmissions. Each year AscoForge Safe produces about 60 million forged steel parts. Most of these parts have a long service life—typically two years of development and a production life that corresponds to the life of the vehicle in which it is placed.

The Old Cost System

AscoForge Safe's previous cost system focused on controlling the direct costs of production. Material costs for each part were calculated based on the steel used, which included adjustments for yield loss. This steel usage was priced out at the purchase cost for steel. Labor costs were tracked based on the time employees spent in the different stages of the production line.

Other direct expenses also were directly linked to products, including typical overhead items such as electricity costs for the workshop and machine depreciation. As Souloumiac explains, "Manufacturing was the subject of in-depth analysis. We could therefore validate the direct costs linked to the entire manufacturing process."

Indirect costs amounted to 150 million francs (US$25 million), yet the indirect costs had never been analyzed in detail. Indirect costs incurred before and after production roughly equaled to one-third of the company's direct costs. These indirect costs included:

- Research and development costs
- Engineering costs
- Quality analysis
- New product costs
- Costs of preparing quotations
- General and administrative expenses (i.e., the cost of general management)

Souloumiac notes, "One very simple rule for indirect costs had applied for a long time. To calculate the total cost price of the parts, the company had decided to apply indirect costs in proportion to direct costs." Applying that proportional ratio to individual parts led to distortions in the product costs estimated for each of the products.

Because each product requires a different effort for design, preparation, production launch, and quality, the actual cost of producing each product varies significantly and is not necessarily proportional to the direct costs incurred. As a result, the company's allocation methods caused high-volume products to be overcosted and low-volume products to be undercosted. (Exhibit 11.1 illustrates this effect by comparing costs generated by a traditional cost system with costs generated by activity-based costing.)

EXHIBIT 11.1   Effect of the Direct Cost Method Compared to ABM Costs

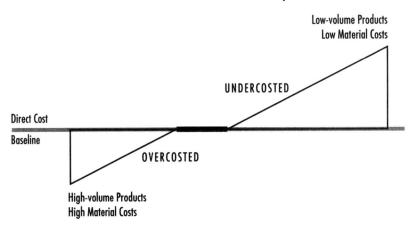

Because of the inaccurate costs, managers at AscoForge Safe could not rely on the costs supplied by the company's management control system. Also, profit margins could not be assessed accurately, which made the bidding and negotiation of contracts even more difficult (and risky).

INITIAL EFFORTS

In an effort to address many of AscoForge Safe's business problems, the company's managing director launched a management initiative called Safe 2000, which established various committees to help with the management of the company. (Exhibit 11.2 shows the organization of the Safe 2000 initiative.) These committees, which ran parallel to the existing management structure, included:

- The Management Committee, which monitored the progress of various other committees

EXHIBIT 11.2   Safe 2000 Organization

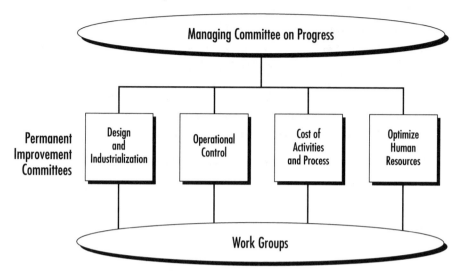

- Numerous Improvement Committees, which had the following objectives:
    - —Design and industrialization
    - —Operational control
    - —Control over the costs of processes and activities
    - —Optimize human resources
- Work Groups that support the Improvement Committees

Souloumiac leads the Cost Improvement Committee. Based on his prior experience with ABM at another company, he believed that an ABM analysis of indirect costs would quickly provide important information managers needed to address AscoForge Safe's business issues. His goals included establishing a permanent ABM system to address the company's ongoing costing needs. In other words, this was not to be a "one-time" project that would disappear after it provided its initial results.

ABM Team

Before kicking off the ABM project, Souloumiac carefully considered whom to include on the team. One option was to have a team made up solely of AscoForge Safe employees. A second option was to include consultants to speed the process. After carefully weighing the pros and cons, he decided to bring in experienced consultants from Arthur Andersen.

The new ABM team included three members from AscoForge Safe (one full-time member and two part-time members) and two Arthur Andersen consultants. The ABM project was launched in September 1996.

The next step was software selection. After a thorough analysis of software available, the company selected *Hyper*ABC by Armstrong Laing as its software modeling tool.

Data Collection

The ABM team's first job was to define activities. Since the project's goals were both strategic and operational in nature, the team had to define activities in great detail. Doing so provided detailed cost management information to aid in reengineering. Before ABM was implemented, all cost reduction efforts occurred across the board, with no detailed analysis of where the cuts would do the most good. In evaluating activities such as processing an invoice, training a new employee, or launching a new product, a detailed analysis of activities is far more helpful in detecting potential cost savings.

The project team went through the following steps to ensure a speedy rollout of ABM:

- Determine project scope
- Collect data
- Build the cost model
- Evaluate the results
- Plan ways to act on the results

The cost model was designed to provide activity-based analyses of the margins for each customer and each product. The cost information also would be used to provide price quotations and cost estimates.

In building a system to provide cost estimates, indirect expenses were analyzed in detail. The objective was to identify quickly the correlation between specific activities and particular products. This information then could be used to trace indirect costs to specific products, thus providing more accurate product costs.

Two examples of this are transportation/storage costs and capital charges. Cost analyses showed that parts sold to U.S. customers should be assigned a greater share of these costs than parts sold to French customers, because U.S. customers' parts have long storage and transportation delays before they reach the United States. French customers' parts, by contrast, usually are sent directly from the factory.

The ABM team also analyzed the indirect cost caused by delayed payments, which is now assigned based on payment patterns of the particular end customers.

By converting to ABM cost assignments, AscoForge Safe has improved and simplified its cost accounting system. Internal costs that previously were allocated arbitrarily are now analyzed and assigned more accurately. Manager reports now focus on the controllable expenses incurred in each section, which has greatly simplified preparing and monitoring the budget.

Detailed ABM information also was used to launch a reconfiguration of the entire production operation. Activity costs were detailed in the ABM model, which also tracks the tasks included in each activity, then the activities involved in each process. These detailed "maps" then were used to support reengineering.

*Hyper*ABC was used to calculate the results of these sophisticated analyses. (See Exhibit 11.3 for the ABM system architecture.) The ABM system included many types of financial and also operational information. (See Exhibit 11.4 for ABM system volumes.)

EXHIBIT 11.3   ABM System Architecture

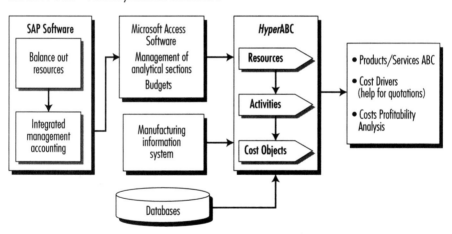

RESULTS AND NEXT STEPS

The ABM project has completely changed AscoForge Safe's cost system. Now more than 75 percent of the company's indirect costs can be traced to products. As Souloumiac explains, "It is not possible to trace all indirect costs to products, because the linkage of costs to products is sometimes so indirect that any cost assignment would be arbitrary." Therefore, items such as general management costs, certain administrative costs, and certain human resources costs were not traced and instead were allocated. Although all costs are still

EXHIBIT 11.4   ABM Model Volumes

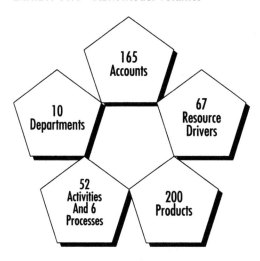

assigned to products, the costs generated by ABM are far more accurate. (See Exhibit 11.5 for the rules of cost assignment.)

The ABM team has thoroughly analyzed all activities to find the most coherent way of assigning their related costs. For example, previously training costs were allocated based on a percentage of labor costs, and following up on contracts was allocated based on sales revenue by product. After ABM was

EXHIBIT 11.5   Rules of Cost Assignment

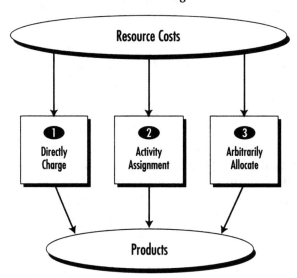

implemented successfully, AscoForge Safe began using the results to set new product prices.

Other information gained included the discovery that 23 percent of the company's products—all previously considered profitable—were actually unprofitable. (See Exhibit 11.6 for a comparison of the ABM results with the results generated by the traditional cost system.) For some products, the margin dropped more than 200 percent. Small-volume products that required very high quality and personalized service became many times more costly, while 5 percent of the products previously considered unprofitable actually proved to be profitable. (See Exhibit 11.7 for differences in margins indicated by the ABM system and the traditional cost system.)

EXHIBIT 11.6   Differences of Results on Costs Calculated with ABM System and with Traditional Accounting Method

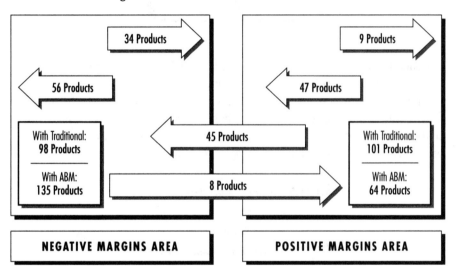

A simple example of why this distortion occurs can be seen by examining the treatment of the cost of quality. The company spends about 9 million francs (US$1.5 million) to ensure quality. Quality assurance activities include the development of quality standards, implementation of those standards, quality audits, and review of quality controls. Previously these quality costs were allocated to each part based on its direct costs. Each part was assigned a quality cost corresponding to 5 percent of its direct costs.

But upon analyzing the quality activities, the ABM team noted that quality costs vary according to end-customer requirements, not according to the direct cost of each part. This was most noticeable for customers from certain

EXHIBIT 11.7   Differences of Margins on Product Costs Calculated with ABM and with Traditional Accounting Method

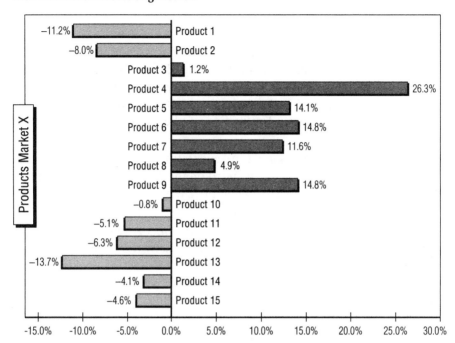

countries that have high quality restrictions. As a result, these parts and customers generated very high quality costs.

The ABM team solved this issue by assigning the cost of quality based on end-customer requirements. They achieved this goal by applying a ratio of quality requirements based on the degree of quality requirements specified by each customer.

The information gained from ABM has led to numerous policy changes. For example, prices are now set according to the policy adopted for each customer, as when the company renegotiates certain sales prices to motivate certain customers to purchase in large quantities. Management is also considering discontinuing some products.

Future Plans

As Souloumiac notes, "We plan to use ABM information for both internal and external benchmarking. We also plan to use the information to continue our process-improvement efforts." Furthermore, AscoForge Safe is continuing to reduce indirect costs.

LESSONS LEARNED

The following lessons have been learned.

- *Simplifying basic accounting is a good first step.* AscoForge Safe began by canceling the internal cost allocations it had used. The various business units were made responsible for controlling the expenses of their own units. This simplified budgeting and monitoring costs. It also set the stage for building an understanding of the cause-and-effect relationships of activities.
- *Use experienced consultants.* Implementation usually goes faster when experienced consultants are included on the ABM team. They bring vital experience and expertise to complete the skill sets brought by internal members of the project team.
- *Across-the-board cost reductions seldom work.* Attempts to cut costs across the board rarely work because some activities are vital. The costs of these activities quickly return in the form of rehired workers, higher outsourcing costs, or higher costs for temporary workers.

  Across-the-board cuts also cause a "hoarding mentality" among managers: Managers tend to hold back (or hoard) excess costs in case another across-the-board cut should occur in the future. This creates a cycle of hoarding that just increases the need for more cost cutting. Detailed activity analysis is needed to identify where costs can be reduced and how to achieve appropriate cost reductions.

ABOUT THE AUTHORS

Henri Tcheng is a Partner with Arthur Andersen in Paris, France.
Isabelle Lacombe is a Consultant with Arthur Andersen in Paris, France.
Carol Cobble is Vice President of Client Services with Armstrong Laing in Atlanta, Georgia.

Note: This case originally appeared in *Cornerstones of Decision Making: Profiles of Enterprise ABM* by Steve Player and Carol Cobble (Greensboro, NC: Oakhill Press, 1999).

12

USING ACTIVITY-BASED MANAGEMENT TO SUPPORT PERFORMANCE MEASURES AND ECONOMIC VALUE ADDED

Francisco Silva and Gema Moreno Vega
Arthur Andersen, Mexico City, Mexico

CASE STUDY: Grupo Casa Autrey, Mexico City, Mexico

SUMMARY

Business Issue

Beginning in 1990, Grupo Casa Autrey embarked on a growth strategy that dramatically altered the landscape of the corporation. Instead of a single channel distribution for one product line, the company expanded to multiple channels and product lines. Competition increased and so did the complexity of the business. Grupo Casa Autrey needed a system to accurately measure costs and profitability of different business units, product lines, and customer channels.

How ABM Was Used

Activity-based management (ABM) was introduced as part of an integrated perspective of the business, which combined a form of Balanced Scorecard and Economic Value Added (EVA) measurements for a holistic management system. The ABM model was used to break down the operating expenses as well as identify and manage the respective profitability levels of customers and products. Pilot development, which included five locations, provided the company with the basis for both strategic and operating decisions.

Grupo Casa Autrey's Results

A multitude of changes—both strategic and operational—were accomplished as a result of the ABM project. In addition to the original objective to measure customer and product profitability, Grupo Casa Autrey created a standard view of the company's processes and activities and established full automation of the model, using standard measurements. Corporate overhead allocation as well as a one-step allocation process to cost centers was addressed. This allowed for quantitative discussions among business units and departments rather than assumptions for charges. In addition, performance indicators based on activities have been linked to a balanced scorecard.

COMPANY BACKGROUND

Grupo Casa Autrey serves as the primary distributor of pharmaceutical products in Mexico. In addition, the company is highly visible in the distribution of health and beauty aids, consumer products, nonperishable foods, publications, videos, and office supplies. By providing the highest level of service in the industry, Grupo Casa Autrey is regarded by the markets it serves as an efficient and reliable company.

Grupo Casa Autrey has over 100 years of experience distributing in the pharmaceutical market. The company's product catalog includes 17,000 products offered to the majority of pharmacies and mass merchandisers throughout Mexico. These products also are offered to convenience, grocery, and government stores, bookstores and magazine stands, and specialized wholesalers and corporate customers. The company establishes commercial partnerships with suppliers, based on openness and an exchange of knowledge. Through this constant exchange of information and ideas, the company adds value to its services and can, along with suppliers, take advantage of the growth opportunities.

Grupo Casa Autrey's strategy is based on the knowledge of the market channels it serves. This knowledge enables the company to understand and meet its customers' needs properly. Led by President and Chief Executive Officer Sergio Autrey, the company is organized with both brand and regional managers. Brand managers handle four product categories: pharmaceutical, consumer, entertainment, and office. Operations are handled by 7,000 employees working in 28 Distribution Centers throughout Mexico. Each month Grupo Casa Autrey distributes more than 40 million products to its customers. Sales revenues in 1997 were 8,746 million pesos (more than US$1 billion), a 14 percent increase above the previous year. "This is a result," say Rubén G. Camiro, chief financial officer (CFO) of Grupo Casa Autrey, "of having a clear corporate mission and a vision we define as being the preferred supplier to our customers and the preferred customer to our suppliers."[1]

BUSINESS ISSUES, EVOLUTION AND CHALLENGES

From its inception in 1898 until 1990, Grupo Casa Autrey operated through a single channel of distribution, independent pharmacies. The company offered only two product lines—pharmaceutical products and health and beauty products. With a stable domestic market, the company experienced little variation in gross margins or in operating margins.

In 1990, however, things changed. Rather than the former, single channel form of distribution, the company began operating in multiple channels, including not only independent pharmacies but also supermarkets, convenience stores, cash-and-carry stores, and corner food stores, among others. In addition, the product lines expanded substantially with the addition of publications, office products, nonperishable foods, and nondurable high-volume consumer products. At the same time, competition increased in numbers and in strength, taxing the formerly stable position of Grupo Casa Autrey.

Diversification had its own set of challenges. It imposed different restrictions on the company's traditional logistics, including:

- New purchasing strategies
- New warehouse requirements
- New sales and customer service training and support
- New requirements for better, more professional sales forces specialized by channel

Diversification also created a more complex environment in several dimensions, such as:

- Logistics and operating procedures
- Development of commercial and strategic alliances and partnerships
- Management and supervision of a larger, more sophisticated group of professionals

When the company was a one-channel enterprise and dealt only with pharmaceutical products, measuring performance was relatively easy. But handling various types of customers, with multiple products and services, makes the measurement criteria and decision making more complex. According to Camiro, "We had to have an accurate way to measure our activities and processes. The bottom line was to have a better understanding of our profitability in the different business units. The objective for implementing ABC was to better understand our company from every angle."

To achieve its goals and face challenges brought forth by a changing marketplace, Grupo Casa Autrey developed a strong philosophy to guide its actions. The company's mission statement advocates the need: "(1) To satisfy the needs of our customers and commercial partners beyond their expectations; (2) To distribute and market products and services, combining efficiency, technological leadership and knowledge; (3) To expand our current markets and identify and develop new relevant ones; (4) To increase the skills of our people, and to achieve the highest profitability and competitiveness for the company."

HOW ABC/ABM WAS USED TO ACHIEVE GOALS

Camiro developed an integrated perspective of balanced scorecard, activity-based management (ABM), and EVA to define how these concepts should be used and applied to the company. (See Exhibit 12.1.) Grupo Casa Autrey decided to develop a model that incorporated both activity-based costing (ABC) and ABM. The ABC model served to break down all operating expenses by channel, product, sales representative, route, and client. The company also decided to monitor and manage each of its respective profitability levels.

EXHIBIT 12.1   An Integrated Perspective

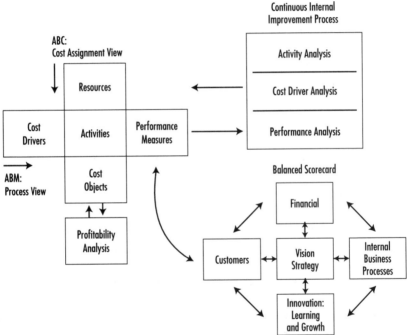

The company's complex operations included:

- 7,000 employees
- 800 vans and trucks (some refrigerated)
- 17,000 products in more than 20 product families
- 28 distribution centers
- 27 operating models
- Consolidated central operating model (corporate activities)

All these operations had to be considered when determining costs and profitability.

Grupo Casa Autrey brought in Arthur Andersen to assist with the implementation. During each phase, a combined Autrey/Arthur Andersen team provided support. Exhibit 12.2 presents team members and their corresponding roles.

EXHIBIT 12.2   Grupo Casa Autrey Team Structure

Autry Member	Team Role	Arthur Andersen Member	Team Role
Rubén Camiro	Sponsor (Autry's CFO)	Francisco Silva, CPA	Partner in charge of the project
Gilberto Ponce, CPA	Project leader (ABC manager)	Gema Moreno, CPA	Manager in charge of the project
Jinsuke Oshino, CPA	Team member (ABC analyst)	Federico Saavedra, CPA	Experienced Consultant, Model developer
		Alberto Trejo	Experienced Consultant, Model automation

The project was developed in three phases. The first phase, conceptual design, included the following steps:

- Identify core and supporting processes.
- Develop activities involved.
- Determine resource and activity drivers.
- Determine cost objects.
- Prepare draft model (detailed and summarized).

During this phase, the conceptual model was designed. "Conceptually, the model is strategic," Camiro comments. "It begins with business strategy, making the big decisions and then defining policies. Once the model is established, it takes on operational characteristics because of the richness of the information it handles."

The first step in the process was to understand the organization within a very complex operational environment. The project team worked with the executive team to identify the core and supporting processes as well as the associated cost impacts, utilizing a high-level map of processes. Once the main processes were identified, there were scheduled focus group sessions with personnel from areas involved within each process. During these sessions the team developed the specific process maps, identified the resources used to perform the activities and evaluated how the cost objects used the activities. For those purposes the team designed and used some tables to gather all the information during the sessions. These tables proved very useful in expediting the information gathering process. Exhibit 12.3 is an example of the tables used.

EXHIBIT 12.3   Example Data Collection Table

RESOURCES					#	Sales Activities	COST OBJECT					
							Products			Channels		
PCs	Payroll	Furniture	Building	Travel Expenses			Pharmaceutical	Beauty	Office supplies	Supermarkets	Convenience	Bookstores
n	y	n	n	y	1	Promotion	y	y	n	n	n	n
y	y	n	n	n	2	Order gathering	y	y	y	y	y	y
n	y	n	n	n	3	Prepare returns, claims, collection form	y	y	n	n	n	n
y	y	n	n	n	4	Input orders, returns, collection	y	y	y	y	y	y
n	y	n	n	y	5	Customer service	y	y	y	y	y	y
y	y	n	n	n	6	Deposit	y	y	n	n	n	n
n	y	y	y	n	7	Supervising	y	y	y	y	y	y

Next the relational map was prepared. The map was so large it covered an entire wall of the room where the team met. During the second phase, however, the team discovered it would have been easier if they had incorporated ABC software support from the onset of the project to reflect the relational map information.

Pitfalls encountered during this first phase included:

- Lack of a clear definition in approach—was a strategic vs. operational model required
- Difficulty in understanding the complexities of the operational environment
- Lack of pilot execution

The second phase was model automation. Specifics of this phase included:

- Software selection (performed internally)
- First data inputting (performed internally)

- Revision of model consistency
- Integration of new cost objects (sales representatives, routes)

At the end of the first phase, the company was finishing the implementation of its enterprise resource planning (ERP) system: Baan. At this time, some information was adjusted, including cost centers and other relevant accounting information. During the same period, the Oros software by ABC Technologies was acquired. The first data was then input using part of the conceptual model information.

At that time, Camiro had also become the official sponsor of ABC efforts within the company. With the CFO as project champion, Grupo Casa Autrey clearly demonstrated commitment to the project and validated future use of results.

The combined Autrey/Arthur Andersen team then revised the model to ensure it was in compliance with the company's current requirements. As a result, the cost objects were increased and the sales representatives and their routes were included. The team also verified the sources of information for resources and drivers, and automated the information charge through table preparations for Oros. At this time, Autrey team member Gilberto Ponce was designated as ABC manager.

The third and final phase was the pilot and roll-out. This phase was comprised of the following activities:

- Pilot development, including five distribution centers
- Model adjustments
- Reports' design
- Roll-out plan

During this phase, the results from the model were tested, primarily using information from the main distribution center and corporate office. Several accounting adjustments were generated as were some adjustments related to driver integrity. After these adjustments, the pilot was increased to four additional distribution centers. Automation fine-tuning was also made during phase 3, and the profitability and activities' reports were designed.

In the technical implementation, there were obstacles to overcome, interfaces that needed to be generated, and other technical problems to be solved. These problems, which were anticipated, were few and workable. The main difficulty was that people were not accustomed to coding their activities in detail. It was an attitude problem of breaking obsolete paradigms. Camiro notes, "It was interesting to see we all did not have the same vision of the enterprise. Creating our model was an exercise in standardization. With the adoption of ABC, the benefits have outweighed the implementation difficulties, and things now flow much more smoothly and there is consistency through the enterprise."

KEY RESULTS

The implementation created a standard view of the company's processes and activities. Before implementation, responsible personnel in several departments did not understand more than 1 or 2 percent of their processes. Now all top executives share the same knowledge and agree on cause-effect relationships.

The chart of accounts suffered several sensitive changes as a result of information generated by the project. Some of the improvements were:

- The creation of new cost centers in accordance with process/activity classification
- Payroll updating, to identify each cost center member correctly
- Linkage between routes' operative registration and accounting records
- Basis development for general expenses allocation

In addition, a one-step allocation of overhead to cost centers was performed outside the ABC model for resources such as rent and power, while the model itself addressed allocation of corporation overhead. Historically, the services provided by the corporate center to its branches were calculated on a sales basis. Consequently the branches generating greater revenues for the group received heavier charges from corporate services. At the end of the project, the company was able to understand exactly the efforts devoted by the corporate center to the different branches through the use of the model.

One of the primary objectives of the company was total automation of the model. A great deal of effort was put into building an accurate model with the data resources available. As a general trend, the company elected to take standard measurements for time-based drivers. Using standards in time-related drivers allowed for easier model maintenance.

Streamlined modeling allowed the company to take advantage of current computing resources. The company has an amazing volume of data on line—two years' worth of daily transactions—controlled through REDBRICK, a powerful data warehousing tool. This tool allowed the project team automatically to obtain a high amount of operational drivers that enriched the results of the strategic model. The information linked perfectly with accounting records. The database contains every transaction, which provides a range of drivers. Grupo Casa Autrey can analyze activities in detail and continually update knowledge of the processes. The model is simple in scope but deep in reach.

Knowledge development regarding ABC and performance measurement was crucial. At the beginning of the project, the company wanted to measure channels and product profitability; at the end of the project, it was clearly more important to measure what was actually administered, such as routes, sales representatives, warehouse teams, as means of determining product and client profitability.

For the continuous internal improvement process, the current ABC model provides an economic map of the organization. Using the process view analysis, Grupo Casa Autrey can establish the necessary performance policies to produce improvement. The performance indicators based on activities are dynamically linked to a balanced scorecard.

LESSONS LEARNED

Grupo Casa Autrey learned a number of valuable lessons during the pilot and subsequent project roll-out.

- It is very important to evaluate an organization's current resources and to take advantage of those resources. While improvements are always possible, they may never materialize. Therefore, make the best use of resources on hand.
- Begin with cost allocation and accounting alignment. Without this it is extremely difficult or even impossible to implement ABM accurately.
- Driver selection is a significant issue during any ABM project development. A poor selection of drivers can damage the results of the model.
- Take advantage of data-warehousing tools such as REDBRICK to support driver and profitability generation. Drivers are the keys to enrich the results from an ABC model and increase its accuracy. Drivers allow the correct application of resources to the activities and reflect the activity contribution to each cost object.
- It is highly recommended that ABC software be selected before the conceptual design of the model is created. The software support expedites the conceptual design phase and allows users to obtain tangible results from the beginning of the project.
- Begin with a strategic view and expand to an operational view. The strategic view allows the team to understand the organization, while the

operational view might be very difficult to manage from the beginning. The operational view comes afterward as a result of a deeper understanding of the organization.

- Control and manage the ABC model in a centralized manner first. After controlling the model, it can be decentralized naturally.
- Create a standard model at first to allow for exceptions as the project develops. Creating a standard model enables the company to manage and improve activity performance as well as to identify potential exceptions to be controlled. It is easier to integrate those exceptions after having the standard model applicable to the whole organization. A standard model represents the general map of the company. (See Exhibit 12.4.)

EXHIBIT 12.4   General Map of Activities and Cost Centers for Corporate Office

915 General Director	904 Commercial Corporate Direction	940 Grocery Sales Direction	968 Independent Channel Coordinator
Presidence and General Direction	Commercial Corporate Direction	Grocery Sales Direction	Coordinator
Commercial Supervision	Grocery Sales Supervision	Grocery Sales Supervision	Coordinate and Supervise
Finance Supervision	Consumer Products Sales Supervision	Convenience Stores Sales Supervision	Sales Training
Operations Supervision	Office Suppliers Sales Supervision		
Legal Supervision	Branches Supervision		969 Convenience Stores Coordinator
Planning Supervision	Marketing Supervision		Coordinator
Other Business Supervision	Citem Supervision		Coordinate and Supervise
			Sales Training

- Having a map of the organization also supports the inputs for standardization.
- Best practices involvement is crucial. Visiting and talking with other ABC users offers new insights on the project, including knowledge about how to use it, how to implement it, and how to improve it.
- It is highly recommended that the internal ABM team be created at the beginning of the project and be placed in-charge of model administration. Assigning this responsibility ensures knowledge transfer, including building detailed modeling experience.
- Model documentation should be performed in parallel with model design to avoid intensive documentation efforts at the end of the project

and to support correct and complete documentation, reducing the risk of undocumented details.

- There must be a strong commitment from the information technology (IT) area and its personnel from the beginning. This commitment will support the automation of source information for the ABC model. IT leaders should be one of the sponsors of the ABC project and should gain "ownership" of supporting the driver feeds to the model.
- All potential users must be involved from the beginning of the project to cover all information requirements with the model. A lack of involvement could cause inaccuracies in the model structure.
- The purpose of an ABM model is to support strategic and operational decision making. As such, the model administrator should be aware of all significant issues related to the cost objects both at a strategic and an operational level. This makes possible delivery of a complete analysis of the ABC information to the executive team.

ABOUT THE AUTHORS

Francisco Silva is a Partner with Arthur Andersen in Mexico City, Mexico. Gema Morena Vega is a Manager with Arthur Andersen in Mexico City, Mexico.

NOTE

1. For additional information on the project and an interview with Rubén Camiro, please refer to: Jorge Medina More. "Grupo Casa Autrey's CFO Drives Profitability Using ABC," *As Easy As ABC* 33 (Summer 1998): 1, 10.

13

IMPROVING PROFITABILITY AND CLIENT RELATIONS WITH COST MANAGEMENT

Olivier Meltzer and Hein ter Meulen
Arthur Andersen, Amsterdam, The Netherlands

CASE STUDY: Hallmark Greeting Cards, The Netherlands

SUMMARY

Business Issue

Hallmark faced increasing competition coupled with a powerful retail network that allows for slim margins. Retailers increasingly demand more information about customer preferences and products rather than simply selecting an image on a greeting card. To protect margins, Hallmark embarked on a brand image initiative.

How ABM Was Used

The company used activity-based management to measure the effects of investments on the business. ABM enabled Hallmark to analyze customer profitability as well as identify and reduce non–value-added activities.

Hallmark's Results

Upon analysis, the company found that many customers were overserviced at the expense of more profitable customers. More important, Hallmark determined which products perform well at which retailers. This information allowed Hallmark to initiate more productive sales discussions with customers to create a win-win partnership.

Unlike the loving image created by their products, the world of the greeting card industry is fiercely competitive. From a production point of view, entry into the market is relatively simple. Anyone who designs an image on paper can have a product to sell. The competition comes on the marketing side fighting for retail shelf space and capturing what the public wants to buy. It is here that Hallmark has made this dynamic market its own.

This chapter demonstrates how Hallmark Netherlands is reinventing itself and the Dutch greeting card market, which is shaped by powerful retailers and strong competition. There are numerous low-cost producers. Market pressure is intensified by the fact that greeting cards often are available free of charge in Dutch bars and restaurants. Hallmark's task was to be successful in this challenging market.

BUSINESS ISSUES

Hallmark Netherlands, a part of the Hallmark Company, produces and markets greeting cards in The Netherlands and Belgium. The most difficult issue in The Netherlands greeting card industry revolves around powerful retailers that control the distribution network for consumer goods. Two large department stores and several retail chains control more than 70 percent of the market. Smaller shops selling greeting cards are organized in buying cooperatives. In The Netherlands, Hallmark faces customers with strong buying power and experience in using that buying power to their best advantage. Many consumer goods producers have had their margins diminished because of the pricing pressure within the distribution network.

For many retailers, greeting cards are not the main product or even a product that attracts their primary customers. This status has two effects:

1. Greeting cards are a side product, and retailers tend not to know much about them. Retailers rely on information provided by the producer or publisher.
2. Greeting cards are easily changed. Therefore, greeting card companies also face competition for the same floor space from products such as newspapers and magazines.

Changes in the Retail Trade

The retail trade in The Netherlands continues to be competitive with regard to information and technology. Through point-of-sales scanning, retailers have gained much knowledge regarding consumer behavior, giving them an advantage over producers. Furthermore, only a few large retail groups have access to prime real estate in The Netherlands, so the retailers are powerful when negotiating prices, which decreases the producers' margins. As a result, retailers determine whether the product will be accessible for the customer and the price paid, which determines the margin for the producer.

Information about customer preferences and products become key drivers of successful distribution. Retailers, for instance, not only look at the quality of the product but also to the producer's value-added activities, such as the product's profit per meter of space used, the level of shop traffic the product generates, the advertising support the producer will supply, and the optimal product assortment (category management). Retailers demand that producers provide specific product information even before merchandise is placed on the shop floor.

For producers this means retailers will be increasingly critical of information provided to them. Producers will be challenged to provide more accurate information about their products than in the past. Not only does this information have to be of a better quality, but it also must be supplied more frequently. In the past, contracts were made for a year. Today product performance is monitored on a daily basis.

Retailers are less likely to accept greeting cards solely on the basis of their image. Information about the product's performance potential also will be necessary. In addition, retailers will want to understand what effect individual greeting cards will have on the entire assortment or category. Increasingly producers are asked to provide more than just the product itself; however, the capability to provide this information is expensive.

The Increasing Role of Marketing

In The Netherlands, marketing greeting cards has long been classified as a sales support function. However, Hallmark is rapidly changing this paradigm by building a brand image for its greeting cards. The goal is to increase awareness of the Hallmark product, which in turn increases the relations with the retailers. A product with a higher awareness and a consumer preference due to a brand name is able to extract higher margins for both producer and retailer.

The concept of brand image allows for the protection of margins made on greeting cards rather than merely focusing on additional sales. Building a brand image is an investment and should be valued as such. Yet measuring the return on an investment in brand equity is difficult.

Publishing Images

The product selected by the end consumer is an image on paper. Creating sellable images requires substantial work as well as an investment in establishing relationships with artists—both of which do not come cheaply. As with brand equity, the return on the investment per artist also should be measured.

An added difficulty is the fact that popular images often vary by market. While a large spectrum of universally accepted images exists, occasionally an extremely popular image is also necessary to boost market share and build brand image. However, this particular image varies greatly market by market.

HOW ACTIVITY-BASED MANAGEMENT WAS USED

The increasing indirect costs of building brand equity while publishing new attractive images has become a never-ending cycle. Consequently, Hallmark needed a good analysis to measure the effects of investments into the business and to determine which retailers would offer the company the most value for its investment. As such a joint Arthur Andersen/Hallmark team embarked on a comprehensive activity-based management (ABM) initiative to address these challenges.

The ABM team consisted of a steering committee, including two of the project's main sponsors, the general manager and financial manager of Hallmark and Olivier Meltzer, an experienced manager with Arthur Andersen, participated in the committee.

Data analysts and the information technology (IT) department were recruited to work closely with the ABM team to provide support for the project. This relationship was crucial to obtain the right data and to work with employees who would lead the activity-based costing (ABC) calculations for Hallmark.

Management wanted to understand the dynamic relation among retail sales, margins, and the company's new investment into the business. The need was greater than a static return on investment or cost analysis could provide. Management wanted to build a simulation model and role-play several scenarios. It was thought simultaneous analysis would provide to a better understanding of the issues than a single analysis.

The enabling tool for role-playing was the NetProphet Activity-Based Management tool from Sapling. NetProphet enables management to define activities and resources. These are related in a software model that then allows simulations based on documented assumptions or facts. Scenarios analyzing the results of small customers vs. the larger customers proved to be very interesting. A commonly used argument is that small customers provide higher margins than large customers. Although this is generally true for gross margin, the amount of "invisible activities," such as planning and travel time for salespeople, often results in a lower net margin. Rather than exclude small customers, the scenarios were designed to answer the question of how to service small customers in a more efficient manner. Initiatives such as telesales and Internet ordering were explored to lower costs in serving smaller customers.

Customer Analysis

The starting point for model building included every individual customer of Hallmark Netherlands. In the past, such an analysis would have been too cumbersome, but with new technologies such as data warehousing, this type of analysis is possible. The results of such a close analysis led to new conclusions and a questioning of the implicit assumptions management had concerning the business.

The most important insight was, of course, the profitability of small customers vs. large customers. Another assumption was that one unit was extremely profitable; however, when the extra hidden-activities were calculated, the operation was not as efficient as expected.

Next, the focus was turned to the products sold to various retailers and all the activities performed to satisfy which customers. Product costs were easily calculated; however, far more difficult to determine was the cost of all additional services performed for customers, such as differences in customer invoice requirements. These activities were recorded in a closely defined activity dictionary and quantified in the software tool. The analysis revealed interesting information. Large retail customers often made special requests that were demanding on supporting departments, such as the information technology (IT) and finance departments, causing extra consumption of resources. Opportunities for improvement were found in the sales process organization. In some cases customers who used several different products from Hallmark were visited by different salespeople.

The process of activity analysis, customer analysis, and gathering the quantifiable operational data was set up in a very structured way and documented to validate the results. Everyone involved in this process was educated and informed in order to facilitate progress in the project.

Value-added Activities vs. Non–Value-added Activities

One of the benefits of a thorough customer and activity analysis is the realization of which activities add value and which do not. The identification of non–value-added activities gives management the opportunity either to cut costs or to improve service. The basis of the distinction between value-added activities and non–value-added ones is always the customer analysis. Without a clear picture of what is valuable to customers, this distinction cannot be made.

A number of non–value-added activities were uncovered that provided management with opportunities to cut costs and gain a better insight into cost structures and causes. As a result of this, Hallmark could modify its approach to the retail trade. For example, non–value-added activities were a result of the sales force operating from three different locations and covering different products within the same territory. These non–value-added duplicating activities took a considerable percentage of the sales force's capacity.

Case for Change

The ABC project provided Hallmark with a new angle of approach to the way of selling products. After the model was built using current financial and operational data, the first results became clear. Management observed the activities that added value and the individual customers who added or subtracted from the bottom line. This understanding, presented in quantifiable numbers, served as an eye opener for everyone involved in the project. It offered strong evidence for management to change the way the organization did business.

According to Arjan den Boer, financial manager for Hallmark Netherlands, "Activity-based management is not just about cost management, it is about really understanding your business. The insights from the ABM analysis are a catalyst for strategic change. It shows you with such a clear picture of what can be improved you just can't resist implementing."

Organizational changes are difficult. There must be a clear reason for change, and it must be understood by the key decision makers in the organization. A good, quantified cost model can provide the necessary reasons. An example of such a major change occurred in the sales department.

The sales department operated on a product-by-product basis. A salesperson would visit clients, show them the catalog of greeting cards, and either take orders or write quotes. The salesperson visited all clients in his or her region based on the prevailing idea of serving all customers equally well. The cost model challenged this approach. The model revealed that:

- Many customers prefer to place their orders by phone.
- Many large retailers did not buy on a product-by-product basis. Instead, they purchased an entire concept, complete with displays, category management, and advertising to support the product. A salesperson could not provide all of this support.
- Many small customers required such difficult services that they took a disproportionate amount of time.

The results of the model showed that many customers were overserviced at the expense of more profitable customers. This information provided management with the evidence to reorganize and professionalize the sales department.

Profitable Client Relations

The cost model also gave insights into what products perform well at which retailers. This information is also critical for the retailer, who must fill valuable floor space and would prefer to fill it with a successful product. Retailers know the approximate performance of greeting cards but may not know about greeting card categories. They may know less about the performance of certain images on their floor space. With the results of the ABM analysis, Hallmark Netherlands management is better able to advise retailers on how an assortment of greeting cards will perform at a particular retailer. This knowledge always has been implicitly present in the minds of marketers and merchandisers. Large retailers often do not accept suppliers who cannot supply adequate information about product performance. But now, management is able to better quantify this knowledge and to share it with retailers. Today products are individually tracked and cost and sales information is used to create assortments specific to each individual customer. Using information about product performance helps build better relationships with retailers as well as a profitable relationship for both parties.

RESULTS OF ACTIVITY-BASED MANAGEMENT

The results of the ABM analysis at Hallmark have been used in a number of areas. Based on the results, two organizational improvement projects were begun, one in the area of sales reorganization and the other in reengineering a business unit's performance. The marketing and sales areas gained additional knowledge that will benefit Hallmark's customers as well. There are future opportunities to work with customers to improve the value chain between supplier and retailer, an initiative already under way in fast-moving consumer goods. It also can benefit the greeting cards business.

The ultimate compliment for the ABM analysis has been Hallmark's intent to roll out this initiative to its markets in the United Kingdom and Australia during 1999.

LESSONS LEARNED

The following lessons were learned during this project.

- *Top management support is crucial.* Work closely with top management to identify, document, and publicize the project. A good business case understood by key personnel is crucial.
- *Involve an IT authority from the onset.* An IT analyst can help develop workable activity definitions. The analyst knows the capabilities of the current system, which avoids creating activity definitions that are not workable because information on these activities is impossible to get.
- *Constantly involve employees in the implementation process.* In order to achieve acceptance of the project, key managers must communicate as much as possible with the organization while the central project team continues the analysis. Open communication will dramatically improve acceptance, understanding and insight providing a solid base for active future use of ABM techniques.
- *The flexibility of an ABC system enables operational and strategic decision-making.* ABC proved to be a unique and powerful tool for looking simultaneously at the cost of processes, product lines, and customer segments. The flexibility of ABC allows organizations to build the bridge between internal cost management and external revenue enhancement. ABC scenario analyses provides a solid set of tools to gain understanding of cause and effect of business decisions and developments.

ABOUT THE AUTHORS

Olivier Meltzer is a Manager with Arthur Andersen in Amsterdam, The Netherlands.
Hein ter Meulen is a Consultant with Arthur Andersen in Amsterdam, The Netherlands.

14

ACTIVITY-BASED MANAGEMENT TURNS A TELEPHONE MONOPOLY INTO A MARKET-BASED COMPETITOR

Paulo Salgado, Nuno Belo, and Margarida Bajanca
Arthur Andersen, Lisbon, Portugal

Carol Cobble
Armstrong Laing, Atlanta, Georgia

CASE STUDY: Portugal Telecom, Lisbon, Portugal

SUMMARY

Business Issues
Deregulation of the telecommunications industry in Europe signaled the rapid introduction of competition across the continent. Competition brought significant challenges as companies needed to adapt to the new environment to survive and managers needed a better grasp of their costs to price products and create value.

How ABM Is Used
In addition to regulatory requirements, Portugal Telecom's managers realized the need to understand the company's costs. The activity-based management (ABM) cost information would enable Portugal Telecom to set appropriate prices, compare its own cost data with competitive benchmarks, and reduce costs to keep prices competitive.

Portugal Telecom's Results
With a mandate to meet regulatory needs, Portugal Telecom built an enterprise-wide ABM system in seven months. Portugal Telecom uses ABM information for price negotiations and support for cost reductions to keep prices competitive. The company plans to enhance existing corporate planning infrastructure to include activity-based budgeting.

Around the globe, countries are introducing market competition into industries previously dominated by regulated or state-owned monopolies. The telecommunications industry has been a major target of these privatization efforts. Indeed, the European Union has agreed to fully liberalize telecommunications throughout Europe, which will mean the rapid introduction of competition across the continent.

But competition will bring significant challenges to all involved:

- Governments will have to ensure that high standards of customer service continue to be met.
- Telecommunications companies will have to adapt to the new environment to survive.
- Managers will have to know more about their costs to price products and create value—information that their existing cost systems simply cannot provide.

Moreover, all of these challenges will have to be met quickly.

This chapter discusses how Portugal Telecom used activity-based management (ABM) to address these competitive challenges. The company, which was formed by the merger of Portugal's two main telephone companies and its main broadcasting service, managed to implement ABM in all parts of the business in just 20 months. The initial enterprise-wide ABM system for regulatory needs was built in seven months, an extraordinarily fast time for a company of its size. This case study explains how the company managed this feat.

BUSINESS ISSUES

The merger that created Portugal Telecom in 1994 was undertaken to facilitate lowering costs and obtaining higher levels of customer service. New rules from the European Commission have paved the way for increased competition. As a result, achieving these goals was critical to the company's survival.

While the merger that created Portugal Telecom was necessary for the survival of the three companies involved, it raised concerns about the potential for monopolistic pricing, particularly in the interconnection business. Therefore, the Regulator—Instituto das Comunicações de Portugal (ICP)—and the Directorate General of Competition and Prices (DGCP) required the company to provide cost data.

While the regulatory requirements were reason enough to implement ABM, Portugal Telecom's managers saw an even greater need—the need to understand the company's costs. Specifically, Portugal Telecom needed cost information that would help it achieve the following:

- Set appropriate prices.
- Compare its own cost data with competitive benchmarks.
- Reduce costs to keep prices competitive.

Failure to understand costs would have left Portugal Telecom vulnerable to competition, which was becoming increasingly intense throughout Europe. Benchmark data from other countries already had indicated that Portugal Telecom would need to reduce its costs to be competitive with what other companies were charging. Thus, understanding the company's costs became essential to cost reduction efforts and to the company's long-term viability.

BACKGROUND

Portugal Telecom was formed in June 1994 by the merger of Telefones de Lisbon e Porto (TLP, which operated telephone service in Lisbon and Porto) and Telecom Portugal (TP, which operated telephone service in the rest of the country). The merger also included Portugal's main broadcasting service, Teledifusora de Portugal (TDP).

In 1998 Portugal Telecom's revenues were 620 billion Portuguese escudos—about US$3.3 billion. The company now has approximately 17,500 employees in both fixed and mobile communications. It operates in four regional areas (recently consolidated from 10) and has branch offices throughout Portugal.

Portugal Telecom operates all public exchanges, the network of local telephone lines, and both domestic and international (through its subsidiary, Marconi) transmission facilities in Portugal. The company also provides telex, leased lines, and television broadcasting. Its subsidiaries provide mobile telephone service, paging, data communications, and cable television services.

ABM PROJECT ROLLOUT

In June 1995 Portugal Telecom engaged Arthur Andersen's Lisbon office to develop a conceptual design for a cost model that Portugal Telecom could use to meet both its regulatory and management accounting needs.

Exhibit 14.1 shows the ABM project time line for Portugal Telecom. By October 1995, after many different approaches had been discussed and analyzed, the conceptual design for the company's ABM project was completed. Manuel Palma, the leader of the ABM project, describes the design as follows:

"The conceptual design described the steps necessary to implement ABM. It showed how resource drivers would trace resources to activities. It explained how individual activities would be grouped into network activities, customer-facing ac-

EXHIBIT 14.1   Portugal Telecom's ABM Project Timeline

Project Milestone	1994	1995	1996	1997	1998
1. Merger created Portugal Telecom.	1				
2. PT signed price convention agreement with the regulator agreeing to define the cost of telecommunication services.		2			
3. PT engages Arthur Andersen to develop the cost model conceptual design.		3			
4. Conceptual design was completed recommending an ABM approach.		4			
5. Approach and treatment of costs discussed.		5 ⟹			
6. Began implementation of the enterprise-wide ABM system.			6		
7. HyperABC software selected.			7		
8. Implementation completed and detailed methodologies sent to the Regulator.			8		
9. Presented the results of tests performed (using 1995 data) to the Board.			9		
10. Presented the results (using 1996 data) to the Board.				10	
11. Results sent to the regulator showing costs of products and services including access lines, traffic, and lease lines.				11	
12. Developed model for interconnection costs to support proposals as well as other services.				12	
13. Summarized activity costs by general direction area.				13	
14. Convert budgets to activity view by general direction and implement activity-based budgets for going into 1999.					14 ⟹

tivities, and so forth. The conceptual design helped us to understand how back-office activities, general office activities, and switching activities would be treated."

The conceptual design gave management much to consider and received considerable attention. It stimulated many discussions. There were many meetings with members of the board, other company managers, and Arthur Andersen to discuss the details of how costs should be treated.

By May 1996 management agreed to stop the debate and start implementing. Agreements with ICP (the regulator) required that a system be put in place to assign costs to all products by the end of 1996. In effect, an enterprise-wide ABM implementation had to take place in Portugal Telecom within seven months. The following sections discuss the structure of the ABM team and the model design used to achieve this objective.

By working at a furious pace, the team met its deadlines. At the end of December 1996, the team sent the regulator the detailed ABM methodology for assigning all costs to products. It included all the resources of the organization, all the drivers, and an explanation of the treatment of network resources for all the products.

TESTING WITH HISTORICAL DATA

In January 1997 the financial results for 1995 were tested in the ABM model the team had designed. In April the team modeled and presented the 1996 results. After reviewing these results, the company forwarded the reports to the regulator in June 1997. The information, which covered the costs of access lines, traffic (including international and long distance), and leased lines, among others, met the initial regulatory requirements.

After this test of the new system, the ABM team used the model to support the interconnection proposals that Portugal Telecom used in its fee negotiations with mobile operations. Cost modeling to support interconnection pricing was completed in October 1997. Nonetheless, Portugal Telecom continues to refine its ABM model to understand and support the pricing of other services, including telex and broadcasting.

In 1997 Portugal Telecom began to obtain the ABM information needed to understand the costs associated with each business unit—for example, business markets, residential markets, and infrastructures. The company also will start using the ABM system information for activity-based budgeting.

ABM TEAM STRUCTURE

Palma, the full-time leader of the ABM effort at Portugal Telecom, is the company's ABM "champion."

ABM was identified as a strategic project by the company's long-term strategic planning initiative called Portugal Telecom 2000 (PT 2000). As such, it received the attention of Portugal Telecom's senior management, many of whom participated on the PT 2000 steering committees.

During the conceptual design phase for the ABM project, a steering committee was created composed of three board members and some company managers. Later the composition of this committee changed. As ABM was being implemented, the project team reported instead to a steering committee that included one board member and all company general managers, among others.

NETWORK TEAM

During the implementation, the ABM project team had two major subcommittees: (1) a *network* team and (2) a *customer-facing activities* team. (Exhibit 14.2 shows the structure of the ABM project team.)

The network team had responsibility for assigning the costs of the network activities (which were defined as activities developed for generic capacity) available to any product or customer. In effect, network facilities are a huge shared resource. The network team consisted mainly of engineers—three full-time engineers—but also one full-time member from the finance department. This team also included three part-time engineers.

EXHIBIT 14.2   Portugal Telecom Implementation Project Team Structure

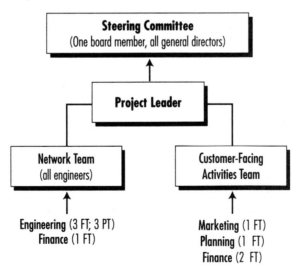

The challenge facing the network team was how to determine the costs of the infrastructure and related support activities. This included understanding the following:

- Where each of the network components was used
- How the network enabled sales
- How individual calls consumed the network's capacity in terms of how many calls it could handle at a given time

The network team analyzed these questions by conducting interviews, sampling, and studying traffic and switching patterns.

CUSTOMER-FACING ACTIVITIES TEAM

Customer-facing activities are those activities performed for the benefit of customers, in response to a customer request, or for a specific product. Examples of customer-facing activities include connecting a customer phone line, handling customer repairs, or supporting a call-waiting function. The customer-facing activities team analyzed these costs and the cost of support activities. Support activities (or *business sustaining activities*) are necessary for managing the business, but they do not relate to any specific products or customers. Examples of support activities include grounds maintenance, governmental compliance, and preparing financial statements. The customer-facing team also was responsible for the organization and study of other resource pools, such as buildings, vehicles, and information systems.

The customer-facing activities team included four full-time people—one each from marketing and planning, and two from finance. This team also used specialized consultants on a part-time basis to address specific issues.

After the initial implementation was complete, most members of the ABM project team returned to their previous jobs. Palma became the manager of the newly created cost system department. (See Exhibit 14.3 for the structure of the department.) Luis Oliveira, the leader of the network team, also remained and now manages three full-time members, two from engineering and one from finance.

The rest of the members of the customer-facing activities team became part of three teams: systems, collection and treatment of information, and reporting. These teams consist of one full-time modeler, two full-time analysts, one full-time person from marketing, and another from finance, as well as two part-time members from planning. The analysts were hired directly from the university. Consultants also are used as needed. With ABM as a component of ongoing management, a separate steering committee is no longer needed for the ABM program.

The cost system department has embedded ABM in the permanent infrastructure of the finance function. It is primarily responsible for maintaining

EXHIBIT 14.3   Portugal Telecom Structure of Ongoing Cost System Development

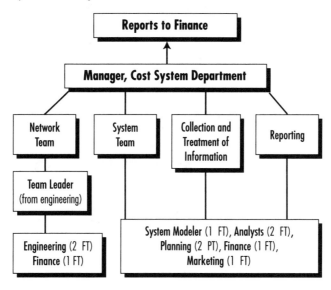

Responsibilities: Maintaining ABM model, data collection, modeling and reporting, and providing analysis and business support, including responding to regulatory requests.

the ABM infrastructure, including data collection, modeling, and reporting. It also provides analysis and business support, including responses to regulatory requests. The department serves to support front-line managers in understanding their costs and in teaching people to think in terms of long-term incremental costing.

SYSTEM ARCHITECTURE

Portugal Telecom runs its enterprise-wide ABM system using *Hyper*ABC software. Because the centralized ABM team tightly controls the model, a single model version can be used for both management and regulatory reporting. Exhibit 14.4 diagrams the system architecture. The team requires that activity and driver definitions be consistent across the organization. It has tightly controlled the model to ensure consistency and comparative reporting.

The system receives data from the company's general ledger, which runs on SAP's version R/2. It also pulls data from other operating systems in Portugal Telecom. The ABM system provides outputs for both regulatory and management information needs. SAS is used to give access to departmental information and to report and analyze all information.

EXHIBIT 14.4   System Architecture

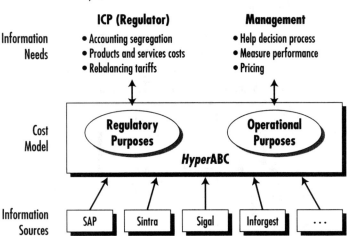

To provide access to the user department, Portugal Telecom is designing a data warehouse. Data for the model flow in from the company's 1,400 departments throughout Portugal. These departments are aggregated into 400 for input into the model.

The Portugal Telecom system includes 580 activities, which are assigned to cost objects by means of 40 activity drivers. Examples of activity drivers used include the number of access lines installed, the minutes in peak hours, the number of repair requests, and the number of invoices. The model has been used to produce annual results beginning in 1995 (prepared in early 1997). In 1999 the team expects to run the model quarterly for management reporting purposes and annually for regulatory purposes.

RESULTS AND NEXT STEPS

Portugal Telecom has come a long way in a short time frame. With a mandate to meet regulatory needs, the company built an enterprise-wide ABM system in seven months. This was achieved due to the clear management mandate, the firm foundation from the conceptual design process, and the time spent aligning management prior to launching systems development.

In 1997 and 1998 this ABM information has been used not only for regulatory purposes but also to meet critical management information needs. These include price negotiations and support for cost reductions to keep these prices competitive.

Portugal Telecom plans to continue using its ABM system to support regulatory requests and to provide management information about product costs. The company also plans to enhance the existing corporate planning infrastructure to include activity-based budgeting.

Management expects the 1999 budget to be based on activities. Implementation of ABM also was completed in January 1998 at Portugal Telecom's Marconi subsidiary, which carries all the international traffic, incoming and outgoing. Also, an implementation is in process at the TMN subsidiary, which houses the company's cellular operations.

LESSONS LEARNED

In completing its ABM system, Portugal Telecom overcame many obstacles. The ABM team had to deal with the merger of multiple cultures as several companies were brought together. The scope of the project—the entire company—was also challenging, as was the problem of completing the implementation in only seven months. Finally, much of the driver data needed for the new ABM system was unavailable.

In dealing with these issues, the implementation team learned the following lessons:

- *A sense of urgency accelerates the process.* The requirement to meet the regulator's deadlines created a sense of urgency in the ABM team and the entire company. Any implementation team should clearly identify the reasons for a speedy implementation, whether they are new regulations, competitive threats, or management vision. Setting deadlines helps to focus ABM teams on the action that must be completed.

- *Top management leadership is crucial.* Portugal Telecom's speedy implementation occurred in large part because of top management's commitment, active leadership, and participation in the process. Because top management was interested and involved, everyone else supported the effort.

- *Communicate milestones.* Even with the commitment from top management and a sense of urgency, those on the ABM team need to publicize milestones as they are reached. This requires having a plan that lays out the milestones, the ultimate objectives, and the expected completion dates. Design a communication plan for getting this information to employees and managers alike.

- *Finance and operations departments must work together to understand the business.* Understanding cost behavior can be far more difficult than just reading financial statements. Often it requires close interaction with operational managers and workers. This is especially true for complex areas such as telephone networks. Techniques such as traffic studies and switching analysis may need to be employed. Therefore, multidisciplinary teams are crucial to developing an adequate understanding of costs. A multidisciplinary approach requires:

—Integrating information (both physical and financial measures)

—Collecting information from nonfinancial sources

—Collecting important performance information not currently captured

- *Budgets ultimately should be determined by customer requirements.* ABM systems help everyone understand that customers and their demands are the most important factors to consider when creating a budget. Changes in customer requirements (or the standard products and services being sold to those customers) can change the activities needed to satisfy customers. The changes in activity requirements change the resources that are needed to be successful.

ABOUT THE AUTHORS

Paula Salgado is Partner with Arthur Andersen in Lisbon, Portugal.

Nuno Belo is a Senior Manager with Arthur Andersen in Lisbon, Portugal.

Margarida Bajanca is a Senior Manager with Arthur Andersen in Lisbon, Portugal.

Carol Cobble is Vice President of Client Services for Armstrong Laing in Atlanta, Georgia.

Note: This case originally appeared in *Cornerstones of Decision Making: Profiles of Enterprise ABM* by Steve Player and Carol Cobble (Greensboro, NC: Oakhill Press, 1999).

15

MAKING THE RIGHT DECISIONS WITH ACTIVITY-BASED MANAGEMENT

Michelle Behrenwald
Arthur Andersen, Grand Rapids, Michigan

Carol Cobble
Armstrong Laing, Atlanta, Georgia

CASE STUDY: American Seating, Grand Rapids, Michigan

SUMMARY

Business Issues

Faced with increasing competition, American Seating wanted a better way to identify product profitability information and to strategically pursue certain areas of the business. Management needed better information to make both strategic and operational decisions such as how to reduce non–value-added costs and enhance value-added services to customers.

How ABM Is Used

American Seating developed an activity-based performance management solution to more accurately mirror resource consumption by process, product and customer. ABM supports economic justification for new products, cost estimates and target costing, pricing practices, and continuous improvement efforts.

American Seating's Results

American Seating successfully created cost and profitability reports by customer group, product line, and segment. After identification of non–value-added activities, the product engineering group achieved a 40 percent reduction in the special sales order processing cycle. Likewise, American Seating was able to redirect resources to provide higher-value service to customers. ABM information is incorporated into continuous improvement efforts, planning sessions, and the budgeting process.

Competition is forcing changes in the direction and growth of the seating industry, as in many industries today. In transportation seating, for example, companies from Mexico now compete heavily with U.S. companies. And in the stadium-seating arena, an Australian company has made significant inroads into the market share of U.S. companies. These are just some of the issues facing American Seating, a leading U.S. manufacturer and assembler of seating products, which is headquartered in Grand Rapids, Michigan.

BUSINESS ISSUES

"We were like many leading-edge manufacturers around the world," says Edward Clark, president and chief executive officer of American Seating. "We needed better information to make both strategic and operational business decisions." But when the company turned to existing data, it discovered that—when it came to good cost information—it was data rich yet information poor.

"Our interest in activity-based management (ABM) began during an executive meeting on profitability," says Thomas Bush, chief financial officer of American Seating. "Because our product line is so large, we had concerns with the accuracy of our standard cost system which provided us with our margins. Our executive team needed a better way to identify product profitability information and to strategically pursue certain areas of the business."

Particular product lines and business segments were not achieving their revenue and profit targets, due, in part, to changing needs in the marketplace and to the commoditization of certain products. Bush adds, "To be successful, we needed to reduce our non–valued-added costs and thereby enhance value-added services to customers. As this became more evident, we began to reevaluate cost and performance management practices."

Because of the diversity and complexity of its products and product segments, the company needed:

- Economic justification for new product ventures and proposed capital investments
- Insight into underlying cost structures to support cost estimates and target costing
- Improved understanding of new product launch costs and the life-cycle impact on profitability
- Pricing practices separate from standard costs
- Benchmarking of operations and quantification of continuous improvement
- Improved information to help managers make more informed strategic and operational business decisions

American Seating researched management tools that might provide the information needed. After a site visit to another company that had implemented an integrated cost management system successfully, management decided to launch an activity-based performance management system to provide the answers. Clark explains: "Performance management offered us a dynamic and flexible process to organize and integrate financial and operational data into meaningful information. It was information we could use to meet our own needs and also the needs of our customers in the marketplace."

ABM STEERING COMMITTEE

Twelve top executives from various parts of the business formed a steering committee to identify the key issues. (See Exhibit 15.1 for a list of steering committee members.) They defined a shared vision and developed specific expectations.

EXHIBIT 15.1   American Seating Steering Team Members

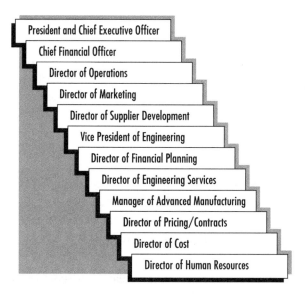

According to Bush, American Seating wanted to understand how to maximize profitability and enhance customer satisfaction despite the growth it was experiencing. To do so, the company needed to understand its product cost structure, which was impossible given the company's standard cost system.

The steering committee wanted ABM to answer the following questions:

- Which products, customers, and segments should we target?
- How can American Seating enhance revenue and increase profitability by product and by customer?
- What are our core competencies?
- Are resources being deployed effectively to achieve strategies and improve profits?
- What is the impact of the improvement efforts?

With help from Arthur Andersen, American Seating developed an activity-based performance management solution. The system sought to accurately mirror resource consumption by process, product, and customer.

BACKGROUND

American Seating Company, a midsize manufacturer founded in 1885 in Grand Rapids, Michigan, has a proud heritage based on the simple idea to develop products that provide a comfortable and productive environment at school, at work, and in public facilities. The company, which has approximately 900 employees, is a leading manufacturer of seating for buses and light-rail systems. It also makes stadium and auditorium seating, office furniture, and ergonomic seating products. These products are manufactured in four facilities and sold throughout North America. Since American Seating is privately held, revenues are not disclosed.

The company's history includes many firsts:

- Adjustable-height furniture
- Angle-adjustable desks
- Desks for both left- and right-handed students
- Tilt-back and automatic-rising theater seats
- Self-leveling glides to eliminate table wobble
- Laminated desktops
- Body-conforming materials to make seats more comfortable
- Cantilevered bus seating

Each of these innovations has become standard in the seating industry.

American Seating began in schoolrooms and theaters. After World War II, however, the company expanded to meet the growing demand in the transportation market. By the 1960s the company also had become the leading manufacturer of architectural seating. Later it entered the office furniture market, again offering innovations previously unmatched. The company now operates in three primary areas or groups:

1. *Interior Systems:* contract seating, tables, and furniture systems
2. *Transportation Products:* bus and light-rail seating
3. *Architectural Products:* auditorium and stadium seating

ABM PROJECT ROLLOUT

In July 1996 American Seating launched an ABM pilot. The objective was to design a performance management framework that would provide more accurate operational and financial information. Exhibit 15.2 provides an overview of milestones achieved during the 20-week implementation.

EXHIBIT 15.2   American Seating Project Implementation Milestones

Requirements Assessment ....Weeks 1–2

Team Training .... Weeks 1–2

Interviews & Activity Effort Worksheets ...... Weeks 3–6

Process Analysis & Schematics .... Weeks 7–8

Software Selection .... Weeks 9–10

Software Training .... Weeks 11–12

Build Model .... Weeks 13–15

Interpret Results .... Weeks 14–18

Implementation & Integration Planning   ...... Week 19

Total elapsed time: 20 weeks

Since completion of the project, this information from the new ABM system has been used for continuous improvement and decision making for issues relating to customer and product profitability. CEO Clark championed the project.

ABM Project Team

The ABM project team included six employees from American Seating and three consultants from Arthur Andersen. The members from American Seating included:

- Director of Cost, who served as the ABM project manager
- Operations Manager
- Director of Engineering Services
- Sales and Marketing Education Director
- Two financial and cost analysts

The team worked together over six months to identify leading practices in cost and performance management practices. They also developed skills and tools on process and project management to help implement the pilot project.

The ABM team was dedicated full time to the successful completion and validation of this project. As Bush says, "We were committed to this project from the CEO down and throughout the organization. We targeted some of our top performers for participation on the ABM team. Although they would be dedicated for about six months, this project was deemed a top priority, and cross-functional leadership and team members were critical to success."

Initial Efforts

Properly training the ABM team was essential. Initial training sessions covered:

- ABM definitions
- Techniques that would be used
- How interviews would be conducted
- Other project tasks and tools

The project team then held a series of kickoff meetings, which were open to the entire company.

Team members and executives gave presentations to define ABM and explain why ABM was being implemented. Communicating the objectives to the entire organization prevented misconceptions later about the project's structure and goals. The combination of early involvement of employees and visible support of top management allowed the project team to move swiftly in implementation.

Next, the cross-functional steering committee conducted a "requirements assessment" to finalize key objectives and questions. The focus included the following:

- Assessing company's culture
- Identifying core competencies
- Matching resources with strategy

- Targeting key products and services
- Enhancing profitability and revenues
- Measuring the impact of improvement initiatives

Interviews

Interviews were the next step. The project team began by identifying who would be interviewed and who would conduct which interviews. From the interviews, activity effort worksheets were completed. (See Exhibits 15.3 and 15.4 for samples of an activity effort worksheet and a completed departmental summary of the forms.) The worksheets showed primary activities for each area, time splits for activities, activity drivers, and the resources other than labor that went into the activities.

About 125 people from every work area and various work centers in the manufacturing facilities were interviewed, including managers from functional areas outside of manufacturing. The team used both group and individual interviews, depending on the preference of the manager of each particular area. Before each interview, those who would be interviewed received guidelines, such as the number and significance of activities to be discussed. Using this interview framework made compilation of results quick and consistent.

The project team was divided into three interview teams, each of which had one or two team members from American Seating and one Arthur Andersen consultant. The interviews generally took about 90 minutes to complete, followed by another hour to document and validate the information. Finishing all of the interviews took about four weeks.

Activity Definition

Initially, the people interviewed were allowed to define the activities they wanted in the model, but their inexperience often caused activities to be defined in too much detail. So the process was divided into two stages. The second, or "schematic" phase, rolled activities up to a higher level that would be modeled and maintained. As a result, ultimately a total of 228 unique activities were defined. Activity drivers then were chosen to trace these activities to cost objects.

Software Selection and Model Building

After the schematic phase was complete, the team evaluated the different software products available, weighing the pros and cons of each given American

EXHIBIT 15.3 Activity Effort Worksheet

Input	Output	Activity	Activity Description	Driver	Names/Individuals/Groups				
					% Time	% Time	% Time	% Time	% Time
					100%	100%	100%	100%	100%

Nonlabor resources:

EXHIBIT 15.4 Activity Effort Summary: Sales Department View

Labor w/ Fringes	Total Department $	Total Hours	Average Hourly Rate
	$187,002	6,240	$29.97
Nonlabor Dollars Allocated	$351,718	6,240	$56.37

Activity	Business Process	Total Hours	Total Labor	Total Nonlabor	Total Dollars	Hours			Driver Volume	Driver Unit $
						Value Added	Management Required	Non–value-added		
Contacting prospects	3a	1,404	$42,075	$52,651	$94,726		1,404		100	$947
Presenting features and benefits of company product and services	6c	1,092	$32,725	$40,951	$73,676		1,092		1,092	$67
Identifying and resolving warranty and nonquality product	13b	858	$25,713	$32,175	$57,888	858			25	$2,316
Developing dealer needs	5a	702	$21,038	$26,325	$47,363		702		5	$9,473
Managing and coordinating area	6c	858	$25,713	$32,175	$57,888		858		9	$6,432
Managing the showroom	6c	0	$0	$117,397	$117,397		0		1	$117,397
Performing administrative responsibilities	10b	1,326	$39,738	$49,726	$88,750		1,326		1,326	$67
Performing independent representative duties	6c	0	$0	$318	$318		0		20	$16
Total		6,240	$187,002	$351,718	$538,720	858	5,382	0		

a Data included are for illustrative purposes only and not reflective of actual company numbers.
b Breakdown of nonlabor dollars includes sales and product literature, showroom, samples, training, and travel and entertainment.

Seating's needs. *Hyper*ABC was selected for its import capabilities, the way it handles multidimensional cost objects, and its reporting flexibility. After the team learned how to use the software, model building began. The selection, training, and model-building steps took six weeks to complete.

Validation

Model building was quickly followed by validation of the data. According to Bush, the model was checked to "make sure everything flowed through properly. Then the results could be analyzed." Once costs were traced to the activities, the ABM team returned to the interview groups for final review and approval.

Validation was extremely important to ensure buy-in from the individuals and groups interviewed. The interviewees needed to understand the results as the ABM project progressed. As Bush states, "We wanted everybody to believe the integrity of the numbers when we got to the end." Since the cost objects were identified during the initial executive sessions, they needed only to be finalized during this stage of the project.

Sixty-eight production work cells were costed during the project. These included areas such as the injection molding department, stamping, assembly, and welding. (See Exhibit 15.5 for an example of a work center activity costing report.) Costing began at the work-cell level, then rolled up into products, which were summarized into product lines. From there, the product lines were accumulated into customer groups, then from customer groups to business segments.

For the initial pilot project, there were 28 product lines, 16 customer groups, and two fully costed business segments. In general, all costs were included in the model. The only area not completed in detail was the transportation business segment, which was partially costed and will be completed in the future. Costs for the transportation work cells were aggregated together.

RESULTS AND NEXT STEPS

About 14 weeks into the project, the team began to build reports, interpret data, and prepare presentations. The efforts were well rewarded. The following major milestones were accomplished throughout different phases of the pilot:

- Completed an assessment of the company's culture and identified a change management strategy to minimize resistance and ensure lasting

EXHIBIT 15.5   Workcenter Activity Costing Report

Activity Costs

Value Class	Activity	Actual Period Dollars	% of Total Cost	Period Unit Rate	Target Unit Rate	Unit Variance	Cost Driver	Cost Driver Rate	Target Driver Rate	Driver Rate Variance
N	ABCD Rework	$10,000	1%	$0.02		$0.02	Rework Hours	$25.00		$25.00
N	ABCD Downtime	$40,000	6%	$0.07		$0.07	Downtime Hours	$400.00		$400.00
V	ABCD Run Production	$150,000	21%	$0.26		$0.26	Run Hours	$60.00		$60.00
N	ABCD Setup	$180,000	26%	$0.31		$0.31	Setup Hours	$60.00		$60.00
N	ABCD Materials Handling	$20,000	3%	$0.03		$0.03	Shop Orders	$3.33		$3.33
N	ABCD Housekeeping	$5,000	1%	$0.01		$0.01	Calculated Machine Hours	$2.50		$2.50
M	ABCD Machine-related Cost	$300,000	43%	$0.52		$0.52	Calculated Machine Hours	$150.00		$150.00
	Workcenter Total	**$705,000**	100%	$1.22	$0.00					

Key: N = Non-value-added   V = Value added   M = Management required

Detailed Account Cost Information

Account Type		ABCD Rework	ABCD Downtime	ABCD Run Production	ABCD Setup	ABCD Materials Handling	ABCD Housekeeping	ABCD Machine-Related Costs	Account Totals
VR	Department AB-shared Mfg. Supplies	$0	$0	$10,000	$0	$0	$0	$0	$10,000
VR	ABCD Direct Labor	$10,000	$40,000	$140,000	$180,000	$20,000	$5,000	$0	$395,000
F	ABCD Machine Depreciation	$0	$0	$0	$0	$0	$0	$250,000	$250,000
VR	Perform Preventive Maintenance	$0	$0	$0	$0	$0	$0	$5,000	$5,000
VR	Perform FWO Requests	$0	$0	$0	$0	$0	$0	$15,000	$15,000
V	Troubleshoot Machinery	$0	$0	$0	$0	$0	$0	$30,000	$30,000
	Activity Total	$10,000	$40,000	$150,000	$180,000	$20,000	$5,000	$300,000	**$705,000**

Workcell Driver Volume Information

	Machine Hours	Run Hours	Downtime Hours	Rework Hours	Setup Hours	Shop Orders
Actuals	2,000	2,500	100	400	3,000	6,000
Planned						
Standard						

Product Mix Information

Product Line Group	Actual Units	Planned Units
Product A	500,000	
Product B	23,100	
Product C	45,000	
Product D	11,000	
	579,100	

Data included in this example are for illustrative purposes only and are not reflective of actual company numbers.

change. The assessment was completed on the front end of the project to manage the change process in the pilot.

- Developed an activity-based business model with documented model logic. This included a schematic diagram of business processes that identified how resources are consumed. (See Exhibit 15.6 for the business model.)
- Prepared process-based activity information for each area. This also included an overall management report indicating resource allocation and the relationship of activities to processes.
- Created cost and profitability reports by customer group, product line, and segment.
- Implemented activity-based reporting for each work cell that the shop-floor work teams could use in analyzing and improving their own performance.
- Identified future enhancements, including the desired criteria for performance measurement, such as key customer satisfaction measures, project profitability tracking, alignment of marketing codes and customer groups, and tracking of key cost drivers.
- Identified short- and long-term operational improvements. Those include reduction of non–value-added activities in each area, elimination of ad-hoc reporting, and identification of additional value-added services to help the company exceed customer expectations.

The team's findings were presented to the cross-functional steering committee. Response to the project was extremely positive. According to Bush, the steering committee was surprised not so much about the profitability of certain product segments as it was about activities. As Bush explains: "The surprises were in terms of how people were spending their time, how much time we were really spending on planning, and how much time was really dedicated to non–value-added activities."

Value-Added Vs. Non–value-Added Analysis

For analysis, activities were classified as either value-added, management required, or non–value-added. A *value-added* activity was defined as adding value from the customer's point of view and represented activities that the customer was willing to pay for. A *management-required* activity neither added value (from the customer's point of view) nor was anything the customer was willing to pay for, yet nevertheless it was an activity required to op-

EXHIBIT 15.6   Business Process Model

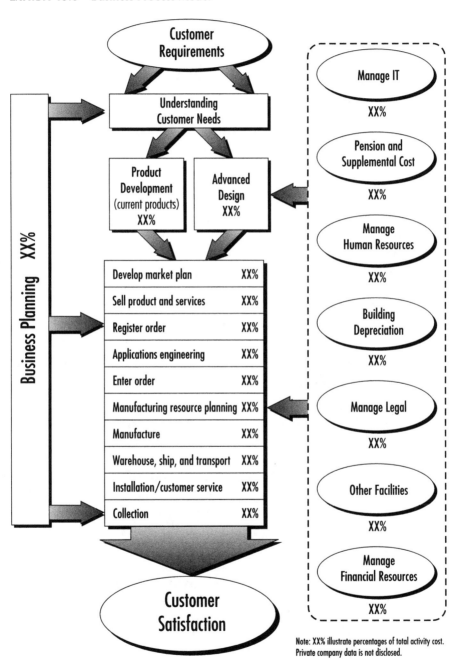

Note: XX% illustrate percentages of total activity cost.
Private company data is not disclosed.

erate the business effectively (e.g., maintaining ISO 9000 certification documents). Finally, a *non–value-added* activity did not add value from the customer's point of view, the customer was not willing to pay for it, and the activity was not even required to operate the business.

According to Bush, "We identified, minimized, and in some cases eliminated non–value-added activities in several areas." The product engineering area began monitoring some of its key cost drivers, which led to a two-day—or 40 percent—reduction in the special sales order processing cycle. This gave the company a competitive edge in an industry where lead times are compressed and quick response rates are imperative.

Continuous Improvement Efforts

American Seating operates under a "minicompany" concept to focus on continuous improvement. Each team within the concept operates as a minicompany, which means that it defines its business plan to support the company's overall strategy. The minicompany teams also initiates benchmarking and improvement efforts, such as machine setup reduction efforts. Performance measures with respect to quality, safety, morale, and cost are evaluated and monitored. The minicompany team improvements bring increased manufacturing flexibility to meet customer requirements and improve capital-investment analysis for new manufacturing technologies.

The information gained by this initiative enabled American Seating to streamline and standardize its product offerings. The company decided to outsource "noncore" manufacturing competencies. This lowered cost, increased efficiency, and thus provided comparable products to customers at a lower overall cost of production.

By using the performance management process and its new tools and knowledge, American Seating can now examine specific segments of its product line strategically (e.g., auditorium seating), to determine if product proliferation has become a problem. The company then may make more accurate decisions about product options that customers truly value. This allows the company to match resources with those high-value product options. It also can use the performance management process to eliminate non–value-added work and focus efforts on product standardization.

The ABM team began to investigate how many resources were spent on non–value-added functions and their related cost. They incorporated the information into planning sessions, into the budgeting process, and into their ongoing process improvement efforts.

The process is continuing. As Bush notes: "Our planning sessions really focus on technology and on how to improve our business processes. Initially I was worried our people would only think about cost reductions. That is not the case. While the objective is to reduce costs in response to competitive pressures, the business process improvements are also about 'doing more with the resources available.'"

Organizational Support and Action

Because of the up-front training and education, reaction to the analysis of non–value-added vs. value-added activities was very positive at all levels of the organization. The training emphasized the fact that classifying an activity as non–value-added was not a personal assessment of the individual worker. According to Clark: "The information we gained through the pilot project helped us redeploy resources to better match our strategy and to increase return on investment by focusing limited resources on key business processes."

For example, customer service redeployed resources to focus on the high-value activities through a redesigned process. A specific service administrator is now assigned to each customer order to increase satisfaction and service levels while also reducing inquiry response time. In this way, customer service can concentrate its efforts in areas most important to customers.

Customer-Focused Product Decisions

According to Bush, the entire ABM process helped in making decisions to reduce American Seating's product offerings, which had an impact on both bottom-line and top-line results. ABM helped managers identify value-added services and products from the customer's point of view. This knowledge ensured that the company would provide these services and, more important, that the value received and the price paid were in line. American Seating ultimately modified its pricing strategies based on what customers consider valuable. As Bush explains: "A lot of companies look at revenue growth as a way to increase profitability. That wasn't necessarily true for us. We found that we could actually sell less and make more in some instances. So the emphasis is really on how we manage the bottom-line of our company, and how we manage our balance sheet. We don't put the emphasis on the increase in sales as much as we had in the past."

FUTURE PLANS

A follow-up executive session focused on how to use the ABM data in the future and what the next steps and priorities should be. Finance was tasked to maintain and improve the ABM database. It also was asked to determine how to make ABM an integral part of the company's culture.

ABM information continues to be used for planning purposes, return-on-asset measurements, pricing strategies, and continuous process improvement. According to Bush, the primary focus continues to be on process improvements. "We prioritized the biggest opportunities, and we are working our way down." Future modeling plans call for completing the rollout of ABM throughout the transportation product segment, which is a large growth area for American Seating. Since the company is considering expansion, it is important to complete this analysis soon.

The ABM team, as it was originally structured, no longer exists, because ABM is no longer considered a project. Instead it is now integrated into management decision making. Finance also uses the ABM model to provide data to other functional areas. The information is shared throughout the organization and used by executives in various functions.

"We quickly recognized that this new approach was a vast improvement over traditional cost management techniques," says Clark. "We are integrating it with current systems to maximize our capabilities. The information we gain is our basis for business planning, resource redeployment, performance measurement, and increasing stakeholder value."

In the future, American Seating intends to incorporate performance management strategies into its plans for focusing and deploying resources on key customer requirements and specific strategies by segment. As the minicompany concept extends throughout the organization, ABM information will be used to develop strategic plans for each minicompany.

LESSONS LEARNED

Some of the key lessons learned by American Seating were:

- *Executive buy-in is the key to the success of an ABM project.* A senior management group championed by the CEO spearheaded the ABM project at American Seating. Such high-level interest and support ensured a successful project and caused ABM information to be used for daily decision making.

- *Dedicate appropriate resources for the job at hand.* According to Bush, "We wanted a dedicated, full-time team from the beginning and we went after our top people. Even though it took them out of their regular jobs for up to six months, ABM was a priority, and we wanted to do it the right way." To be successful, the appropriate resources must be dedicated. Don't go halfway. The team was critical to achieving an enterprise rollout quickly.

- *Select a cross-functional team.* Cross-functional representation is needed on the ABM team. Such representation will greatly facilitate gaining buy-in from the organization. The functional areas will view it as their project if they have adequate representation. A cross-functional mix will also provide a wealth of knowledge, especially when activities and cost drivers are being defined and validated.

- *Experienced consultants speed the rollout.* Experienced consultants from Arthur Andersen played a critical role in focusing the team. "Having Arthur Andersen involved was a key enabler to our success," notes Bush. "The integration of consultants into the cross-functional team helped us to avoid many of the pitfalls we might have otherwise experienced. They kept us on track as we rolled out the project in an extremely short time frame and transferred knowledge to our team members."

- *Do not make ABM a finance project.* From the beginning, the ABM project was championed by the operational side of the business. This emphasis enabled the ABM team to hit the ground running.

- *Perform a requirements assessment at the outset.* Work with management from across the organization to understand their needs and expectations. For the system to be successful and the information it provides actually to be used, management expectations must be solicited up front, *not* at the conclusion of the project.

- *Clearly communicate goals, objectives, and strategy to the organization.* Make sure that people clearly understand the objectives. Communication helps obtain buy-in from the organization. It also ensures that people will not misunderstand the goals that are trying to be accomplished. When information is used to eliminate non–value-added activities, employees should understand that the purpose is not to eliminate their jobs. Make sure they know the aim is to make them more effective and efficient. Provide examples of how the time saved from the elimination of non–value-added work will be redeployed into value-adding efforts.

- *Focus on integration.* Finding and retaining a dedicated management information services (MIS) person for model maintenance and updates can be difficult—and crippling when the proper skill set is lacking.

- *Keep it simple.* Do not build any more complexity into the system than what is needed to accomplish the goals. More does not mean better. If Bush had one piece of advice to give on implementing an ABM project, it would be to keep the project as simple as possible: "The information is more valuable if people can understand it and can use it."

ABOUT THE AUTHORS

Michelle Behrenwald is a Senior Manager with Arthur Andersen in Grand
   Rapids, Michigan.
Carol Cobble is Vice President of Client Services for Armstrong Laing in At-
   lanta, Georgia.

Note: This case originally appeared in *Cornerstones of Decision Making: Profiles of Enterprise ABM* by Steve Player and Carol Cobble (Greensboro, NC:
Oakhill Press, 1999).

16

CUSTOMER AND PRODUCT PROFITABILITY

Scott W. Smith and James D. Castille
Arthur Andersen, Cleveland, Ohio

CASE STUDY: Manco, Cleveland, Ohio

SUMMARY

Business Issue

Manco is constantly challenging itself to obtain accurate, timely information to manage operations. During its rapid growth, the customer base and product offerings have expanded, leaving Manco with the need for better information to support strategic decision making. Previously, profitability management focused on gross margin, with the "costs below the line" assigned as a percentage of sales dollars. Manco established that the available information was inadequate and chose to integrate activity-based costing (ABC) concepts during its new system implementation.

How ABC Was Used

Manco utilized existing data sources to develop and design the ABC model and then recast product and customer profitability. The ABC system was incorporated into their new enterprise resource planning (ERP) system and data warehouse to generate new profitability reporting.

Manco's Results

The company now understands the financial implications of customer ordering patterns and product mix and uses that information to manage and improve profitability. The company is now able to better quantify and leverage customer profitability information. The results are allowing Manco to target improvement areas in its operating processes in the distribution area as well as redesign its pricing methodologies and tools.

While businesses spend considerable time and effort measuring the gross margin derived from products sold, this information often falls short in providing complete information needed to support strategic and operational profitability management. Because most financial systems provide information focused solely on the products sold, customer and channel-specific costs often are not captured or reported in a meaningful manner. The information, therefore, typically lacks meaning for effective profitability management for the following reasons:

- It is too summarized.
- It is tied to generally accepted accounting principles (GAAP) and the related financial reporting.
- It contains too many general allocations.

Most companies, even manufacturers, now find themselves competing in some part on customer service. Through unique delivery, packaging, or marketing activities, businesses attempt to differentiate themselves. As customers become more demanding, these costs are becoming a larger portion of the total cost structure. Despite these trends, surprisingly few companies have systems in place to capture and assign the cost of these "services" to products and customers.

Best-practice companies are developing profitability management systems that go beyond the gross margin level to include all relevant costs of the business. Because the 80–20 rule (80 percent of a company's profits come from 20 percent of its customers and products) usually applies when true profitability is analyzed, knowing which customers and products are in the 80 percent bracket and which are in the 20 percent bracket is critical. This information then can be used to determine ways to improve profitability management and target customers, products, and channels for growth.

COMPANY BACKGROUND

Manco manufactures and distributes specialty tapes, stationery, housewares, and mailing consumer products. With over $160 million in annual sales, Manco offers a broad line of branded consumer products to the retail market and office supply channels, including its signature "Duck Tape" product line. Led by its entrepreneurial founder, Jack Kahl, Manco has achieved significant growth in the last decade. The key factor behind Manco's success has been a continuous focus on the needs of the consumer and retailer. A partnership based on service and the creation of innovative products anchors the strong Manco culture. At Manco's headquarters outside Cleveland, Ohio, the sign along "Just Imagine Drive" reads: "You are now entering into the land of imagination. From this point, turn on your imagination."

Behind Manco's creativity and imagination, however, resides a world-class system of people, processes, and technology. The company's expertise historically has been sales and marketing, and it has taken tremendous work over the last three years for the infrastructure to catch up. Now that infrastructure, particularly the profitability management system, helps to reinforce and drive continued growth.

BUSINESS ISSUES

Manco faced challenges to provide information and manage operations as it grew rapidly. As a result, the company found itself operating with multiple systems and a financial group that was focused primarily on closing the books and traditional financial reporting. As stated by Raj Aggarwal, chair of the Finance and Audit Committee of Manco's Board, "Manco had tremendous top-line sales growth but did not have commensurate growth in overall profitability. Management and sales lacked the information to distinguish between profitable and unprofitable customers and products."

Manco launched its "Navigator" project to implement a new Enterprise Resource Planning (ERP) system and Data Warehousing project to address several key issues: the need to consolidate systems, address year 2000 issues, and improve the quality of information available to managers. "We recognized the need to improve the speed and accuracy of our decision making processes by establishing a strong foundation of integrated business systems. We believe this is a key to enabling continued profitable business growth," stated Jeff Shear, vice president of Information Systems.

Like many businesses, Manco's customer base and product offering changed over time. Instead of relying on its traditional product line of Duck Tape, Manco introduced new products in such categories as seasonal weatherproofing, packaging and mailing materials, shelf liners, and bath mats. The profile of customers changed as well and now includes not only large general retailers but also specialty retailers in office and home products. In addition, Manco was acquired by Henkel Corporation and is integrating its consumer adhesives businesses (Loctite Group in North America and LePage in Canada) into Manco. This integration effort creates an even greater diversity of products and customers.

In the past, Manco focused its profitability management primarily on gross margin. The company's view of customer profitability was built into the general ledger structure, but attaining product profitability numbers was cumbersome. In both cases, full profit and loss statements were generated, but the costs "below the line" were assigned as a percentage of sales dollars. To assume all of the costs varied proportionately with sales volume was clearly erroneous. While everyone knew differences among customers and products translated to different activities—from order entry to distribution and customer service—the financial impact of these activities was not being captured. The business changes and growing diversity of products and customers served only to accentuate these problems. Faced with inadequate information, Manco decided to use activity-based costing (ABC) concepts as it deployed new systems.

Before beginning its profitability management effort, the company developed a clear set of guiding principles. One of these principles was to create a system that would provide up-to-date information within the core transaction systems of the company. As Jack Kahl says, "Information is like eggs; the fresher the better." The company wanted to use the data capture systems within the ERP system, where possible, to minimize off-line data collection and analysis. Finally, the system had to provide more accurate costing, while being simple enough to be understood by a diverse group of users.

HOW ABC WAS USED

The company engaged Arthur Andersen to assist with the implementation of the Navigator project as well as to help design and implement the ABC system. The chief financial officer and the vice president of Logistics championed the project, with participation from distribution, finance, inventory accounting, sales, and marketing working on the ABC team.

To balance the objectives of full integration, simplicity, and accuracy, the team followed a basic approach that included:

- Prototype the "conceptual" system in spreadsheet models
- Weigh the technical implementation issues, including simplifying the conceptual model and modifying the ERP or developing a data warehousing application
- Understand the impact of the new costing method on customers and products
- Obtain buy-in and implement the new system

In general, the approach was to use existing data sources to design the ABC models and then recast product and customer profitability. Ultimately the goal was to incorporate the ABC system in the ERP and data warehouse to generate this new profitability reporting. As depicted in Exhibit 16.1, this process is a continuous cycle of improvement.

The project involved three major areas: distribution, SG&A (selling, general, and administrative), and freight costing. The following sections outline the analysis and implementation approach for each area.

EXHIBIT 16.1   Integrated Profitability Reporting: A Continuous Improvement Cycle

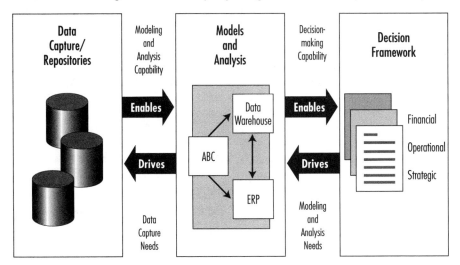

Distribution: Analysis and Implementation

Shipping over 6.8 million cases of product a year, warehousing and distribution (excluding freight) represents a large portion of Manco's costs. The existing system did not adequately relate these costs to customers and products. The company tried traditional methods: a flat charge per case, which penalized the large orders that were in fact quite efficient to handle; and a percent of sales price, which penalized the higher-value products, but not necessarily the most inefficient. Inherently, Manco management understood each order required different amounts of effort and thus should be charged based on such effort.

The team identified three major activities in distribution—receiving, storing, and picking—and identified the breakdown of all distribution costs with one of these activities. It was determined that every pallet took the same effort to receive. The storing activity had a direct relationship to the cubic size of space occupied and the inventory turns or velocity through the warehouse. Because of the wide variation in the cubic size and inventory turns of the different products, assignment of costs based on these new methods had a significant impact on profitability.

Picking, which represents over 80 percent of the total distribution costs, provided the single largest area for improvement of cost assignment. The cost to pick an order relates to its profile—meaning the mix of lines, how many different products and cases, the volume of products—on the order. The challenge was to relate the order profile statistics with the effort to pick an order (and thus its cost), while keeping the approach simple.

A time study and subsequent regression analysis revealed a direct correlation between the time required to pick an order and the number of lines on that order. In other words, for Manco's typical range of orders, it took about the same amount of time and effort to pick a line regardless of the quantity of the product. Using a simple driver of lines picked not only captured the cost relationship, it also simplified communication and implementation. A summary of the distribution cost pools, activities, and drivers is shown in Exhibit 16.2.

EXHIBIT 16.2   Method for Determining Cost per Driver

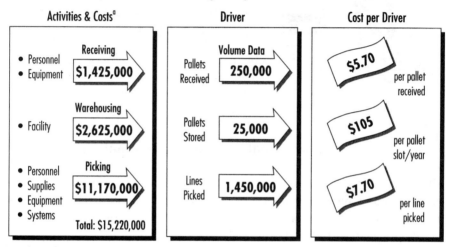

ª Numbers are for illustrative purposes only and do not reflect actuals.

After determining the costs, activities and drivers, the team then collected the relevant data by product and customer. This enabled a spreadsheet model to be developed to demonstrate the profitability impact of the new cost assignments. As seen in Exhibit 16.3, the results were striking. Gene Obrock, director of Customer Logistics, said: "We always believed the customers' ordering pattern and order profile had a significant influence on the activities and cost to serve them. When the impact is actually quantified in terms of profit margin, the contrast among customers is even greater than we intuitively anticipated." The change in cost assignment methods from percentage of sales dollars to a transaction (per line) charge for picking was the key driver of these profitability changes. This was a result of two key factors:

1. Different order profiles of customers. Some customers placed few orders with a high volume of product on each order, while other customers ordered more frequently and in smaller volumes. As Exhibit 16.4 shows,

EXHIBIT 16.3   Percentage Change in Gross Margin by Customer

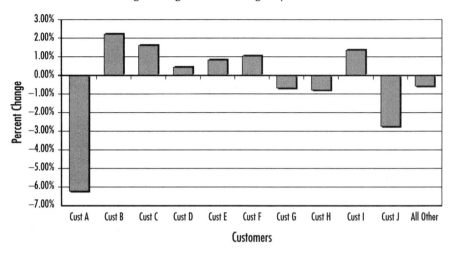

EXHIBIT 16.4   Customer Comparison of Standard Cost versus Lines

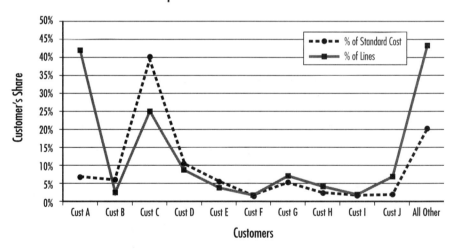

Customer A represents 40 percent of the value of products picked but less than 20 percent of the picking transactions. Therefore, the new cost method based on activity reduced Customer A's distribution cost assignment significantly.

2. Different value of products. The change in method had the greatest impact on low-value products. The chief financial officer, Marc Fedor, noted: "It brings focus to the value of the products we sell. If we pick an order line of coal and an order line of diamonds, which product has the

ability to absorb the cost of picking and still remain profitable? Similarly, which customer orders have the volume to absorb the picking transaction cost most profitably?"

Selling, General and Administrative: Analysis and Implementation

As with distribution, the team developed a methodology to assign selling, general and administrative (SG&A) expenses to customers and products based on the actual consumption of resources. The previous method used a percentage of sales dollars as the single method for allocating costs, which greatly distorted product and customer profitability information.

Given the multitude of activities performed, the team took a slightly different approach to manage the level of detail in the model and ultimate system. Instead of measuring all activities separately, they were grouped into three main driver categories—sales order transaction volume, direct relationship (to products or customers), and sales dollar volume. This minimized the number of drivers while improving on the single-allocation method used in the past. Exhibit 16.5 provides a view of the assignment process.

EXHIBIT 16.5   Understanding the Assignment Process

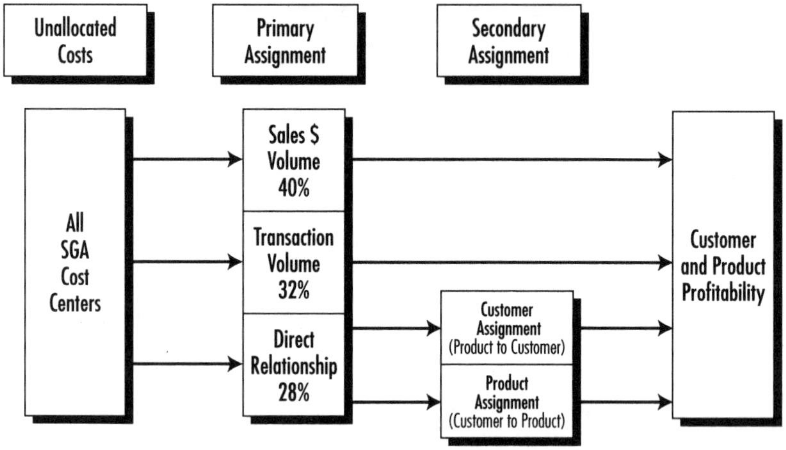

The results of the SG&A area also resulted in changes to the reported profitability of customers and products:

- Direct relationship (28 percent of SG&A). Analysis of these costs (primarily marketing, graphics, and product development) revealed that certain products required a greater-than-average level of support. The prior method of assigning costs based on a percentage of sales dollars tended to penalize existing, high-volume products. The results showed, however, that the low-volume and new products cost just as much, if not more, to support.

- Sales dollar volume (40 percent of SG&A). A portion of the costs (primarily administrative, human resources, legal, etc.) could not be associated with a driver other than a general assignment method.
- Sales order transaction volume (32 percent of SG&A). Similar to the picking analysis, customers who placed orders more frequently received an increase in cost assignment for the activities (primarily customer service related) associated with this driver.

Freight: Analysis and Implementation

Freight costs represent a significant portion of standard product cost. Because of the diversity in products and customers, these costs could distort the view of profitability under the traditional cost assignment methodology (percentage of sales dollars). This method did not reflect the key drivers of freight cost: distance, order size, and product characteristics.

Thus the new allocation method needed to reflect how products and the customer order profile influence freight costs. While new system developments would allow Manco to track freight costs directly to the customer (i.e., receipt of electronic bill of lading), the team needed to assign freight to products as well. During the freight study, the key product characteristics—weight, density, and cubic feet—were tested to determine their relationship to the drivers of cost. The final model used cubic feet as the product cost driver. While all of the factors contributed to the overall freight cost, this method represented a cost-effective answer that yielded more accurate results.

As a result of the ABC analysis, cost assignment was shifted from the more dense, high-value products such as Duck Tape to the less dense, low-value products such as packaging materials. Again, this method correlates logically with the true drivers of cost—shipping larger products, regardless of the product's value.

RESULTS

The combined profit margin impact of the new ABC system for all three areas ranged from –12.8 percent to +3.8 percent for some customers and products. These results are significant for any business, but especially for one selling into the highly competitive retail market. These results have had a dramatic impact on the way Manco manages profitability. "Incorporating these improved costing methods into our core systems keeps us focused on the key elements for improving our profitability and increasing value to our customers: operational methods and efficiencies, product mix and pricing, and the operational relationship between Manco and our customers," stated John Kahl, Manco's president.

For example, Exhibit 16.6 shows a sample of the portfolio of customers and illustrates the importance of evaluating the business on full profitability, not gross margin. In the chart, Customers A and B have similar gross margins, but the "cost to serve" is much less for Customer A. (Note the size of the circle represents sales dollars.)

EXHIBIT 16.6   Customer Profitability: Gross Margin versus Cost to Serve

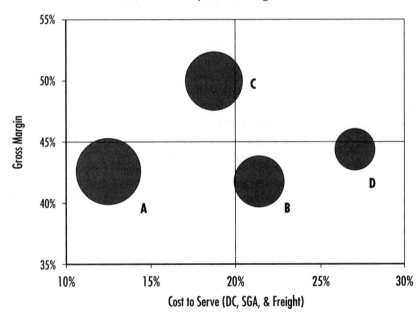

Manco is using the ABC information to change the way it manages the business and makes decisions. Some of the applications have included:

- New information allows Manco to better understand the economic realities of what and how the customer purchases. Manco shares this information with customers in an open dialogue to alter purchasing activities and create a win-win situation for the company and customer.

- High cost-to-serve customers pay an increased price for those activities. In other situations, Manco now can determine to what extent product prices can be reduced and still remain profitable.
- Based on findings in the distribution area, Manco is addressing how the company can change its operating processes to fill small orders more efficiently.
- Manco is redesigning its pricing tools to incorporate the drivers from the ABC models to cost products more accurately at the time pricing decisions are made.
- The company is able to more aggressively price products sold to customers who have a more optimal order profile more aggressively.

LESSONS LEARNED

Several key lessons can be applied by other businesses looking to improve their profitability management systems.

Strategy

A cost management strategy and well-developed approach to the design of the profitability system is required. To ensure the system and tools provide the right information and decision support, several factors should be considered:

- What should be the balance among maintenance, complexity, and accuracy?
- How detailed is the required reporting (i.e., customer, segment, channel, etc.)?
- What decisions will be made or impacted by the new information?
- Who are the key users of the information?
- How often will the information need to be updated?

Technology

Information systems are making multidimensional (product, customer, channel) analysis more feasible. There are several options for the creation of profitability analysis, ranging from spreadsheets and PC models, to custom-built applications. The choice of technology should be based on the profitability management strategy. Additional factors to consider include:

- The ability of the existing general ledger and transaction systems to capture data
- The desired or acceptable level of detail vs. the available level of detail
- The existing data sources (i.e., manufacturing or distribution) and accessibility
- The technology options given the organization's skills and resources
- The timing of reporting and data collection

People

People ultimately determine the success and acceptance of any change initiative; implementation of this type of system should be considered a major change effort. As new information is gathered and reported, there will be product and customer "winners" and "losers"; the impact on stakeholders should not be ignored. Considerations include:

- The impact on performance measures and incentive plans
- Resistance to what could be perceived as another "accounting" project
- Ability to relate the initiative to the strategy of the company and communicate the business value of the information
- Training and education on how to use information
- The ability to obtain cross-functional support with a visible project sponsor

Companies need a better understanding of the drivers of cost and value in their business. This requires a systematic approach to determining, collecting, and providing data that is different from traditional financial reporting. While profitability information is not the sole solution, it should be a key part of the management reporting system and decision-making process. In too many companies, decisions about customers and products are based on instinct alone. Business conditions demand a better approach—technology and best-practice companies are delivering it.

ABOUT THE AUTHORS

Scott W. Smith is a Partner with Arthur Andersen in Cleveland, Ohio.
James D. Castille is a Manager with Arthur Andersen in Cleveland, Ohio.

17

STRATEGIC USE OF ACTIVITY-BASED MANAGEMENT TO DETERMINE PRODUCT PROFITABILITY

Andrew Marchus
Arthur Andersen, Miami, Florida

Jay Collins
Arthur Andersen, Tampa, Florida

CASE STUDY: National Council on Compensation Insurance, Boca Raton, Florida

SUMMARY

Business Issue

National Council on Compensation Insurance (NCCI), the nation's largest worker's compensation data, statistical, and research corporation, is facing increasing competition from data service companies and even insurance companies that consider this business attractive. Although NCCI has a 70-year history of providing quality services and products, it recognized the need for an activity and process view of its organization to continue providing cost-efficient services.

How ABC Was Used

Using activity-based costing (ABC), management sought to provide a different view of cost information to managers in every functional area. The goal was to enable more informed decision making. In the near term, management's objectives were twofold:

1. Improve the user-friendliness of its product profitability and cost information which is used to make pricing and product management decisions.
2. Determine process and activity costs to enable the identification and pursuit of streamlining opportunities and cost savings.

Management's long-term objectives included both activity-based management (ABM) and activity-based budgeting (ABB).

NCCI's Results

In addition to its original project goals, the ABC effort benefited NCCI in several additional ways. The ABC system has replaced costly, manual time reporting of activities. It has also proved useful for Human Resources by providing a true understanding of the cost of recruiting (i.e., time, processing of new hires, training). One unique result was a comprehensive understanding of the disaster recovery cost. Beyond identifying the equipment and out-of-pocket costs to rebuild after a hurricane, NCCI was able to identify the activities and processes to quantify total costs to rebuild in the event of a natural disaster.

Facing increased competition, NCCI needed to better understand the cost of its products and processes. Activity-based costing (ABC) offered a new alternative to examining costs in lieu of using the traditional overhead allocation methodologies. Past efforts at providing profitability and cost information involved very little direct costs and several levels of overhead allocations. Externally, NCCI's largest customers claimed they were paying proportionally more for the same services that NCCI provided to its smaller customers, since pricing was based on premium levels rather than usage.

Under the guidance of its new chief executive officer, NCCI has undertaken a company-wide cost improvement effort. Task forces have been assembled for processes, product costs, and pricing. An ABC model provides the task forces with activity cost information so the company can explore ways to efficiently process data and produce core products.

Knowing which processes cost $300,000 vs. those costing only $10,000 allows the company to prioritize efforts. Theresa Alvarado, manager of the ABC process, stated: "In the past, we would investigate large revenue items first, identify the processes involved in producing the product, and analyze if any inefficiencies exist. With ABC, we can focus directly on the activities, identifying large expense items as well as non–value-added items and work to achieve greater efficiency, reducing the costs quicker and more effectively."

BACKGROUND

NCCI is the nation's largest worker's compensation data, statistical, and research corporation. Founded in 1927, the company provides database products, software, publications, and consultation services to businesses, labor associations, state funds, self-insureds, independent bureaus, agents, regulatory authorities, legislatures, and over 700 insurance companies. Actuaries, underwriters, and other experts provide the value-added element to NCCI's products and services, which are used by worker's compensation providers in making key decisions to minimize risks and improve profits. To its customers—and others in the industry—NCCI is the information company that:

- Collects, analyzes, and adds value to information covering more than $20 billion in annual worker's compensation premiums

- Compiles and provides individual company experience rating to 400,000 employers annually
- Compiles and analyzes loss cost estimates for more than 600 business classifications in 37 states
- Joins with national and local businesses to prevent workplace injuries and reduce worker's compensation costs

Headquartered in Boca Raton, Florida, the company employs 1,100 people. In addition, several satellite offices around the country serve their respective local markets. Several aspects of NCCI made it a unique candidate for ABC:

- Its labor force is predominantly white collar, consisting of actuaries, underwriters, publishers, worker's compensation experts, and management information systems (MIS) developers. In fact, a major portion of its total expenditures and one-third of the employees are MIS-related.
- Several members of NCCI's board of directors are executives from its *customers*. As a result, even though the company is a not-for-profit organization, it must efficiently manage costs while producing value-added products.
- There are numerous variations to many of its products, thus leading to potential cost distortions. For example, a publication sold to a customer in Texas may also be sold to a customer in another state, but the structure and data content of the publication could vary significantly based on different legislation and regulatory requirements.

CONDUCTING A BUSINESS IMPACT ANALYSIS

NCCI began a major effort to conduct a business impact analysis. The company began by understanding the nature and cost of the processes conducted by the organization as a whole. The core product and activity costs were needed to help NCCI achieve its long-term objectives.

Product Cost

For example, a product cost dilemma faced by management might involve two products, Manual A and Manual B. To produce Manual B, NCCI begins with Manual A as its base and modifies it so that the manual can be used by customers in different states or by different types of customers. Product managers intuitively know it costs much more to produce Manual B because of the additional effort and resources required. How much more is the issue. In many cases, managers can approximate the cost of additional labor and materials, but there are many hidden overhead costs, such as occupancy, indirect labor, database maintenance, and development. These costs cannot be properly traced without significant investigation. As a consequence, the company is hard-pressed to answer important questions such as:

- Is it effectively recovering the incremental costs of producing Manual B?
- What is the margin on product B vs. A? If competition exists, what is the flexibility in B's price?

In the past, overhead allocations were analyzed at both the division and company level and charged to products equally on the basis of direct expense. The existing system relied on the integrity of the time reporting system and the information provided to accounts payable for all vendor payments. The percentage of product costs reflected as direct expenses was minimal when compared to the percentage related to the overhead allocations. Managers wanted to see the total direct expense as the product costs and reduce the amount of allocations.

Product Profitability

As depicted in Exhibit 17.1, the old method allowed NCCI to identify the labor and other direct expenses related to the product. The problem was that the majority of the expense, over 50 percent, was left unidentified and there-

Exhibit 17.1   Product Profitability

Old Method—Traditional Cost		New Method—ABC Cost	
Revenue:	$1,300,000	Revenue:	$1,300,000
Expenses:		Expenses:	
Direct Labor	$200,000	Produce Exp Mod	$650,000
		Support Desktop Publishing	$50,000
Division Overhead	$400,000	Support Mainframe Systems	$100,000
		Support Legal—External	$50,000
Other Direct Expenses	$150,000	Respond to Mod—Phone	$100,000
Total Direct Expenses	$750,000	Total Direct Expenses	$950,000
G&A Overhead	$300,000	G&A Overhead	$100,000
Total Expenses:	$1,050,000	Total Expenses:	$1,050,000
Margin:	$250,000	Margin:	$250,000

fore allocated as part of divisional or general and administrative overhead. These overhead expenses were allocated to all direct expenses on the basis of total direct expense, which may have been inaccurate for many products. With the new method of ABC, NCCI has been able to trace more expenses directly to the product, limiting the general and administrative costs to reflect the true business sustaining costs for the corporation. This has provided a more accurate reflection of each product's profitability and provided product managers with the necessary information to effect changes where possible.

Process Improvement

Understanding the activity cost of producing a manual for a single state was certainly a top priority in pursuing ABC. But to respond to this new information, the company would need to pinpoint the right processes and people that support the end products. Inherently, management could identify many process improvements and cost reduction possibilities. They also knew (but not to what extent) that many of the perceived problems crossed departmental lines, thus adding to complexity. To quantify these issues, NCCI needed fully loaded activity costs—costs that reflected the true consumption of resources (i.e., salary, occupancy, technology, and travel) and support services such as MIS, Human Resources, and information systems.

PROJECT ROLLOUT

NCCI realized implementing an ABC system was a comprehensive effort with many variables. Management desired a speedy implementation so the company could benefit from the improved cost information quickly. Accordingly, NCCI brought in Arthur Andersen to assist in the ABC model design and implementation.

An implementation team was assembled consisting of five NCCI members and four consultants from Arthur Andersen. The NCCI team was composed of members of the planning and analysis group, which reported to the chief financial officer. Each project participant from the planning and analysis group had an internal consulting relationship with at least one of the company's seven divisions, and thus had relationships with the people in each division as well as a working knowledge of specific activities, issues, and challenges.

Additional support was provided by business unit managers from each division, who felt that they would benefit from this project as well. Six months was established as the time frame to implement an enterprise-wide ABC model, using the historical prior full year's expenses as the initial data set to work with. The decision was made to use this as a baseline upon which the current year's actuals could be built once the project was completed.

The project began with the assistance of Arthur Andersen identifying and defining all the activities of the company (by division and cost center) into an activity dictionary.

Thorough data collection is essential to implementation. The project was on a very aggressive timetable; thus the team pushed hard to develop the data collection templates and to begin the interviews. Initially the team was not able to obtain the detail of nonpayroll expenses by cost center until about two weeks into the interview process. Although the team knew the labor costs, which were the majority of each cost center's budget, the team did not know which cost centers had significant nonpayroll costs. After receiving the nonpayroll expenses, the team had to go back to some centers and determine which activities consumed those costs.

Some of the key areas that contributed greatly to the success of the project included project planning, training, project communications, and data gathering.

Project Planning

A two-day visioning session with the project team launched the effort. NCCI's long-term vision and strategy was articulated at the outset of the meeting and used as a guide to the discussion; one conclusion was that ABC had to clearly support and be consistent with the direction of the company. The theme of the offsite meeting was to envision success three years after the completed implementation. Each team member gave his or her personal vision as to how the end result should look. Everyone was encouraged to cite specific examples of success. The result of this planning session included:

- A business case for ABC, linking its benefits to NCCI's near and long-term strategy
- A shared understanding of what a successful ABC implementation would look like
- A list of factors that were critical to the success of the ABC effort

Training

Training was provided at various stages of the project. The training, led by an Arthur Andersen representative, was especially effective because it combined three elements: (1) knowledge of activity-based costing, (2) specific training on the chosen ABC software, ABC Technologies' Oros product, and (3) an appreciation of NCCI's business issues.

At the outset, each project participant plus key senior managers attended a full-day session on the basics of activity-based costing. This course covered ABC terminology, benefits of ABC, how ABC supports other company initiatives, ABC implementation steps, and an ABC case study. A second training course covered the basics of ABC software and presented the merits of each of the main ABC software products. During the project, training was provided on the use of the selected Oros ABC software by ABC Technologies. This training provided comprehensive coverage of ABC modeling, importing/exporting data, and report writing.

As the project neared completion, additional training was provided on the executive information system (EIS) reporting tool, which was from Cognos. This enabled managers to view ABC results in graphical form. For the modeling and EIS training, the Arthur Andersen members also had a working knowledge of the model structure and the implementation issues an outside instructor would not have had.

Project Communication

The willing and active involvement of all the divisions and respective cost centers was crucial. While top management's strong support created a sense of urgency, employees needed to support the effort for their own reasons as well. The joint team sought to communicate the benefits of ABC at all levels of the company. As such, employees understood the importance of their involvement and developed a sense of ownership and support.

With this in mind, the team designed materials to be used in initial meetings with division management. The following areas were covered in the kick-off presentation prior to data gathering:

- Why ABC?—the business case for NCCI
- An overview of ABC basics and terminology
- Project approach and time line
- What to expect in the coming months
- Resource and time needs from each division's participants

Alvarado and the other members of the team realized that if senior management and the divisions did not agree with the concept of ABC, the project would fail. Involvement at all levels of the company would drive ABC forward, and lead to the implementation of ABB and ABM.

Data Gathering

Project participants were paired into teams of two and assigned to specific divisions. At least one person from each team had knowledge of their assigned divisions and a working relationship with key contacts within each division that contained several cost centers. By meeting with the senior people in each division the team gained the support of the cost center managers. Prior to the initial meetings, several templates were developed to facilitate the collection of activity information. Division leaders were encouraged to talk to their people about the reasons for the ABC project and expectations for the coming months.

By virtue of being heavily involved in defining activities and assigning costs, management became increasingly convinced ABC information would make a significant impact. Before Arthur Andersen had even completed a test model, several managers had approached the implementation team to review the model results to analyze their product costs. Since the first distribution of ABC reports, the manager in charge of maintaining and enhancing the ABC model has received a great deal of constructive feedback on the model, and some modifications of the model have been made in response.

BUSINESS IMPACT ANALYSIS

One use of the ABC information was for coordinating business impact analysis such as obtaining a comprehensive understanding of disaster recovery costs.

Using the activity dictionary, the project team was able to quickly pinpoint the activities most vulnerable in the event of a natural disaster such as a hurricane. The activity dictionary allowed the team to bypass all the interviews and identification of activities that normally must be completed in similar process improvement efforts. By using this dictionary as a baseline, the team eliminated months of research and interviews. As a result, the business impact analysis was completed much sooner than originally expected.

RESULTS AND NEXT STEPS

Prior to implementing ABC, biweekly time reporting was a time-consuming but necessary task. Today time reporting will be used only by a handful of people to track hours for the few products that require time reports. Future modifications to the ABC system may provide the time information required and eliminate time reporting completely.

Even with early operational wins and overall momentum, many more opportunities exist for NCCI to benefit from ABC. Discussions are now taking place about setting performance targets based on the ABC information as well as moving toward activity-based budgeting. But to be viewed as an overall success, the model also must help management achieve its long-term objectives. It will take time to realize strategic benefits, but management is confident the model will support key strategic decisions regarding product development, regional operations, and customer profitability. Additional data needs to be gathered, and further segmentation of the products by location and customer should be enhanced.

LESSONS LEARNED

The following lessons were learned by the NCCI implementation team.

- *Devote a consistent implementation team.* The planning and analysis group was going through some major changes during the implementation. As a result, new people were added to the project midstream, without the benefit of having participated in the initial ABC visioning, planning, and training sessions. Although the project team met the implementation deadlines, some people struggled with learning a new discipline in conjunction with new roles with the planning and analysis group.

- *Active involvement from operations spurred the implementation.* Although the implementation was led by the finance function, it was not truly finance "driven." Instead, demand-pull for more accurate cost information arose from every senior manager in the company. The solid relationship between the permanent ABC team and the divisions ensured the continuous involvement and support of operational members throughout the company.

- *Dedicate the right people with the proper knowledge.* Dedicating NCCI people with a lucid knowledge of the key operations and good relationships with division management was a key to success. Data collection and activity analysis went smoothly and the level of enthusiasm by divisional people was much greater. This success underscores the pitfall that if outside consultants are relied upon too heavily, the project's success may be in jeopardy.

- *Employ graphical reporting techniques.* Executive information system tools can provide clear summaries of ABC information for managers, particularly those who prefer graphical displays of data as opposed to numeric reports. As the implementation progressed, it became more evident that top management wanted the flexibility to view information in ways that numerical ABC reports could not accommodate. The project team selected and implemented an EIS tool to extract model data and allow the data to be viewed in numerous graphical or numeric ways. The EIS software allows the user to change the view of the ABC data, perform data drill-downs, construct pie and bar charts, conduct period-to-period comparisons, create customized views, and print custom reports.

ABOUT THE AUTHORS

Jay Collins is a Partner with Arthur Andersen's Advanced Cost Management Team. He is based in Tampa, Florida.
Andrew Marchus is a Manager with Arthur Andersen Business Consulting in Miami, Florida.

18

UNCOVERING OPPORTUNITIES TO IMPROVE THE BUSINESS WITH ACTIVITY-BASED COSTING/MANAGEMENT

Jay Collins
Arthur Andersen, Tampa, Florida

Robert J. Savage
Arthur Andersen, North Plainfield, New Jersey

Nick Curcuru
Arthur Andersen, Tampa, Florida

CASE STUDY: Tampa Electric Company, Tampa, Florida

SUMMARY

Business Issues

Tampa Electric Company (TEC) needed to know the total energy delivery costs of providing various services to different customer groups. The company needed a model to help it better understand the fully loaded process and activity costs for its transmission and distribution business. This would enable TEC to more accurately identify important cost-saving opportunities and target new market expansion in the changing deregulated utility environment.

How ABCM Was Used

TEC used activity-based cost management (ABCM) for strategic customer and service profitability analyses. Its ABCM strategy included software implementation, cost analysis, and data reporting tools. Arthur Andersen and TEC built an ABCM model with an executive information systems (EIS) for reporting that accomplished this objective. Key financial and nonfinancial personnel were trained to effectively understand the information and how to manage for results.

TEC's Results

ABCM has given the Energy Delivery division the ability to know what the total costs are to provide services to customers. It has identified not only the direct costs, but also internal and external overhead costs associated with these services. Knowing these costs have given TEC the ability to better bid nontariffed services. TEC has been able to eliminate sev-

eral nonvalued activities and has improved efficiency in others. TEC is actively benchmarking activities between service areas, incorporating the best performance processes
throughout all service areas. ABCM is being used as a performance tool by tying management compensation to targeted ABCM goals.

One of the key elements of survival in a competitive environment is understanding the true cost of providing products and services to customers. In
1997 Skip Wilson, vice president of Energy Delivery for TEC, launched the
Energy Delivery Financial Services organization within his operating unit.
The mission of the group was to help operational people understand the financial side of the business, including identifying the total cost of providing
services to customers. Tom Salisbury, director of Financial Services for Energy Delivery at Tampa Electric, was selected to lead the new department and
to push ABCM forward.

According to Salisbury, one of his early findings was that he could ask five
different people about the cost of providing a service and get five different answers. This simple query confirmed the company's need for better cost information. As the company moves toward a deregulated environment, profitability
will surely be impacted. The ability to identify costs associated with design, construction, operations, and maintenance as they relate to different services and
customer types will be key to the future success of the company and its shareholders. The company wants to focus on delivering its products and services to
its most profitable customers and markets. "Previously, we've been focused on
reducing expenses and cutting costs. That's still important, but companies don't
grow by cutting too far into expenses," said Wilson.

Additionally, TEC wanted to capitalize on more efficient resource allocation. Spending resources on non–value-added activities limits the company's
ability to spend its resources and money on projects that could have a positive
return for the company. Using ABCM, the company wanted to identify and
eliminate process inefficiencies and redirect resources to more value-added
activities. "Our shareholders expect a good return on their investment.
ABCM allows us to maximize the use of our resources by eliminating non–
value work resulting in increased profitability," stated Salisbury.

BACKGROUND

Tampa Electric Company is the major company within TECO Energy, a $2
billion diversified, energy-related holding company headquartered in Tampa,

Florida. TECO Energy includes Peoples Gas, TECO Transport, TECO Coal, TECO Coalbed Methane, TECO Power Services, Bosek, Gibson Associates, TECO Properties, and TeCom, which is currently marketing an advanced interactive energy management system.

Tampa Electric has a service territory of approximately 2,000 square miles serving the electrical needs of approximately 550,000 customers. Its six generating plants have the capability to produce 3,600 megawatts of electricity. Exhibit 18.1 details TECO Energies Florida service area.

The Energy Delivery division of Tampa Electric is the first to implement activity-based cost management (ABCM). This division is responsible for transporting the energy produced by the generating plants to homes and businesses. Energy Delivery, which is responsible for maintaining nearly 11,000 miles of line, includes two operating functions, Transmission and Distribution. High-voltage transmission lines carry power from the generating plants to a substation or an industrial customer. Distribution lines generally move power from the substations to the end users.

Customers fall into three basic categories: (1) residential, (2) commercial,

EXHIBIT 18.1   TECO Energy: Florida Service Area

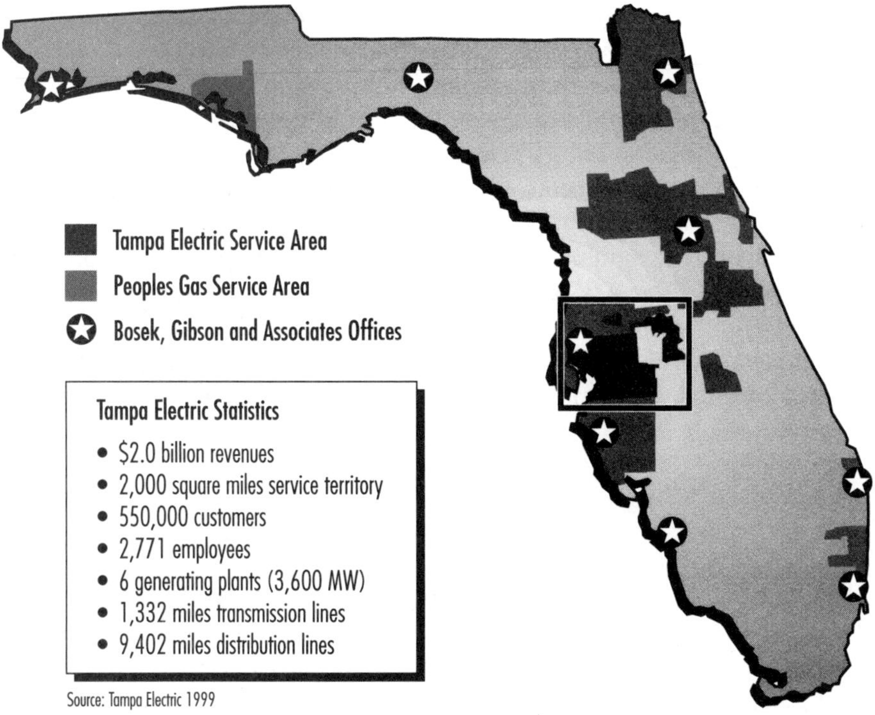

■ Tampa Electric Service Area

■ Peoples Gas Service Area

✪ Bosek, Gibson and Associates Offices

Tampa Electric Statistics

- $2.0 billion revenues
- 2,000 square miles service territory
- 550,000 customers
- 2,771 employees
- 6 generating plants (3,600 MW)
- 1,332 miles transmission lines
- 9,402 miles distribution lines

Source: Tampa Electric 1999

and (3) industrial. With the ABCM, these categories are subdivided into lower levels such as rural, urban, multifamily buildings, single-family residential, and mobile homes. Understanding the true cost of its customer classes and the markets served allows the company to better predict the processes needed to manage costs.

THE APPROACH

In the beginning, several key members of the management team attended a cost management conference to learn the fundamentals of ABCM. Next, several consulting firms were invited to present their credentials, implementation approach, and submit a preliminary bid. Salisbury notes, "During this period we were able to talk with companies who had implemented ABCM successfully. We learned what worked for them and what did not, what they would do differently, and most importantly if they realized the benefits they were seeking. Talking to these groups of people re-enforced our belief that ABCM was the solution to our business issues."

Arthur Andersen was selected to give a presentation to TEC senior management concerning the benefits of an ABCM system implementation and the value the Arthur Andersen team could bring to the company. In addition to a deep skill set and competency, the Arthur Andersen members fit well with TEC personnel assigned to the project, and the company was awarded the contract to help train and implement the ABCM project.

The Tampa Electric Team implemented ABC Technologies' Oros® ABCM software with Cognos Executive Information System (EIS) graphical reporting capability. The system was designed to integrate with the company's newly installed work order management system called STORMS developed by Severn Trent. This new system would enable all direct costs to be captured at the source for approximately 60 percent of the Energy Delivery organization. The team worked closely with key members of the management team to train them on how to use and maintain the ABCM model, including managing for results.

Objectives

The original objective of the team was to identify higher-level activities across Energy Delivery and focus on ABCM activities in the Meter Operations. The meter department was chosen because it was perceived to be an area with the most potential for cost savings in the shortest time. Before the team could begin interviewing people successfully, it had to educate employees on ABCM fundamentals and the business issues to be addressed. Two two-day classes were held for Energy Delivery management. For other employees, several high-level presentations were put together. During the first two weeks, training presentations were held at each location, giving all employees and potential interviewees the opportunity to understand ABCM basics and how it could affect the way they perform their jobs in the future.

In addition, the team was tasked with subdividing the residential, commercial, and industrial customer categories into lower levels. There was also the challenge of interfacing the ABCM software with the new work management system being implemented in parallel. Working with the work management team led by Mike Pearson, manager of technical support, the ABCM team was able to successfully design the new system to feed the Energy Delivery ABCM model with critical cost information. This information provides a more precise measure of labor and materials consumed by an activity.

Implementation Process

One of the challenges for the project team was securing adequate resources for the project implementation. The company's team was relatively small and spread thin because of their day-to-day responsibilities. Additionally, the scope of the implementation was more than doubled to include an Energy Delivery enterprise-wide ABCM implementation rather than simply a pilot in Meter Operations. The original scope included approximately 60 interviews, 70 to 80 activities, and 15 ABM activities within the meter department. Once the team began the interview process, they quickly learned they were gathering so much in-depth detail that it would be an injustice if the ABCM process stopped with the meter department. Therefore, it was decided that ABCM would be implemented across all of Energy Delivery.

The implementation was scheduled to take 16 weeks. However, the increase in scope resulted in a doubling of the number of scheduled interviews with key company personnel, which added only two weeks to the project schedule. The implementation team formed four two-person interview teams. The teams interviewed a statistical sample of 113 people out of a total Energy Delivery workforce consisting of 730 members. The interview process took nearly 11 weeks to complete and was done in parallel with designing the resource database and ABCM model.

The next time-consuming task was compiling and documenting the activity dictionary. Three team members were assigned to complete this task. Over 300 different activities were identified during the initial interview process. This information was pared down to 61 high-level ABC activities and 117 detailed ABM activities. When completed, each member of the management team received a copy of the activity dictionary. The team also placed the dictionary on the Financial Services intranet website so everyone in the company could access it easily.

Still another challenge for the team was to include all overhead costs that are associated with each activity. Many expenses are not charged directly to Energy Delivery. Expenses such as fringes, occupancy, and information technologies had to be manually calculated for inclusion in the model. This gave a more accurate representation of the total cost of performing an activity. Exhibit 18.2 outlines the hierarchy from resources to cost objects.

The Oros ABC software model is used to calculate and report activity cost. Bob Hobkirk, senior performance specialist with TEC, was trained on the model and served as the model builder. He became very proficient with the model within a short time, which was a critical component to the project's success. The team identified that Energy Delivery performed seven major functions. The organizations operate, design, maintain, or construct the transmission and distribution system. They also can be involved in supporting subsidiary businesses, invoice and service customers, or understand markets and customers. This was the structure around which the model was

EXHIBIT 18.2   TECO Sample Cost Hierarchy

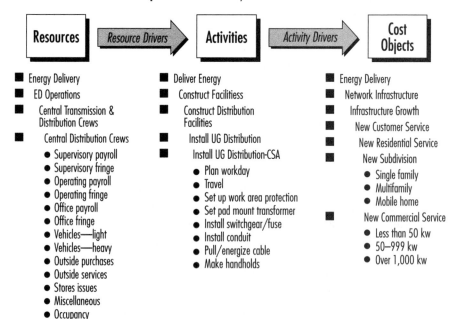

EXHIBIT 18.3 (a) TECO Process Classification Scheme and (b) Top 15 Activity Cost Results

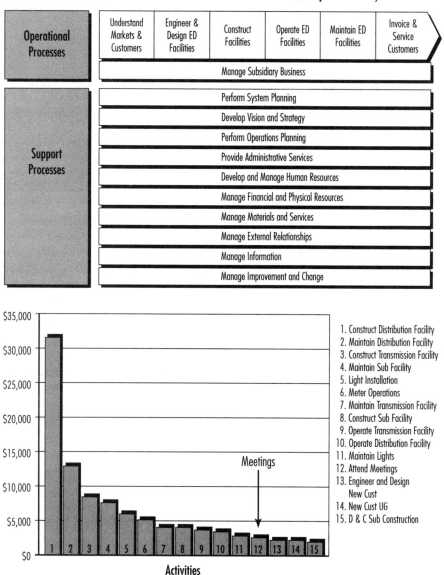

developed. Exhibit 18.3 provides an overview of the process classification scheme and the top 15 activity costs.

All direct costs were added to the model. Next, overhead costs relating to support functions internal to Energy Delivery were added. Finally overhead costs that are external to Energy Delivery were added. The model had to be set up so that management could look at activity costs with any of these costs highlighted or removed. The resulting model was very large and included many attributes, but it provided the needed versatility. One of the other objectives of the model was to give the operating areas the ability to benchmark against themselves. TEC has seven regional service areas, which basically perform the same functions. The model was established creating each of these service areas as separate "business units." "With the work done in ABCM, TEC has the ability to compare activities in these areas and capitalize on the efficiencies one may have that others have not yet identified," according to Joe Campoamor, director of Energy Delivery Operations.

After the model was completed, the first reports of activity cost and activity time matrixes were produced. These reports were included in a presentation to all management in Energy Delivery. The presentations explained how the model was constructed and how to interpret the reports provided. Management was then given the opportunity to verify the information provided and make necessary changes. These changes were then updated in the model, and finalized reports were published for analysis. An Energy Delivery customized Tampa Electric Cognos PowerPlay instruction manual specific to the Energy Delivery Group and a hands-on training class were also prepared. The training included exact screen prints of what the user would see during training sessions. Exhibit 18.4A and 18.4B illustrates a sample of the reporting system and drill-down capabilities.

A key to this project's success was management's commitment, which filtered strongly throughout the organization. Management was dedicated to the success of the project and ensured its people spent the time needed to gather information, be available for interviews, train and learn how to use the model, and manage for results. This commitment resulted in a very comprehensive implementation.

RESULTS

TEC has begun identifying some significant cost savings opportunities using the model. Some examples are as follows:

- Testing of meters in house vs. in the field would save approximately $50,000.
- Travel time between jobs is one of the higher costs included in the installation process of power lines.
- Replacing residential meters is considerably less expensive than repairing them.

EXHIBIT 18.4A   TECO High Level Reporting View

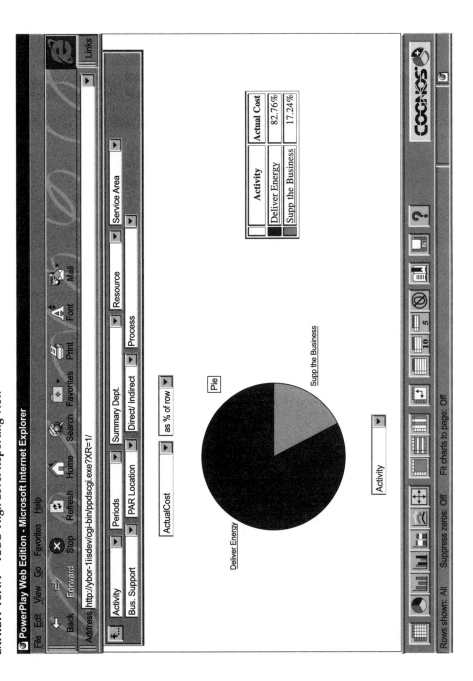

EXHIBIT 18.4B   TECO Drill Down Reporting View

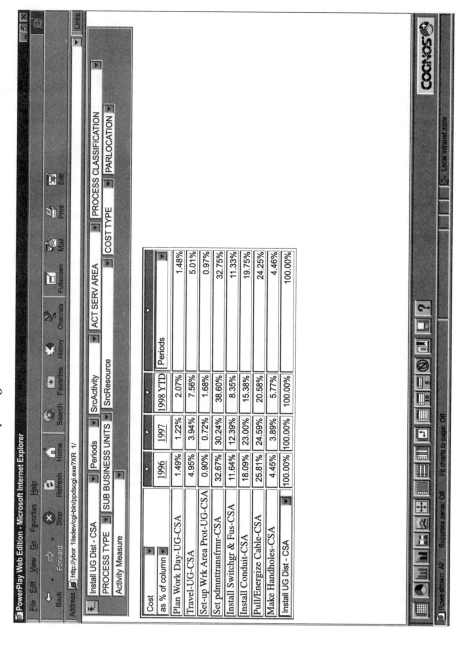

- While reviewing process costs, it was discovered that there was an unusually high activity cost for a component of construction. A large piece of equipment, valued at more than $100,000, was found that had been written off. This presented an opportunity to implement a new process preventing future unwarranted write-offs of equipment.
- Meeting costs for management was one of the 15 highest-cost activities in the company. The company is looking into how to better structure meetings in terms of purpose and attendance.
- The costs of activities are now known and include internal and external overheads.

TEC is fully committed to the success of its ABCM system and has incorporated the results in the evaluation of operational efficiency.

NEXT STEPS

As with many ABCM implementations, a key to the future success of the company is getting its people to understand and use the model results. Being committed to the success of ABCM, Energy Delivery has asked each of its directors to use the information to identify improvement opportunities and report back quarterly. To further ensure this use, it has tied compensation to the overall results of the activity analysis. Energy Delivery has identified a savings target by area to be achieved in 1999 using ABCM. The seven TEC services regional areas already have begun to benchmark results internally across regions to help identify efficiency and best practice. All operating areas are working together to achieve goals this year.

The company is looking to do some innovative things in terms of supplying cost information to parties who need it. To encourage use of the information, the team is using the TEC Intranet to distribute graphical drill-downs of model results in addition to the activity dictionary. The team is also identifying ways to provide all management access to the model itself to gather more detailed information. One problem to overcome is that departments can physically reside in various locations throughout the 2,000-plus-square-mile service territory. Therefore, not all areas have access to the server on which the model resides. TEC is currently refining the PowerPlay modules to provide additional data not originally accessible through the first model.

To provide the best data possible, the Energy Delivery Systems organization has taken a different approach while reviewing its activities. It has embarked on creating its own time collection system. Since nearly all employees in the systems organization have access to a computer, the director has commissioned programmers to develop software to capture actual time spent on activities. "Having the ability to collect precise time spent on an activity," states Bobby Arnold, director of Energy Delivery Systems Controls, "is preferable over using estimated time from a matrix."

The next step will be to implement activity-based budgeting (ABB). This will be easier to accomplish as TEC becomes more proficient with using ABCM. A new financial system for the TECO holding company, which will better support the capturing of activity costs, is under evaluation. Energy Delivery expects to keep ABCM in the forefront and become one of the top best-practice companies in the country using ABCM.

LESSONS LEARNED

The following lessons were learned:

- It is extremely important to have senior management's commitment to an ABCM implementation and have this commitment communicated frequently to ensure buy-in from all levels of management.
- Pick a diverse team of financial and operational people. Provide the team with the resources required to do a quality job.
- Provide training to all levels of the organization. Set the expectations of your organization upfront so that they will know what we will be doing with the information. Communicate the long-range plans, such as activity-based budgeting, profitability analysis, internal and external benchmarking, and so on.
- Validate the model structure in the beginning with people who will be using the data. Once information begins to flow to users, they have a tendency to better understand how the data can be used and want the structures changed. With thousands of attributes, change is more difficult and time consuming after the fact.
- Avoid project scope creep. Have a comprehensive schedule established upfront with milestones identified.
- Have a plan for rolling out the use of ABCM. The "excitement" begins to wear off soon. Be prepared to answer the question, "What's in it for them?" Tying performance objectives to the use of ABCM will increase its ability for success.
- Having users validate the results helped with the buy-in of operational groups. The validation process identified many processes that needed changing, in many cases reducing expenses.

- Communicate the final results of the initial implementation project with everyone involved so that they know how the data was used. Let them know this was not just another management exercise but an ongoing change in the way management will look at the business.

ABOUT THE AUTHORS

Jay Collins is a Partner with Arthur Andersen's Advanced Cost Management Team. He is based in Tampa, Florida.

Robert J. Savage is a Senior Manager with Arthur Andersen's Advanced Cost Management Team. He is based in North Plainfield, New Jersey.

Nick Curcuru is a Consultant with Arthur Andersen's Business Consulting practice in Tampa, Florida.

Summary

Steve Player and Roberto Lacerda

Preparing this book gave us the opportunity to work with clients and colleagues around the globe. What was striking was the similarity of the business issues they were trying to solve. Likewise, we marveled at how quickly the lessons learned traveled.

Best practices are quickly adopted. In many cases the practices were not only adopted but transformed into a better, more usable form. As knowledge flows more quickly, the world is truly becoming smaller. While competition can now come from any corner of the globe, so do opportunities for learning.

If we as authors and editors have achieved our purpose, this book will have helped that learning process. In Part One, Chapter 1 focused on the basic tools and techniques of ABM. Chapter 2 reviewed seven commandments of implementation and some key points from the ABM Best Practice Studies. These studies are an ongoing collaboration between Arthur Andersen, APQC, CAM-I, and individual sponsor companies.

Chapter 3 discussed the recent changes in the software available to support ABM implementations. Enterprise software companies are converging on the analytical applications space and incorporating ABM. These vendors are enhancing their own embedded systems while, in many cases, also teaming with the PC-based ABM solutions. More powerful OLAP tools have come onto the market. In the wake of this, the traditional PC-based tools have also continued to improve. Using funding supplied by venture capitalists or investments from other companies, these vendors have strengthened their products and enhanced their understanding of the needs of ABM implementers. In a nutshell, the system support for ABM implementations continues to get stronger.

The final chapter in Part One reviewed the developments regarding reporting solutions. Ultimately, how information is presented and used is the key to achieving the benefits of using ABM. Well-constructed reports with the ability to highlight as well as detail results have become a key to unlocking the value of ABM insights.

Part Two brought forward the global lessons in ABM by sharing the results of real company implementations. The cases come from Brazil, Canada, Mexico, France, The Netherlands, Portugal, Germany, and the United States. The cases span a variety of industries—banking, telecommunications, discrete manufacturing, process manufacturing, consumer products, insurance, distribution, service bureaus, and utilities. The specific uses are an even greater variety.

In addition to the case studies, the overview of ABM tools and techniques, best practices, evolution in ABM systems, and the changes in reporting, we have also included an appendix and a glossary. The appendix reviews how benchmarking is being performed in the finance and accounting functions. Leveraging ABM information, the appendix reviews how Arthur Andersen is comparing global lessons in these functions. This study began three years ago in Germany and has spread around the world. The Glossary of ABM terms comes primarily from CAM-I. This is a good example of how standardizing terms can be helpful to enhance global understanding.

Activity-based management—understanding the nature of work and the value it creates. It has become a global phenomenon that is as multipurposed and diverse as the geographic realms it operates in. We look forward to hearing from you regarding the lessons you are learning.

Appendix: Benchmarking in Finance and Accounting Functions

Willy G. Hartung
Partner, Arthur Andersen, Frankfurt, Germany

Since 1994 Arthur Andersen Managementberatung GmbH in Germany has conducted an ongoing benchmarking study of the finance and accounting functions. At present, over 1,000 companies worldwide are participating in the continuous research. This appendix addresses three areas within benchmarking: (1) the possibilities and limitations with benchmarking, (2) the collection and evaluation of benchmarking data, and (3) the specific benchmarking results obtained by studying "best-in-class" organizations.

POSSIBILITIES AND LIMITATIONS WITH BENCHMARKING

An efficient method of improving quality and cutting costs in finance and accounting functions is to observe, analyze, evaluate, and compare the efficiency of finance and accounting functions with the "best-in-class" (companies with excellent processes). Important lessons can be learned by studying the aims, approaches, and beneficial aspects of successful companies.

Benchmarking as a New Management Tool

Cost management techniques, such as target costing and activity-based costing (ABC), have long supported the reengineering of companies. Now many companies are realizing that the current strategies of product and cost management are internally focused. But competition takes place outside the company in dealings with other market partners.

In this context, benchmarking opens new prospects by providing an instrument to compare against world-class performance. By continually comparing products, services, processes, and methods with other companies, the aim is to systematically close the performance gap compared with the best-in-

224

class. More than just quantifying the differences in performance such as processing speed or cost incurred, benchmarking is a systematic search for new ideas and solutions. Therefore, methods do not always have to be reinvented. Instead, there is much to be learned from the successful methods implemented by other companies. Efforts and resources can be concentrated on implementing the improvements. The result is often far faster improvements.

Today comparisons are made with best-practice companies across all sectors rather than in a particular industry. For example, the benchmarking concept of the Informationszentrum Benchmarking (IZB, Benchmarking Information Center) of the Fraunhofer Institute in Berlin showed that looking beyond its own industry gives a company strategic competitive advantages over its competitors.[1]

Characteristics of Benchmarking

While many definitions and views of benchmarking exist, the following provides a high-level review of basic attributes followed by common misconceptions.

Benchmarking is:

- A systematic process to show performance deficits and the causes
- A structured approach in order to learn from the practices of leading performers
- The comparison of products, processes, and methods of operational functions
- A regular, continuous process
- Part of the concept of the "learning organization"

Benchmarking is not:

- An instrument used only to depict differences in performance
- Systematic copying and mere imitation of proven methods
- Pure comparison of financial data
- A one-time event
- A quick fix

According to a 1997 survey of the Rationalisierungs-Kuratorium der Deutschen Wirtschaft (RKW), companies in industries particularly exposed to increased international competition have already gained in-depth benchmarking experience. Those include 40 percent of automobile manufacturers,

50 percent in the mechanical engineering and technology sector, and 80 percent of major companies in the electrical industry.[2]

However, these figures must not mask the fact that the majority of companies around the world do not engage in systematic benchmarking. The causes are not just the fear of coming into contact with competitors or the concern that the method may be long and costly. Over 80 percent of the companies surveyed stated that lack of knowledge about benchmarking prevented them from applying this kind of approach.

Limits of Performance Measurement in Finance and Accounting Functions

A company's accounting function plans all commercial transactions in terms of volume and value, records the figures, and controls the processes. The finance and accounting functions also supply information for other organizational units or managers. This makes these functions essential for the success of the company.

Unlike other operating areas such as distribution, finance and accounting functions are not perceived as contributing value; rather they are seen only as cost units. Since low costs are not in themselves a factor for the measurement of performance, there is a lack of criteria covering the total efficiency of this area of responsibility. Thus comparison with the efficiency and quality of the performance of the finance and accounting functions in other successful companies allows for greater transparency. In so doing, the finance and accounting departments may counteract the bad reputation they may hold in the company, where they are seen as producing large amounts of confusing data or "information garbage" and branded as an "impediment to sales."

As evidenced in other operating areas, when it comes to optimizing the process and organizational structure in finance and accounting functions, few comparisons can be made with other successful companies. At most, according to German industrial standards, quality management serves as an external yardstick for the purposes of comparison.

Benchmarking as an Optimization Approach

The classical differentiation between external and internal accounting is important for the optimal use of benchmarking in finance and accounting functions. The increased use of electronic data processing (EDP) assists in evaluating data in any form, such as using management information systems or databases, and increasingly erodes the strict distinction between internal and external. While technology is helping bring the internal and external views together, most finance departments take responsibility to meet legal requirements of their host countries. For instance, the accounting requirements prescribed by German law (e.g., §§ 238 f. of the German Commercial Code) do not give a financial accounting department, as an external accounting function, unlimited scope to redesign the processes in its area of responsibility. According to generally accepted accounting principles (GAAP), all commercial transactions in the company must be recorded chronologically, systematically, completely, and in a proper manner. In fulfilling these quantitative and qualitative minimum requirements for the preparation of annual financial statements, procedures are very similar to those used in accounting departments in other companies. However, rationalization potential can be found along the way, allowing—while still observing the accounting regulations—the efficiency of the department to be enhanced and the costs per performance unit to be improved upon.

For example, by using more commercial software, the number of incoming vendor invoices entered per employee can be increased or the processing time for each creditor reduced. Testing functions built into the program can even improve the quality of the individual entries. Benchmarking the accounting departments of other successful companies in terms of processing volumes and times for purchase and sales invoices can provide important information to optimize business processes. Other typical finance benchmarks include the use of electronic methods of payment, the number of accounts, the use of automatic entries, the number of journal entries, and the time required to process monthly or annual financial statements.

In addition to these quantitative means of comparison within administrative accounting, qualitative benchmarks exist. These include how modern and up-to-date the valuation procedures for annual financial statements are or how they are being enhanced. Qualitative criteria for comparison in the area of finance include such aspects as the structure of cash management, cost accounting, and financial budgets of other companies.

Experience has shown—as in the case of a benchmarking study by Arthur Andersen Managementberatung—the "best-in-class" use the greater portion of their human resources in the area of internal accounting or control. With human resources the most important tool—without a legal foundation—for the planning, control, and supervision of what goes on in the company, particular attention is paid to the key activities of strategic corporate planning, budgeting, profit and loss forecasting and reporting. In this area of responsibility, benchmarking reveals qualitative improvement opportunities. In many companies, the quality and informative value of internal accounting methods are insufficient because conventional methods such as standard costing and full absorption costing are predominant.

Aims of Benchmarking in Finance and Accounting Functions

Benchmarking in finance and accounting functions is designed to provide organizations and managers with fast, improved information at a low cost. Effective benchmarking requires the following:

1. Accounting services are to be made transparent. To do so, the organizational structure and process organization are described in detail.
2. Operational (measurable) performance figures/target values for both quantitative and qualitative measures must be set out and quantified (e.g., the processing times and volumes for purchase orders and sales invoices). In this way, benchmarks can be determined more clearly and future optimization measures can be measured and controlled.
3. Differences in performance—both quantitative and qualitative—compared with other successful companies must be recorded, analyzed, and evaluated. In this context a distinction is made between services prescribed by law and services carried out on behalf or at the request of managers from within the company.
4. Improvement measures considered for accounting services must adapt to the actual requirements of the company.
5. Ongoing surveillance of goal attainment: Optimization measures are prioritized according to improvement potential—such as cost savings or quality enhancement—and the cost involved in the implementation (e.g., investment in electronic data processing systems). The implementation of the measures is followed closely.

Recognizing and Overcoming Resistance to the Introduction of Benchmarking

Employees and department heads often resist the introduction of systematic measurement and the comparative appraisal of processes in their company because they fear losing their jobs or because they believe they are not able to cope with unattainable goals. They often hinder restructuring or improvement measures vital for maintaining the competitiveness of the company.

Common arguments include:

- "It is impossible to compare our company with other companies."
- "The urgency of measurement (appraisal) and the informative value of the measurement results are doubtful."

- "There is no time to collect data because there is more important work to be done."

Experience shows these kinds of arguments are not due to difficulties with the benchmarking tools themselves but have different causes:

- The fear of being made personally responsible for errors
- The fear of change and the related loss of privileges and importance
- Insufficient commitment of management to eliminate weak points consistently

The following measures help overcome this kind of resistance and ensure the successful implementation of benchmarking at the company:

- Ensuring the data can be compared with those of other companies
- Concentrating on the most important processes
- Ensuring the support of management for the implementation of benchmarking
- Integrating the employees involved in each process
- Informing employees on an ongoing basis through the managers responsible for benchmarking

Benchmarking leads to a continual process of adaptation and learning. With this basic understanding of possibilities and challenges available with benchmarking, organizations can effectively move into benchmarking process.

THE BENCHMARKING PROCESS: FROM DATA COLLECTION TO IMPROVEMENT

The benchmarking process consists of four stages: data collection, evaluation, analysis, and improvement.

1. Collection of Data

Since 1994 Arthur Andersen Managementberatung GmbH has been conducting benchmarking studies in finance and accounting functions. To date, more than 1,000 companies worldwide, including more than 300 in Germany, are participating in the study. A special questionnaire was developed for the collection of data to record all the information systematically and in a comparable fashion. However, the benchmarking study is not just a one-time survey; it involves the ongoing and ever-expanding collection of data on finance and accounting functions provided by a growing number of companies.

The questionnaire for the collection of data is completely standardized across the world and differs from the cross-industry standard only with respect to aspects specific to particular countries, such as provisions from the accounting regulations of the German Commercial Code. By structuring the data in an appropriate fashion, the efficiency of the finance and accounting functions of one company can be compared with that of another. Comparisons can be drawn, for example, within a state, according to company size, or by industry as well as across countries or industries.

Benchmarking efforts are facilitated by examining the 10 main processes in finance and accounting functions. These are shown in Exhibit A.1.

EXHIBIT A.1   Ten Main Processes in Finance and Accounting

| Payroll accounting | Accounts payable | Billing | Accounts receivable | Close-the-books and reporting |
| Budgeting/ planning | Fixed assets accounting | Travel and expense accounting | Tax | Internal audit |

Delimitation of the Processes in Finance and Accounting Functions

To ensure general comparability, the core activities of finance and accounting functions are divided into 10 main processes independent of the industry concerned. The tasks of the main processes are defined precisely with regard to the beginning and the end of a process and the method of measurement within one process. For example, the following main tasks have been assigned to the process of "accounts payable":

- Setting up and maintaining master data on creditors
- Checking purchase invoices
- Clarifying invoice discrepancies
- Classifying purchase invoices
- Posting invoices
- Preparing and performing monthly payments
- Paying invoices either manually or mechanically

- Processing of return debits or credits
- Filing and archiving invoices

Explanations and examples are given for each of the main tasks, allowing the precise allocation of each process. For example, any entry of a purchase invoice, a payment transaction, or other slips is an accounting event irrespective of the number items it is based on or of the fact that compound entries are to be regarded as just one accounting event. Regardless of how the individual accounting processses are organized in the company, evaluations of corporate data are comparable. For the ongoing Arthur Andersen benchmarking study, an Arthur Andersen consultant reviews the content of the forms for completeness and plausibility. A sample questionnaire for accounts payable appears in Exhibit A.2.

Completion of the forms takes between a half day and two days per process, depending on the functionality of the company's information system. Completing the questionnaire can create a sense of awareness; the detailed and systematic catalog of questions allows the respondent to reflect on the organization of management and work, which enables strengths and weaknesses to be identified.

Measurement Criteria

The efficiency of finance and accounting systems is measured on the basis of cost, quality, and time. They are not calculated solely on the basis of the cost incurred but also on the basis of the quality and speed of the services rendered. These measurement criteria allow the localization of strengths and weaknesses of management and work in finance and accounting functions with respect to individual processes. Performance is measured on the basis of process and output-related ratios. Exhibit A.3 highlights benchmarking measurement criteria for three performance factors: quality, cost, and time. For example, to measure the performance criteria of "quality", is the number of corrections for every 100 entries is benchmarked.

Data on cost (for staff, supplies, and information technology support), performance volumes (number of invoices, payments received, entries), and the factors influencing performance (number of active vendors, errors, days until payment is received) must be collected for each process.

2. Evaluation

Once the data are collected and entered into a computer-aided evaluation system, the individual position of each company is compared with the bench-

EXHIBIT A.2 Questionnaire for Accounts Payable

Standard Questionnaire Supports the Systemic Recording of Cost and Performance Data (in US$)

1. Total labor cost of Accounts Payable — US$3,162,500
   (salaries, overtime, benefits, incidental labor costs, etc.)

2. Cost of temporary labor — $27,500
   (contract and temporary labor not belonging to the permanent staff)

3. Cost of materials and other variable costs of Accounts Payable — $247,500
   (overhead cost of materials, training, and other variable costs—
   excluding rent, depreciation, or allocations)

4. External services, including annual and monthly fees — $2,750
   Specify the total cost of the IT support to Accounts Payable (labor
   cost, cost of materials, license fees and system maintenance
   cost for the provision of data processing times, software, hardware,
   and the utilization of management information services)

5. Labor cost of the IT department used predominantly/exclusively by Accounts Payable — $110,000
   (salaries, overtime, and incidental labor costs for system support and
   operative/technical support)

6. Cost of materials and other variable costs of the IT department for Accounts Payable — $247,500

7. Annual license fees and system maintenance fees — $55,000

8. Total cost of accounts payable (total of questions 1 to 7) — US$3,852,750

9. How many invoices are processed annually? — 200,000

10. How many accounting events are processed annually? — 250,000

11. How many accounts payable payments are issued annually? — 120,000

12. What is the value of the total number of annual accounts payable payments? — US$544,572,050

13. On Average, each month, how many accounts payable errors are detected — 520
    (e.g., incoming voucher errors, processing errors, incorrect payments)?

14. How many active suppliers do you have? — 6,200

Complete the following questions in terms of fulltime equivalents (FTEs). For example, a part-time
staff member working 20 hours per week would be counted as 0.5 FTE and a head of Controlling/
Accounting spending only one day per week on Accounts Payable would count as 0.2 FTE.
Some management time must be specified in order to calculate a leverage ratio.

	Management/ supervisory	Other staff	Total
15. Fulltime equivalents (FTEs) in corporate Accounts Payable	5.00	60.20	65.20
16. FTEs in Accounts Payable not employed by corporate A/P	2.05	4.20	6.25
17. Total FTEs	7.05	64.40	71.45

EXHIBIT A.3   Benchmarking Measurement Criteria for Three Performance Factors

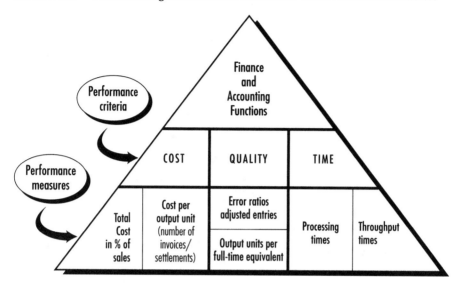

mark group (based on characteristics such as the same industry, sales volume, country). The results are presented visually—mainly in the form of quartile charts. (See Exhibit A.4.) These graphs show the performance of the company investigated for each measurement criterion (cost, quality, time) as compared to the performance of the benchmark group. Each quartile represents the performance spread of 25 percent of all companies from the chosen database. The higher a company is positioned in the chart, the more efficient its finance and accounting functions are in comparison with the benchmark group. The median shows the value of the company positioned exactly in the middle (50 percent) of all companies.

Differences in cost and performance are simple to locate using this form of presentation. The shortcomings compared to the "best" can then be quantified. For example, the preparation of monthly financial statements takes the "best-in-class" two and one-half days whereas other companies take more than 17 days.

Between eight and 15 measurements are provided for each accounting process. For example, measurements for "accounts payable" include the number of purchase invoices processed per employee and year and processing costs per purchase invoice. Performance in finance and accounting functions can be studied in more depth by viewing several comparative diagrams. In addition, the starting points for optimizing work processes are identified and may lead to improvement measures. In the accounts payable department, for instance, the increased use of electronic payment systems and the automatic

EXHIBIT A.4   Quartile Chart

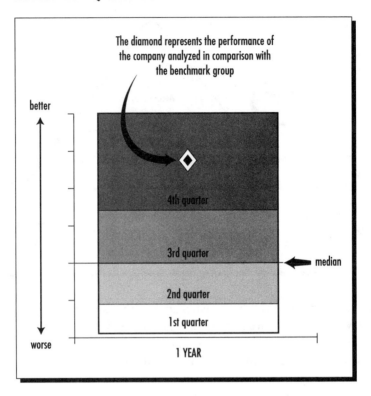

comparison of invoices with orders and deliveries can help optimize work
processes with regard to cost, processing time, and correctness.

3. Analysis

The goal of this stage is to determine the causes of performance differences
in comparison with other companies such as the appropriate use of EDP
in accounts payable. For example, in Exhibit A.4, the diamond shows the
performance of the company analyzed in comparison with the benchmark
group.

Key issues to consider in determining the location or position in comparison with best-in-class companies involve choices such as organizational, personnel, technical and legal structures. For example, what is the effect of legal
or statutory provisions such as GAAP on the accounting department's performance?

The aim of this discussion is to identify the elements of a process responsible for the difference compared with the top performers. A flow chart creates transparency and forms the basis for process analysis. Exhibit A.5 provides a sample flow chart using an accounts payable example.

Another important tool in connection with analysis is activity-based costing. With the help of ABC, analysis can be focused on the cost-intensive activities making up some 80 percent of activity costs. This especially includes checking and auditing invoices, correcting entries and payments, resolving outstanding payments, and processing dunning letters from vendors.

For example, an activity-based costing view of accounts payable is documented Exhibit A.6. The graph depicts those cost-intensive items that can be streamlined and reduced. Thus improvement measures can aim directly at those activities.

4. Improvement

The comparative examination and analysis of differences in performance reveal the need for action and improvement opportunities. By quantifying the potential for optimization and the expense of implementation, measures to bring about change can be prioritized. In addition, target values or guidelines for internal services can be established, such as halving the number of correcting entries in one year with specific training measures, and the degree of goal attainment can be assessed in an objective manner.

Without target values and measurements, results cannot be improved. Experience has shown that measurements are key. If something cannot be measured, it cannot be controlled. If it cannot be controlled, it cannot be managed. If it cannot be managed, it cannot be improved.[3]

RESULTS AND VALUE OF BENCHMARKING

In February 1997 almost 1,000 companies from different industries, countries, and sizes were involved in Arthur Andersen Managementberatung GmbH's benchmarking study for finance and accounting functions. The largest number of participants are from the United States—with over 500 companies—because benchmarking has been common there since the end of the 1980s. The initial reserve shown toward this management tool in Germany is now giving way to growing interest and increased participation. While only 200 German companies were participating in the benchmarking study in February 1997, the number increased to more than 300 German participants by August of that year. Other European countries had 48 companies participat-

EXHIBIT A.5   Sample Flowchart of Procedures

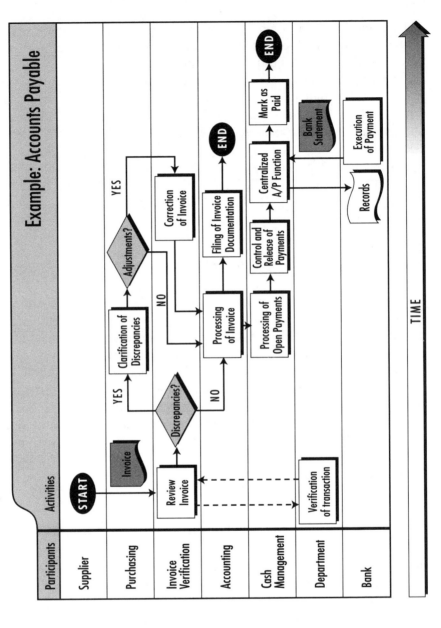

Example: Accounts Payable

EXHIBIT A.6 ABC for Accounts Payable

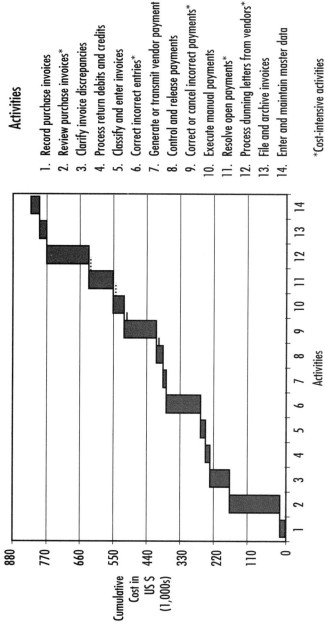

Activities

1. Record purchase invoices
2. Review purchase invoices*
3. Clarify invoice discrepancies
4. Process return debits and credits
5. Classify and enter invoices
6. Correct incorrect entries*
7. Generate or transmit vendor payment
8. Control and release payments
9. Correct or cancel incorrect payments*
10. Execute manual payments
11. Resolve open payments*
12. Process dunning letters from vendors*
13. File and archive invoices
14. Enter and maintain master data

*Cost-intensive activities

ing with an additional 34 from Australia, and 23 from Canada pushing the total over 1,000.

Of the 40 industries defined on a uniform basis worldwide, nine industries in Germany comprise most of the participants in the benchmarking study. In terms of size, most companies participating in the study are small to medium size. Almost one-half of the companies have sales of DM 100 to 500 million (US$55 to $277 million), one-third from DM 500 million to 2 billion (US$277 million to $1.1 billion). Exhibit A.7 highlights the industry mix and size of the Germany portion of the benchmark group.

In addition, the majority of participating companies are midsize organizations. (See Exhibit A.8.)

Functions of the Future

The results of Arthur Andersen Managementberatung GmbH's benchmarking study show that in the future the organization, management, and work in finance and accounting functions will be fundamentally different from that of today.

Best-practice companies—those that have the best procedures and results in comparison with all the rest—show the following trends:

- A new range of responsibilities and image as an internal service provider exists.
- Currently more than 90 percent of personnel capacities in finance and accounting functions are used for routine work, such as recording and processing data, historical reporting, and monitoring and control of the accounting systems.
- The new technological and organizational requirements (client-server technology, process orientation, activity-based costing) and increasing pressure from competition (market orientation, target costing) require a shift in responsibilities in finance and accounting functions.
- In more successful companies, the main focus is now on supporting management through the supply of significant and reliable data and the measurement of the factors that determine the company's success. A leading mechanical engineering company, for example, assumes that only 8 percent of all complaints actually are reported to the company, while more than 90 percent of all cases of customer dissatisfaction are discussed at home or at work or are not reported at all. This means that potential for improvement of the product or service is not identified or not recognized in time, and it is harder to retain customers. The only

EXHIBIT A.7   Industry Examples from Germany in the National Benchmark Group

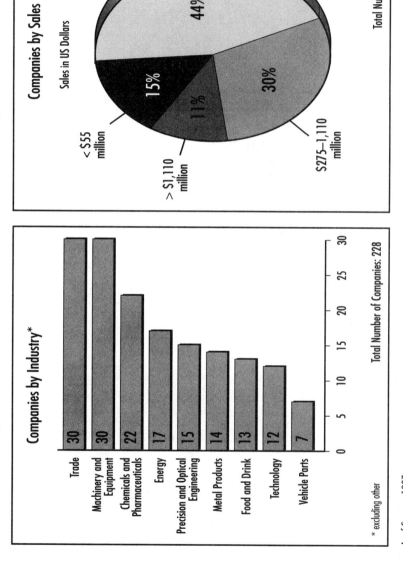

Companies by Industry*

Industry	Value
Trade	30
Machinery and Equipment	30
Chemicals and Pharmaceuticals	22
Energy	17
Precision and Optical Engineering	15
Metal Products	14
Food and Drink	13
Technology	12
Vehicle Parts	7

Total Number of Companies: 228

Companies by Sales

Sales in US Dollars

$55–275 million

< $55 million — 15%

> $1,110 million — 11%

$275–1,110 million — 30%

44%

Total Number of Companies: 228

* excluding other

As of Summer 1997

EXHIBIT A.8   Size of German Companies in Study

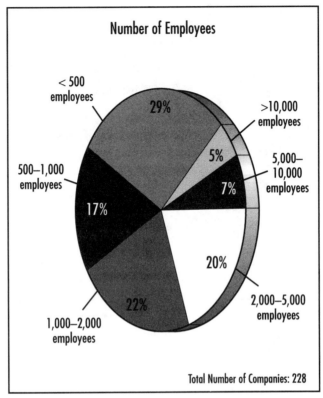

As of Summer 1997

remedy is to intensify the measurement of customer satisfaction by the finance and accounting functions.

Advantages from Continuous Improvement

The results of the study also illustrate that better performance in finance and accounting functions is already being achieved by the "best-in-class," typically at a lower cost. In some cases, the difference in cost is more than 50 percent. Improvements in performance at leading companies often are achieved in terms of cost, quality, and time simultaneously. For example, process speeds for the preparation of the annual financial statements at a major German service company are 30 percent lower in comparison with other companies from the same industry. At the same time, the cost of preparation is lower and the quality of the work better.

Concentrating on Value-Added Work

Leading companies make use of the opportunities provided by modern data processing by consistently automating large tasks and routine work (i.e., mechanical comparison of open items in payment transactions) and concentrating to an increasing extent on the analysis and interpretation of accounting results (i.e., the structure of overdue receivables). Manual work, such as recording data or correcting errors, is steadily consuming less of employees available capacity.

Pragmatism and Recipient Orientation

The organization of management and work in finance and accounting functions of the "best-in-class" is simple and pragmatic. For example, complex cost unit structures with difficult cost allocation procedures are avoided. Instead, the allocation of costs and proceeds focuses on important business processes, such as components per period. Qualitative performance characteristics such as employee satisfaction play an important role. At the same time, there is a strong focus on the needs of management. The decisive criterion is the timely provision of important and reliable information or key performance indicators.

Cost

The evaluation of the database with regard to cost led to a number of new findings, including total costs as a percentage of sales. For example, total costs for the 10 processes measured in the finance and accounting functions expressed as a percentage of sales vary from 0.18 percent to 3 percent. Twenty-five percent of participants had costs as a percentage of sales of between 1.75 percent and 3 percent. For 50 percent of participating companies costs ranged from 0.18 percent to 1 percent (as a percentage of sales).

What is surprising is that, contrary to all expectations, there are no interrelations relating to size and industry; companies of the same size or industry have different cost positions. The opinion often prevalent in the business world that publicly traded companies generally do better in terms of cost as a percentage of sales is unfounded.

Cost Structure

Personnel expenses account for the greatest costs in finance and accounting functions. On average, these costs amount to 76 percent of expenditure. The cost of data processing averages 16 percent, which means the remaining costs (e.g., office materials) are an average of 8 percent. Apart from minor exceptions, this distribution also applies for the cost allocation to the individual business processes of finance and accounting functions. An average 85 percent of total costs can be attributed to five core activities:

- Invoicing (21 percent)
- Payroll accounting (18 percent)
- Accounts receivable (17 percent)
- Accounts payable (17 percent)
- Financial statements (11 percent)

However, company or industry differences show there are sometimes considerable deviations from these average figures. For example, the cost of finance and accounting functions for publicly traded companies (compared to the averages) are:

- Accounts payable (31 percent)
- Payroll accounting (17 percent)
- Accounts receivable (16 percent)
- Invoicing (13 percent)
- Financial statements (8 percent)

Relationship Among Cost, Quality, and Time

Companies with high costs for services in finance and accounting functions do not necessarily achieve a corresponding level of quality and speed. In fact, according to the results of the benchmarking study, companies with relatively low total costs also excel in the performance factors of "quality" (i.e., low incidence of error) and "time" (i.e., automatic entry of payments received, faster preparation of annual financial statements). Exhibit A.9 provides a list of measures used in the analysis of efficiency of accounts receivable accounting according to the factors of cost, quality, and time.

Longer processing times, such as longer times between invoicing and entry of payment (several weeks), or beginning to work on annual financial statements and presentation of the statements (several months) usually lead to higher costs. The coordination and streamlining of the accounting tasks at the beginning and during the process virtually eliminates repetition.

Causes of Inefficiencies

According to the results of the benchmarking study, most deficiencies in performance described, such as incorrect classification, are not caused by the

EXHIBIT A.9 Analysis of the Capacity of Accounts Receivable

COSTS

- Total costs of accounts receivable as a percent of revenue
- Total costs of accounts receivable per employee (FTE)
- Total costs of accounts receivable by cost category
- Processing costs per transaction
- Costs of credit rating/dunning procedures per A/P
- FTE per DM1 million of revenue
- Bad debt loss as a percent of revenue
- Bad debt loss as a percent of receivables
- Average amount of lost receivables

QUALITY

- Annual number of payments received per FTE
- Number of payments received per diem
- Percent of incorrect payments received
- Percent of number of correct payments received
- Percent of on-time payments received
- Percent of utilization of electronic data processing
- Number of active debtors per FTE
- Percent of debtors with credit check
- Percent of debtors past due
- Percent of debtors processed by collection agencies

TIME

- Percent of payments received and entered the same day
- Number of days between invoicing and receiving payment
- Turnover rate of receivables
- Time it takes to process a credit application
- Total cycle time

finance and accounting functions. Often there is a lack of coordination between a company's departments with regard to responsibilities for processes. For example, the counting of an inventory as of the cut-off date in the process of annual financial statements are not clearly defined.

The efficiency of accounting processes can be determined on the basis of more than 20 measurement criteria—divided into cost, quality, and time. Exhibits A.10 and A.11 provide examples of this criteria for the process of accounts receivable.

RESULTS

The costs for processing payments received range from DM1 to 25 (US$0.55 to $14.00) per payment. For 50 percent of German participants—i.e., some 150 companies—costs are less than DM5 (US$2.70) per payment received. The number of days between invoicing and receipt of payment varies from 10 to 180 days. Fifty percent of all German companies participating register receipt of payment 10 to 50 days after invoicing. The results can be presented in the form of a quarter chart. Each quarter represents the performance spread of 25 percent of all companies from the chosen database. The higher the analyzed company is positioned in the diagram, the more efficient (more cost-effective, faster) its finance and accounting functions are compared to the rest.

The evaluation in connection with bad debt loss is interesting. Twenty-five percent of German participants put their bad debt loss at 2 to 6 percent of total receivables. The average amount per receivable lost is between DM12,000 and 40,000 (US$6,700 and $22,222) for 25 percent of German participants.

For companies registering later receipt of payment—50 to 180 days after invoicing—the share of bad debt loss is similar.

Companies performing particularly well in the measurement values stand out above all because they:

- Use a scoring model for the evaluation of creditworthiness during sales negotiations
- Analyze the payment behavior of customers on a regular basis and inform the distribution department
- Have and use predefined sets of measures or standards for the identification and handling of overdue receivables
- Enter payments received in the accounts receivable account on the same day

The analysis and evaluation of the measurement values (cost, quality, time) in context gives the companies participating in Arthur Andersen Manage-

Evaluation of Accounts Receivable

Total Costs of Accounts Receivable as a Percent of Revenue

0.0%
0.2%
0.4%
0.6%
0.8%
1.0%
1.2%
1.4%

Processing Costs per Transaction

In US $

0
3
6
9
12
15
18

Annual Number of Payments Received per FTE

80,000
60,000
40,000
20,000
0

Costs of Credit Rating/Dunning Procedures per A/P

In US $

0
110
220
330
440

Number of Days Between Invoicing and Receiving Payment

Days

0
40
80
120
160

FTE per US$550,000 of Revenue

0.00
0.02
0.04
0.06
0.08
0.10
0.12
0.14
0.16

EXHIBIT A.11 Results of Accounts Receivable Analysis

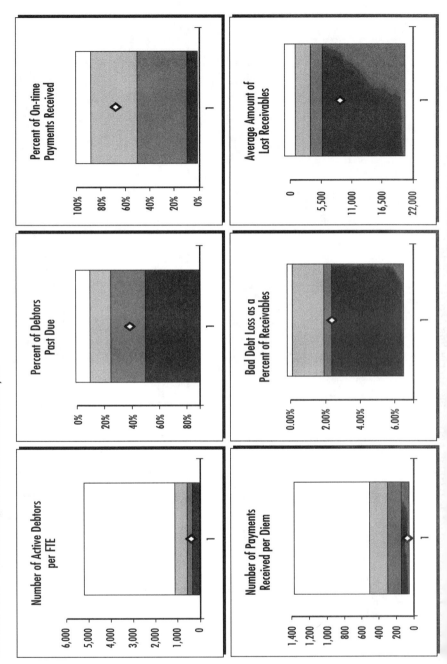

mentberatung GmbH's benchmarking study a precise and subtle view of where their finance and accounting functions stand.

As a result, the costs for "services" in accounting and controlling can be reduced in future. At the same time, the task profile in this area will undergo a fundamental change.

ABOUT THE AUTHOR

Willy G. Hartung is a Partner with Arthur Andersen in Eschborn/Frankfurt, Germany. He is responsible for the area of finance and accounting and leads Arthur Andersen's benchmarking process in this area.

NOTES

1. Informationszentrum Benchmarking, "Blick durch die Wirtschaft" (Berlin: Fraunhofer Institute, April 25, 1996).

2. Rationalisierungs-Kuratorium der Deutschen Wirtschaft, "Blick durch die Wirtschaft," April 21, 1997.

3. J. J. Harrington, Business Process Improvement (New York: McGraw-Hill, 1991).

Vignette: Leybold Systems GmbH

Willy G. Hartung, Partner, Frankfurt, Germany

Leybold Systems (LS) GmbH, with its registered office in Hanau, Germany, is an independent business unit of the Balzers and Leybold Group, which belongs to the Swiss Oerlikon-Bührle Group. The company develops, produces and sells equipment for vacuum production procedures primarily in large area coating, optics, and compact disc lines. LS ranks as a worldwide leader in these particular areas.

LS generates annual sales of more than DM350 million (US$194 million) and has approximately 800 employees. LS and other companies of the Balzers and Leybold Group long ago made the decision to become an excellent company on all measures in terms of total quality management. The companies made this commitment so they could not only remain profitable, but also maintain the high quality requirements they faced both internally and externally.

BUSINESS ISSUES FOR BENCHMARKING

The first step in achieving the high quality goals set by LS was to establish the appropriate methods and procedures for all business units and divisions. The level of implementation of each area was determined on a ratio basis in the context of assessments. This ensured that comparisons with other companies were appropriate. It also provided the possibility to attain further knowledge of and information on best methods and processes. For this reason, individual divisions of LS, such as the purchasing department, finance, and accounting, initialized their own independent benchmarking analysis.

OBJECTIVES AND EXECUTION OF THE BENCHMARKING ANALYSIS

LS established an organization that operates as an internal service center for several group companies. Benchmarking finance and accounting is provided to meet the following objectives:

- Assess the performance of finance and accounting as relates to costs, quality, and time compared to other companies on a cross-industry and industry-related basis
- Identify starting points for improvement and their quantification
- Obtain objective and factually traceable criteria for the assessment of the department's own performance

LS worked with consulting firms to accomplish its benchmarking analysis most effectively. Arthur Andersen Managementberatung met the following criteria and was selected to assist the company. The measures included:

- Availability of relevant and reliable comparative values
- Knowledge of best methods and procedures of how to reach record performance
- Proven methodical know-how in benchmarking
- Favorable price/performance ratio

Once Arthur Andersen was selected, the group established an internal coordination of the procedure, such as scheduling and job allocation. In addition, tasks relating to the analysis were established based on both time and contents. These were determined on the basis of the scheduled date of the presentation of results. Finally, the group selected the fiscal year 1996 as the review period.

Arthur Andersen recommended a benchmarking approach consisting of a modular setup comprised of the areas of purchasing, distribution, and marketing in addition to finance and accounting. Within each of these modules, the processes were defined on a standard basis. For example, within the finance and accounting module, 10 processes were precisely defined by main tasks.

A standardized questionnaire was used, along with instruction on how to complete the forms. The questionnaire was completed by managers responsible for each individual process within the module. Each area was given several weeks to complete the process.

Most of those participating in the analysis had never measured information in this manner and experienced some difficulty in the process-related data processing. Because of the process-related approach, employees of other divisions outside finance and accounting were also queried. For example, employees in the distribution department and in the field, among others, participated in completing the travel expense report process, to make adjustments for incomplete expense claims.

Once the questionnaire was complete, it was reviewed and evaluated for completeness, plausibility, and comparability.

RESULTS

The results were presented to the employees and executive officers of LS involved in the examination as well as to customers of the accounting department.

Overall, the comparison with other companies led to an outstanding result for Leybold Systems. In addition to more transparency, LS also has an exact location finding regarding quality, cost, and time. For example, the analysis determined that Leybold is a top performer at certain services, such as providing monthly statements on the third working day of the following month.

The analysis, which provided more than 70 quantitative measuring points in such categories as costs, time, and quality, also made it possible to identify, locate, and quantify a number of starting points for improvements. As a result the process-related benchmarking approach is of particular importance. It showed conclusively and measurably for all persons involved that lasting improvements can be realized only by involvement of and cooperation with employees in upstream and downstream entities who are involved in the respective process. It proved, for example, that by intensifying cooperation with the purchasing department, improvements in the auditing process can be achieved.

GOING FORWARD

Additional areas of change included improvement potentials and the costs of implementation. These areas were quantified through the results of the benchmarking analysis, which also helped to prioritize improvement measures. The "settlement of business trips" was selected during the first stage as pilot project for a deliberate optimization.

A project team consisting of employees from different areas of LS further analyzed the business trip process. They were supported in their effort by Lufthansa AirPlus and confirmed the improvement potentials, for example, of throughput time and error rate.

Improvement potentials continue to be realized with:

- The support of a corresponding software
- The integration and reorientation of all administrative procedures of the

business trip process, including the filing of a travel application, procurement of trip funding, advance payments, approval, and filing of travel expense reports with accounting

At present LS is still in the introduction stage, but significant improvements are already visible.

At the same time an ongoing project team is reviewing the "accounts payable" process for improvement possibilities. Only by visualizing the course of the process can further potential weaknesses, such as duplication, random disturbances, standby, and delay time, be identified by the company. In the future, further processes will be analyzed in detail and ideas will be implemented to optimize the process.

Leybold Systems found that the benchmarking analysis in finance and accounting constituted an important milestone on its way to business excellence and to achieving the high quality set forth in its commitment to total quality management.

ABOUT THE AUTHOR

Willy G. Hartung is a Partner with Arthur Andersen in Eschborn/Frankfurt, Germany. He is responsible for the area of finance and accounting and leads Arthur Andersen's benchmarking process in this area.

GLOSSARY

ABC   See *activity-based costing.*

Absorption costing   A method of costing that assigns all or a portion of the manufacturing costs to products or other cost objects. The costs assigned include those that do and do not vary with the level of activity performed.

Activity   1. Work performed within an organization. 2. The aggregations of actions performed within an organization that are useful for purposes of activity-based costing.

Activity analysis   The identification and description of activities in an organization. Activity analysis involves determining what activities are done within a department, how many people perform the activities, how much time they spend performing the activities, what resources are required to perform the activities, what operational data best reflect the performance of the activities, and what value the activity has for the organization. Activity analysis is accomplished by means of interviews, questionnaires, observations, and reviews of physical records of work.

Activity attributes   Characteristics of individual activities. Attributes include cost drivers, cycle time, capacity, and performance measures. For example, a measure of the elapsed time required to complete an activity is an attribute. (See *cost driver, performance measures.*)

Activity-based costing   A methodology that measures the cost and performance of activities, resources, and cost objects. Resources are assigned to activities, then activities are assigned to cost objects based on their use. Activity-based costing recognizes the causal relationships of cost drivers to activities.

Activity-based cost system   A system that maintains and processes financial and operating data on a firm's resources, activities, cost objects, cost drivers, and activity performance measures. It also assigns cost to activities and cost objects.

Activity-based management   A discipline that focuses on the management of activities as the route to improving the value received by the customer and the profit achieved by providing this value. This discipline includes cost driver analysis, activity analysis, and performance measurement. Activity-based management draws on activity-based costing as its major source of information. (See *customer value.*)

Terms were adapted with permission from the Consortium for Advanced Manufacturing—Raffish, Norm and Peter B. B. Turney, ed., "The CAM-I Glossary of Activity-Based Management, version 1.2," Arlington, TX: The Consortium for Advanced Manufacturing International, 1992.

Activity capacity   The demonstrated or expected capacity of an activity under normal operating conditions, assuming a specified set of resources and over a long period of time. An example of this would be a rate of output for an activity expressed as 500 cycles per hour.

Activity cost assignment   The process in which the cost of activities is attached to cost objects using activity drivers. (See *activity driver, cost object.*)

Activity cost pool   A grouping of all cost elements associated with an activity. (See *cost element.*)

Activity driver   A measure of the frequency and intensity of the demands placed on activities by cost objects. An activity driver is used to assign costs to cost objects. It represents a line item on the bill of activities for a product or customer. An example is the number of part numbers, which is used to measure the consumption of material-related activities by each product, material type, or component. The number of customer orders measures the consumption of order-entry activities by each customer. Sometimes an activity driver is used as an indicator of the output of an activity, such as the number of purchase orders prepared by the purchasing activity. (See *bill of activities, cost object, intensity.*)

Activity driver analysis   The identification and evaluation of the activity drivers used to trace the cost of activities to cost objects. Activity driver analysis also may involve selecting activity drivers with a potential for cost reduction. (See *Pareto analysis.*)

Activity level   A description of how an activity is used by a cost object or other activity. Some activity levels describe the cost object that uses the activity and the nature of this use. These levels include activities that are traceable to the product (i.e., unit-level, batch-level, and product-level costs), to the customer (customer-level costs), to a market (market-level costs), to a distribution channel (channel-level costs), and to a project, such as a research and development project (project-level costs).

Allocation   1. An apportionment or distribution. 2. A process of assigning cost to an activity or cost object when a direct measure does not exist. For example, assigning the cost of power to a machine activity by means of machine hours is an allocation, because machine hours are an indirect measure of power consumption. In some cases, allocations can be converted to tracing by incurring additional measurement costs. Instead of using machine hours to allocate power consumption, for example, a company can place a power meter on machines to measure actual power consumption. (See *tracing.*)

Assignment   See *cost assignment.*

Attributes   Characteristics of activities, such as cost drivers and performance measures. (See *cost driver, performance measure.*)

Attribution   See *tracing.*

Avoidable cost   A cost associated with an activity that would not be incurred if the activity was not required. The telephone cost associated with vendor support, for example, could be avoided if the activity were not performed.

Backflush costing   1. A costing method that applies costs based on the output of a process. The process uses a bill of material or a bill of activities explosion to draw quantities from inventory, through work-in-process, to finished goods; at any intermediate stage, using the output quantity as the basis. These quantities are generally costed using standard costs. The process assumes that the bill of material (or bill of activities) and the standard costs at the time of backflushing represent the actual quantities and resources used in the manufacture of the product. This is important, since usually no shop orders are maintained to collect costs. 2. A costing method generally associated with repetitive manufacturing. (See *repetitive manufacturing, standard costing*.)

Benchmarking   See *best practices*.

Best practices   A methodology that identifies an activity as the benchmark by which a similar activity will be judged. This methodology is used to assist in identifying a process or technique that can increase the effectiveness or efficiency of an activity. The source may be internal (e.g., taken from another part of the company) or external (e.g., taken from a competitor). Another term used is competitive benchmarking.

Bill of activities   A listing of the activities required (and, optionally, the associated costs of the resources consumed) by a product or other cost object.

Budget   1. A projected amount of cost or revenue for an activity or organizational unit covering a specific period of time. 2. Any plan for the coordination and control of resources and expenditures.

Capital decay   1. A quantification of the lost revenues or reduction in net cash flows sustained by an entity due to obsolete technology. 2. A measure of uncompetitiveness.

Carrying cost   See *holding cost*.

Competitive benchmarking   See *best practices*.

Continuous improvement program   A program to eliminate waste, reduce response time, simplify the design of both products and processes, and improve quality.

Cost Accounting Standards   1. Rules promulgated by the Cost Accounting Standards Board of the United States Government to ensure contractor compliance in the accounting of government contracts. 2. A set of rules issued by any of several authorized organizations or agencies, such as the American Institute of Certified Public Accountants (AICPA) or the Association of Chartered Accountants (ACA), dealing with the determination of costs to be allocated, inventoried, or expensed.

Cost assignment   The tracing or allocation of resources to activities or cost objects. (See *allocation, tracing*.)

Cost center   The basic unit of responsibility in an organization for which costs are accumulated.

Cost driver   Any factor that causes a change in the cost of an activity. For example, the quality of parts received by an activity (e.g., the percent that are defective) is a determining factor in the work required by that activity, because the quality of parts received affects the resources required to perform the activity. An activity may have multiple cost drivers associated with it.

Cost driver analysis   The examination, quantification, and explanation of the effects of cost drivers. Management often uses the results of cost driver analyses in continuous improvement programs to help reduce throughput time, improve quality, and reduce cost. (See *continuous improvement program, cost driver.*)

Cost element   An amount paid for a resource consumed by an activity and included in an activity cost pool. For example, power cost, engineering cost, and depreciation may be cost elements in the activity cost pool for a machine activity. (See *activity cost pool, bill of activities, resource.*)

Cost object   Any customer, product, service, contract, project, or other work unit for which a separate cost measurement is desired.

Cost of quality   All the resources expended for appraisal costs, prevention costs, and both internal and external failure costs of activities and cost objects.

Cost pool   See *activity cost pool.*

Cross-subsidy   The improper assignment of costs among cost objects such that certain cost objects are overcosted while other cost objects are undercosted relative to the activity costs assigned. For example, traditional cost accounting systems tend to overcost high-volume products and undercost low-volume products.

Customer value   The difference between customer realization and sacrifice. Realization is what the customer receives, including product features, quality, and service. This takes into account the customer's cost to use, maintain, and dispose of the product or service. Sacrifice is what the customer gives up, including the amount the customer pays for the product plus time and effort spent acquiring the product and learning how to use it. Maximizing customer value means maximizing the difference between realization and sacrifice.

Differential cost   See *incremental cost.*

Direct cost   A cost that is traced directly to an activity or a cost object. For example, the material issued to a particular work order or the engineering time devoted to a specific product is a direct cost to the work orders or products. (See *tracing.*)

Direct tracing   See *tracing.*

Discounted cash flow   A technique used to evaluate the future cash flows generated by a capital investment. Discounted cash flow is computed by discounting cash flows to determine their present value.

Diversity   Conditions in which cost objects place different demands on activities or activities place different demands on resources. This situation arises, for example, when there is a difference in mix or volume of products that causes an uneven assignment of costs. Different types of diversity include batch size, customer, market, product mix, distribution channel, and volume.

Financial accounting   1. The accounting for assets, liabilities, equities, revenues, and expenses as a basis for reports to external parties. 2. A methodology that focuses on reporting financial information primarily for use by owners, external organizations, and financial institutions. This methodology is constrained by rule-making bodies such as the Financial Accounting Standards Board (FASB), the Securities Exchange Commission (SEC), and the American Institute of Certified Public Accountants (AICPA).

First-stage allocation   See *resource cost assignment.*

Fixed cost   A cost element of an activity that does not vary with changes in the volume of cost drivers or activity drivers. The depreciation of a machine, for example, may be directly related to a particular activity, but it is fixed with respect to changes in the number of units of the activity driver. The designation of a cost element as fixed or variable may vary depending on the time frame of the decision in question and the extent to which the volume of production, activity drivers, or cost drivers changes.

Flexible factory   The objective of a flexible factory is to provide a wide range of services across many product lines in a timely manner. An example is a fabrication plant with several integrated manufacturing cells that can perform many functions for unrelated product lines with relatively short lead times.

Focused factory   The objective of a focused factory is to organize around a specific set of resources to provide low cost and high throughput over a narrow range of products.

Forcing   Allocating the costs of a sustaining activity to a cost object even though that cost object may not clearly consume or causally relate to that activity. Allocating a plant-level activity (i.e., heating) to product units using an activity driver such as direct labor hours, for example, forces the cost of this activity to the product. (See *sustaining activity.*)

Full absorption costing   See *absorption costing.*

Functional decomposition   Identifies the activities performed in the organization. It yields a hierarchical representation of the organization and shows the relationship between the different levels of the organization and its activities. For example, a hierarchy may start with the division and move down through the plant, function, process, activity, and task levels.

Holding cost   A financial technique that calculates the cost of retaining an asset (e.g., finished goods inventory or a building). Generally, the calculation includes a cost of capital in addition to other costs such as insurance, taxes, and space.

Homogeneity   A situation in which all the cost elements in an activity's cost pool are consumed in proportion to an activity driver by all cost objects. (See *activity cost pool, activity driver, cost element.*)

Incremental cost   1. The cost associated with increasing the output of an activity or project above some base level. 2. The additional cost associated with selecting one economic or business alternative over another, such as the difference between working overtime or subcontracting the work. 3. The cost associated with increasing the quantity of a cost driver. (Also known as differential cost.)

Indirect cost   The cost that is allocated—as opposed to being traced—to an activity or a cost object. For example, the costs of supervision or heat may be allocated to an activity on the basis of direct labor hours. (See *allocation.*)

Intensity   The cost consumed by each unit of the activity driver. It is assumed that the intensity of each unit of the activity driver for a single activity is equal. Unequal intensity means that the activity should be broken into smaller activities or that a different activity driver should be chosen. (See *diversity.*)

Life cycle   See *product life cycle.*

Net present value   A method that evaluates the difference between the present value of all cash inflows and outflows of an investment using a given rate of discount. If the discounted cash inflow exceeds the discounted outflow, the investment is considered economically feasible.

Non–value-added activity   An activity that is considered not to contribute to customer value or to the organization's needs. The designation non–value-added reflects a belief that the activity can be redesigned, reduced, or eliminated without reducing the quantity, responsiveness, or quality of the output required by the customer or the organization. (See *customer value, value analysis.*)

Obsolescence   A product or service that has lost its value to the customer due to changes in need or technology.

Opportunity cost   The economic value of a benefit that is sacrificed when an alternative course of action is selected.

Pareto analysis   The identification and interpretation of significant factors using Pareto's rule that 20 percent of a set of independent variables is responsible for 80 percent of the result. Pareto analysis can be used to identify cost drivers or activity drivers that are responsible for the majority of cost incurred by ranking the cost drivers in order of value. (See *activity driver analysis, cost driver analysis.*)

Performance measures   Indicators of the work performed and the results achieved in an activity, process, or organizational unit. Performance measures may be financial or nonfinancial. An example of a performance measure of an activity is the number of defective parts per million. An example of a performance measure of an organizational unit is return on sales.

Present value   The discounted value of a future sum or stream of cash flows.

Process   A series of activities that are linked to perform a specific objective. For example, the assembly of a television set or the paying of a bill or claim entails several linked activities.

Product family   A group of products or services that have a defined relationship because of physical and production similarities. (The term "product line" is used interchangeably.)

Product life cycle   The period that starts with the initial product specification and ends with the withdrawal of the product from the marketplace. A product life cycle is characterized by certain defined stages, including research, development, introduction, maturity, decline, and abandonment.

Product line   See *product family.*

Profit center   A segment of the business (e.g., a project, program, or business unit) that is accountable for both revenues and expenses.

Project   A planned undertaking, usually related to a specific activity, such as the research and development of a new product or the redesign of the layout of a plant.

Project costing   A cost system that collects information on activities and costs associated with a specific activity, project, or program.

Repetitive manufacturing   The manufacture of identical products (or a family of products) in a continuous flow.

Resource   An economic element that is applied or used in the performance of activities. Salaries and materials, for example, are resources used in the performance of activities. (See *cost element.*)

Resource cost assignment   The process by which cost is attached to activities. This process requires the assignment of cost from general ledger accounts to activities using resource drivers. For example, the chart of accounts may list information services at a plant level. It then becomes necessary to trace (assuming that tracing is practical) or to allocate (when tracing is not practical) the cost of information services to the activities that benefit from the information services by means of appropriate resource drivers. It may be necessary to set up intermediate activity cost pools to accumulate related costs from various resources before the assignment can be made. (See *activity cost pool, resource driver.*)

Resource driver   A measure of the quantity of resources consumed by an activity. An example of a resource driver is the percentage of total square feet of space occupied by an activity. This factor is used to allocate a portion of the cost of operating the facilities to the activity.

Responsibility accounting   An accounting method that focuses on identifying persons or organizational units that are accountable for the performance of revenue or expense plans.

Risk   The subjective assessment of the possible positive or negative consequences of a current or future action. In a business sense, risk is the premium asked or paid for engaging in an investment or venture. Often risk is incorporated into business decisions through such factors as hurdle rates or the interest premium paid over a prevailing base interest rate.

Second-stage allocation   See *activity cost assignment.*

Standard costing   A costing method that attaches costs to cost objects based on reasonable estimates or cost studies and by means of budgeted rates rather according to actual costs incurred.

Sunk costs   Costs that have been invested in assets for which there is little (if any) alternative or continued value except salvage. Using sunk costs as a basis for evaluating alternatives may lead to incorrect decisions. Examples are the invested cost in a scrapped part or the cost of an obsolete machine.

Support costs   Costs of activities not directly associated with production. Examples are the costs of process engineering and purchasing.

Surrogate activity driver   An activity driver that is not descriptive of an activity but that is closely correlated to the performance of the activity. The use of a surrogate activity driver should reduce measurement costs without significantly increasing the costing bias. The number of production runs, for example, is not descriptive of the material disbursing activity, but the number of production runs may be used as an activity driver if material disbursements coincide with production runs.

Sustaining activity   An activity that benefits an organization at some level (e.g., the company as a whole or a division, plant, or department) but not any specific cost object. Examples of such activities are preparation of financial statements, plant management, and the support of community programs.

Target cost   A cost calculated by subtracting a desired profit margin from an estimated (or a market-based) price to arrive at a desired production, engineering, or marketing cost. The target cost may not be the initial production cost but instead the cost that is expected to be achieved during the mature production stage. (See *target costing.*)

Target costing A method used in the analysis of product and process design that involves estimating a target cost and designing the product to meet that cost. (See *target cost.*)

Technology costs A category of cost associated with the development, acquisition, implementation, and maintenance of technology assets. It can include costs such as the depreciation of research equipment, tooling amortization, maintenance, and software development.

Technology valuation A nontraditional approach to valuing technology acquisitions that may incorporate such elements as purchase price, start-up costs, current market value adjustments, and the risk premium of an acquisition.

Throughput The rate of production of a defined process over a stated period of time. Rates may be expressed in terms of units of products, batches produced, dollar turnover, or other meaningful measurements.

Traceability The ability to assign a cost by means of a causal relationship directly to an activity or a cost object in an economically feasible way. (See *tracing.*)

Tracing The assignment of cost to an activity or a cost object using an observable measure of the consumption of resources by the activity or cost object. Tracing is generally preferred to allocation if the data exist or can be obtained at a reasonable cost. For example, if a company's cost accounting system captures the cost of supplies according to which activity uses the supplies, the costs may be traced—as opposed to allocated—to the appropriate activities. Tracing is also called direct tracing.

Unit cost The cost associated with a single unit of the product, including direct costs, indirect costs, traced costs, and allocated costs.

Value-added activity An activity that is judged to contribute to customer value or satisfy an organizational need. The attribute "value added" reflects a belief that the activity cannot be eliminated without reducing the quantity, responsiveness, or quality of output required by a customer or organization. (See *customer value.*)

Value analysis A cost reduction and process improvement tool that utilizes information collected about business processes and examines various attributes of the processes (e.g., diversity, capacity, and complexity) to identify candidates for improvement efforts. (See *activity attribute, cost driver.*)

Value chain The set of activities required to design, procure, produce, market, distribute, and service a product or service.

Value-chain costing An activity-based cost model that contains all activities in the value chain.

Variable cost A cost element of an activity that varies with changes in volume of cost drivers and activity drivers. The cost of material handling to an activity, for example, varies according to the number of material deliveries and pickups to and from that activity. (See *activity driver, cost element, fixed cost.*)

Variance   The difference between an expected and actual result.

Waste   Resources consumed by unessential or inefficient activities.

Willie Sutton rule   Focus on the high-cost activities. The rule is named after bank robber Willie Sutton, who, when asked "Why do you rob banks?" is reputed to have replied, "Because that's where the money is."

Work cell   A physical or logical grouping of resources that performs a defined job or task. The work cell may contain more than one activity. For example, all the tasks associated with the final assembly of a product may be grouped in a work cell.

Work center   A physical area of the plant or factory. It consists of one or more resources where a particular product or process is accomplished.

Index